The Body Productive

The Body Productive

Rethinking Capitalism, Work and the Body

Edited by
Steffan Blayney, Joey Hornsby and Savannah Whaley

BLOOMSBURY ACADEMIC
LONDON • NEW YORK • OXFORD • NEW DELHI • SYDNEY

BLOOMSBURY ACADEMIC
Bloomsbury Publishing Plc
50 Bedford Square, London, WC1B 3DP, UK
1385 Broadway, New York, NY 10018, USA
29 Earlsfort Terrace, Dublin 2, Ireland

BLOOMSBURY, BLOOMSBURY ACADEMIC and the Diana logo are
trademarks of Bloomsbury Publishing Plc

First published in Great Britain 2023
This paperback edition published 2024

Cover design by Adriana Brioso
Cover image: Joe Limon and Charles Weidman performing twin leap in *Dance in
Movement* by Gjon Mili. (© Bettmann/Getty Images)

A catalogue record for this book is available from the British Library.

A catalog record for this title is available from the Library of Congress.

ISBN: PB: 978-0-7556-3955-7
        ePDF: 978-0-7556-3953-3
       eBook: 978-0-7556-3952-6

Typeset by Integra Software Services Pvt. Ltd.

To find out more about our authors and books visit www.bloomsbury.com
and sign up for our newsletters.

Dedicated to the memory of Didier Deleule
(1941–2019)

Contents

Contributors

Philip Barnard is Emeritus Professor of English at University of Kansas. His publications primarily address the cultural politics of the novel during the revolutionary age, US novelist Charles Brockden Brown (1771–1810), and poststructuralism and historical materialism since the 1960s. Recent publications include *Pentecostal Modernism: Lovecraft, Los Angeles, and World-Systems Culture* (2017, co-authored with Stephen Shapiro) and *The Oxford Handbook of Charles Brockden Brown* (2019, co-edited with Hilary Emmett and Stephen Shapiro). He has also translated *The Literary Absolute* by Philippe Lacoue-Labarthe and Jean-Luc Nancy, as well as texts by Philippe Sollers, Alain Kirili, Severo Sarduy and others.

Steffan Blayney works for a trade union in London, and is an honorary research fellow in the Department of History at the University of Sheffield. He is the author of *Health & Efficiency: Fatigue, the Science of Work and the Making of the Working-Class Body* (University of Massachusetts Press, 2022).

Helen Charman teaches in the English Studies department at Durham University. Her first book, *Mother State*, is forthcoming from Allen Lane. Her poetry has been shortlisted for the *White Review* Poetry Prize and the Ivan Juritz Prize for Creative Experiment.

François Guéry born 22 March 1944, alumnus of the École Normale Supérieure, is Professor Emeritus of philosophy and formerly the dean of the Philosophy Faculty at Université Lyon-III. He has participated in several radio programmes on philosophy. His research interests include Marx, notably in *Le Corps productif* (*The Productive Body*), written with Didier Deleule in 1972, and *Industrial Society and Its Enemies*, published in 1989; Heidegger, for his thinking on technology, in *Heidegger rediscuté*

(Heidegger Revisited), published in 1995, and Nietzsche; he translated the second *Untimely Meditation* with commentary, and partially translated *Thus Spake Zarathustra*, to which he returned in *Archéologie du nihilisme* (Archeology of Nihilism), published in 2015. His work engages with civilizational problems, such as ecological crisis (*La politique de précaution*, The politics of precaution, with the minister Corinne Lepage, 2001), and feminism, which he will consider in a forthcoming work, *La loi du plus faible* (The Survival of the Weakest).

Joey Hornsby recently completed a PhD in French Studies at King's College London, her degree being awarded in August 2021. Her research considered the role of economic, labouring relationships in the work of Georges Bataille. She is the author of '"Working Girl": Sex Work and Intersubjectivity in Georges Bataille's *Madame Edwarda*' published in *Nottingham French Studies*, spring 2022.

Arianna Introna received her MLitt and PhD in Scottish Literature from the University of Stirling and is now Associate Lecturer with the Open University. Her research interests range from Scottish literature, disability studies and the medical humanities to Marxist autonomist theory, critical theory and the social history of the welfare state. Her first book, *Autonomist Narratives of Disability in Modern Scottish Writing: Crip Enchantments* (2022), explores the intersection between imaginaries of disability and representations of work, welfare and the nation in twentieth- and twenty-first-century Scottish literature.

Graham Jones is a writer currently based in the Midlands, UK, and is the author of *The Shock Doctrine of the Left* (2018) and *Red Enlightenment: On Socialism, Science, and Spirituality* (forthcoming).

Phil Jones is a researcher for the think tank Autonomy. He regularly writes for publications such as the *London Review of Books*, the *Guardian*, the *New Statesman* and Novara Media. He is the author of *Work Without the Worker: Labour in the Age of Platform Capitalism* (2021).

Christopher Law is a researcher, writer and editor, currently based in Glasgow, Scotland. His research interests tend to revolve around literary theory, black studies and contemporary literature and poetics. He completed his PhD in Comparative Literature at Goldsmiths, University of London, in 2019.

Stephen Shapiro teaches in the Department of English & Comparative Literature at the University of Warwick. With Philip Barnard, he edited the English translation of *The Productive Body*. Author or editor of nineteen books, his most recent work includes *Pentecostal Modernism: Lovecraft, Los Angeles and World-Systems Culture* (with Philip Barnard); *How to Read Marx's Capital* and *How to Read Foucault's Discipline and Punish* (with Anne Schwan). He is also a member of the Warwick Research Collective, which collectively wrote *Combined and Uneven Development: Towards a New Theory of World-Literature*. He does not believe Foucault was ever a neoliberal.

Dan Taylor is Lecturer in Social and Political Thought at the Open University. He works in contemporary political theory and the history of political thought. He's the author of *Spinoza and the Politics of Freedom* (Edinburgh University Press, 2021); *Island Story: Journeys through Unfamiliar Britain* (2016, shortlisted for the Orwell Prize) and *Negative Capitalism: Cynicism in the Neoliberal Era* (2013). For more, see www.dantaylor.blog.

Grace Tillyard is a researcher and writer who recently completed her PhD at Goldsmiths, University of London, in the Department of Media, Communications and Cultural Studies. Grace's research interests encompass reproductive politics, sociology, feminist and decolonial approaches to science and technology studies, digital and internet cultures and migration.

Marina Vishmidt is a writer and lecturer. Her work has appeared in *South Atlantic Quarterly*, *Artforum*, *Afterall*, *Journal of Cultural Economy*, *e-flux journal* and *Radical Philosophy*, among others, as well as a number of edited volumes. She is currently editing a reader on speculation for the Documents of Contemporary Art series (2022). She is the co-author of *Reproducing Autonomy* (with Kerstin Stakemeier) (2016), and the author of *Speculation as a Mode of Production: Forms of Value Subjectivity in Art and Capital* (2018). She is part of the Marxism in Culture collective and the board of the New Perspectives on the Critical Theory of Society series (Bloomsbury Academic). She teaches at Goldsmiths and is currently the Rudolph Arnheim Visiting Professor in Art History at Humboldt University in Berlin.

Savannah Whaley is a researcher in performance studies and critical theory. Her PhD project reread long-standing theorizations of feminist body art since 1970 to make a critique of political economy central to understandings of performance, gender and the body. She has taught across Drama, English, and Culture, Media and Creative Industries departments at Queen Mary, University of London and King's College London.

Dawn Woolley is an artist and a research fellow at Leeds Arts University. Her research examines contemporary consumerism and gender, paying particular attention to the new mechanisms of interaction afforded by social networking sites. Recent solo exhibitions include; 'Consumed: Stilled Lives' bildkultur Gallery, Stuttgart (2022) and 'Consumed: Stilled Lives' Perth Centre for Photography, Australia (2021). Recent publications include: 'The Dissecting Gaze: Fashioned Bodies on Social Networking Sites', in *Revisiting the Gaze: Feminism, Fashion and the Female Body* (London: Bloomsbury, 2020). *Consuming the Body: Capitalism, Social Media and Commodification* is due to be published in 2022 by Bloomsbury.

Acknowledgements

This collection evolved out of a conference of the same name held at Birkbeck, University of London, in December 2018, and it was the interest in and success of that event that encouraged us to take some of the work shared there forward. We would therefore firstly like to thank all of those who chaired panels, presented papers, and attended on the day for generating conversations and sharing ideas without which *The Body Productive* would not exist. It has been a pleasure to watch some of those initial papers develop into the chapters contained in this book. We are also grateful to the various organizations who provided funding for the conference: Birkbeck, the Higher Education, Research and Innovation Department of the French Embassy in the UK, the Institut Français du Royaume-Uni and the Wellcome Trust. Special thanks go to our friend and colleague James Horton, for his support with design, artwork and translation, at the conference and beyond.

We are grateful to everyone at Bloomsbury and Zed who helped to make this book possible: to Kim Walker for her initial interest in the project, and to Melanie Scagliarni and Olivia Dellow for their enthusiastic support and invaluable help along the way. The process of putting this book together has been particularly difficult due to the circumstances of the Covid-19 pandemic, and we are grateful to all of the contributors for their patience, kindness and warmth throughout what has been a longer-than-planned process. We feel lucky to have had the opportunity to work with so many brilliant and generous thinkers, and we are thankful to each of the authors in this collection for their serious and thoughtful engagement with this project. We would also like to mention, and to thank, those contributors who gave their time and thinking to this project at different points along the way and who, for various reasons, were not able to submit chapters for the final collection: Christina Gerantoni, Amelia Horgan, Amber Lascelles, Ana Carolina Minozzo, Annie Olaloku-Teriba and Chrystel Oloukoï. Our warmest thanks also to Rafael Lubner, Erin Maglaque, Christine Okoth and Luke Whaley for their thoughtful comments and words of advice in relation to the editors' introduction.

Compiling this collection has been a first for all three of the editors, and an invaluable learning experience, and we would not have been able to stick with it without the support, love and guidance of friends, family and colleagues, of whom there are too many to mention individually. Special thanks, however, are due to Stephen Shapiro and Philip Barnard, for believing in the project from the start and for giving so much of their time and wisdom, from the earliest plans for a conference to the final stages of the book. Finally of course, none of this would have been possible without François Guéry and Didier Deleule, and we are enormously grateful to both of them for their interest, enthusiasm and willingness to be involved in the project from the outset. While we regret that Deleule was sadly unable to see the book come to fruition, we are immensely glad to have had the encouragement of both *The Productive Body*'s authors for our work. We hope that we have been able to do their original text justice.

Introduction: Rethinking capitalism, work and the body

Steffan Blayney, Joey Hornsby and Savannah Whaley

Capitalism is the sophisticated and materialised form of the hatred of Man and of his body.

François Guéry[1]

Capitalism requires work, work needs bodies and bodies are shaped by capital. Far from being a natural given, the body is therefore a site of continuous mediation and ideological contestation. Starting from the body under capitalism as a primary locus of exploitation and struggle, the central premise of this book is that understanding bodies and their relationship to work is crucial to understanding how capitalism works and how it shapes our lives. Capitalism, driven by accumulation, is characterized by a compulsion to make bodies *productive*: to make them work and work harder, to make them intelligible and knowable, and to integrate them as functional parts within its networks of production, consumption and exchange. As the chapters in this collection show, this drive takes many forms and is met with various kinds of resistance. Struggles over the body operate at a number of levels, from the macroscopic, targeting individuals or populations, to the microscopic, concerned with discrete bodily organs, processes and capacities.

To begin an analysis of capitalism with the body may seem odd, or indeed anachronistic. Do we not, as countless commentators have argued, now live in a post-industrial age of digital, immaterial and fundamentally *disembodied* capitalism, one in which physical work has largely been replaced with various kinds of intellectual, interpersonal, emotional and affective labour? Today, in the Global North at least, fewer of us work 'with our hands' than ever before. In the UK, the percentage of people employed in manufacturing and heavy industries has decreased sharply since the mid-twentieth century, while the service sector now accounts for more than 80 per cent of jobs.[2] Is it not the case, as Franco 'Bifo' Berardi has put it, that while industrial capitalism dealt with 'bodies, muscles and arms', our own post-Fordist moment is more concerned with 'the mind, language and creativity as its primary tools for the production of value'?[3]

Yet not quite all that is solid melts into air. In today's capitalism, it is not difficult to find examples of direct control, exploitation and abuse carried out at the level of the body. The human side of an ostensibly 'digital' economy is manifest not only in the manufacturing centres of the Global South – which produce much of the hardware that allows us to experience capitalism as 'immaterial' – but also in the low-paid and precarious service jobs which underwrite this economy in the Global North.[4] In the giant Foxconn manufacturing facility in Shenzhen, China, where a large proportion of Apple products sold globally are produced, working conditions are reported to be so brutalizing that workers have been required to sign a 'no suicide' pledge, following a series of deaths.[5] In the United States and the United Kingdom workers in Amazon warehouses are subject to automated 'productivity tracking' systems, using GPS tracking and biometric measurement to calculate 'time off task' during shifts, with workers reporting having to urinate in bottles rather than take toilet breaks in order to avoid the system's digital reprimands, which can lead to dismissal.[6] Drivers and couriers for 'platform' services like Uber and Deliveroo have been test subjects at the cutting edge of similar forms of digital surveillance, now being rolled out in a wide range of workplaces, with workers' every move timed and logged to ensure maximum productivity.[7] Even in occupations which are less obviously physical, such as office work, demands and stresses are placed on workers' bodies – from the eye strain and headaches caused by staring at computer screens, to back problems caused by poorly designed seating – while intensifying cultures of overwork and management surveillance, and the increasing blurring of distinctions between work and leisure, take their toll on the body in the form of 'burnout', depression and fatigue.[8]

In considering bodies under capitalism, however, we are not only – or even primarily – concerned with the immediate negative impacts which work can have on our bodies, but with the more fundamental and long-term ways in which capitalism and the demands of work shape ideas of what bodies are and what they are for. Capitalism, in this sense, does not only make bodies productive, but *produces bodies*, and knowledge about bodies, according to its own imperatives. The ways in which we understand health and fitness, the relationship between body and mind, and the various categories of political identity which get attached to and articulated through our bodies – such as race, gender, or sexuality – are all mediated through capitalism's logics of production, consumption and exchange. What is at stake then is more than a narrow question of good or bad work, healthy or unhealthy working practices, or demands that we can make of employers. In rethinking the body within work and capitalism, our aim is also to imagine a body beyond them.

*

The impetus for this rethinking was the publication, in 2014, of the first complete English translation of François Guéry and Didier Deleule's *The Productive Body* (*Le corps productif*). Despite being referenced by Michel Foucault in 1975 in *Discipline & Punish* (*Surveiller et punir*), this short, but suggestive, work had remained largely unknown, particularly to anglophone readers, in the intervening years.[9] First published in 1972 in a Paris still reeling from the after-effects of the 'events' of May 1968, *The Productive Body* reflects the intense theoretical and political debates and controversies of a volatile and intellectually generative period for the French left, such that it can be difficult for contemporary readers – unversed in the arguments between the French Communist Party and the emergent 'Maoist' left, or in the finer points of French structuralism or phenomenology – to orient themselves within its problematic.[10] Its argument is not always straightforward; its tone is sometimes polemical and direct, sometimes ironic and playful, often abstract and obscure. Yet in its attention to the body and bodies as sites of domination and exploitation, to the transformations of human subjectivity through technologies of information, observation and surveillance, and to the potential for resistance in a world in which capital's dominance appears ever more totalizing, it is also a book which is strikingly resonant today.

While the product of a close collaboration between its two authors, *The Productive Body* is structured as two separate essays, one by each contributor, with a co-written foreword setting out the shared objectives of the project. One of these objectives, as Guéry further elaborates in his contribution to the present volume, is a return to Marx, and in particular to the chapters in Part Four of *Capital*, Volume I, which deal with the historical development of the labour process under capitalism, and from which the concept of a 'productive body' is taken. While not used systematically in *Capital*, the term 'productive body' (or 'productive organism') is deployed by Marx in these chapters to describe the collective organization of labour-power as it is brought under the control of capital. Though the coordination of workers to perform particular tasks is a phenomenon which predates the emergence of capitalism, the need for increasingly complex divisions of labour creates an opportunity for early capitalists to assert their control over production:

> All directly social or communal labour requires, to a greater or lesser degree, a directing authority, in order to secure the harmonious co-operation of the activities of individuals, and to perform the general functions that have their origin in the motion of *the total productive organism*, as distinguished from the motion of its separate organs.[11]

As a result, the work of 'directing, superintending and adjusting becomes one of the functions of capital, from the moment that the labour under capital's control becomes co-operative'. While wage labourers, like pre-capitalist workers, continue to participate in a 'social labour process', their cooperation is now 'entirely brought about by the capital that employs them'. Thus, 'their unification into *one single productive body*, and the establishment of a connection between their functions' is a process which is now entirely outside of their control.[12] In *The Productive Body*, Guéry and Deleule seek both to explain historically how this unified body coheres through successive stages of capitalist development, and to explore the effects of such a process on our understandings of bodies, work and subjectivity under capitalism in the present.

Guéry and Deleule's interest in 'the body' then is not as a biological given, nor as an essential grounding for human subjectivity, but as an object which emerges historically. Fundamentally, they argue, the history of the body is a history of *production*. The body – as the original means by which humans produced their own subsistence – is the prototypical means of production and, as such, 'the privileged instrument from which all developed technology, including machines, may be derived.'[13] At the same time, it follows, the history of the body is necessarily a *social* history. Production requires a division of labour, which in turn brings people into social relations. The 'biological body' of the individual is thus necessarily brought into a 'social body': an organic combination of bodies, in which each individual performs discrete tasks towards a collective end or ends. The 'productive body' is the particular form that this process takes under capitalism.

For Guéry and Deleule, following Marx, the 'productivity' of the productive body refers not simply to the capacity to produce, but to the specifically capitalist phenomenon of the production of wealth for another in the form of surplus-value – that value which is produced by the labourer in excess of the wage they receive, and which is realized as profit by the employer. Rising productivity, in these terms, means a greater proportion of the value produced accruing to the capitalist and a smaller proportion received in wages. 'To be a productive worker,' as Marx concludes, 'is therefore not a piece of luck, but a misfortune.'[14] Under capitalism, Guéry and Deleule argue, this misfortune is intensified through a progressive 'tendency… towards the conversion of human material into productive-form'. With the rise of modern industry, as work is reorganized in order to obtain the maximum possible surplus from the available workers, individual bodies in turn become progressively more 'integrated into the productive body as elements of production'.[15]

The first half of *The Productive Body*, written by Guéry, traces in broad terms the development of the productive body (implicitly in Western Europe), from the first incursions of capitalist practices into the closed structures of the medieval guild, to the mechanized factories of the twentieth century. Here, the progression (in Marx's terminology) from the era of 'handicrafts' through 'manufacture' to 'large-scale industry' entails at each stage new relationships between work, the body and society. With capitalist control over the labour process becoming ever more dominant, the social body is increasingly reorganized according to a rationality of productivity. While the earliest capitalists, still constrained by feudal restrictions on the organization of work, could only seek to increase their profits by extending the working day, the transition to the era of 'manufacture' sees an increasingly powerful capitalist class beginning to transform the work process itself. The need for an ever-greater surplus leads the capitalist to pursue ever-larger economies of scale, entailing the accumulation of larger numbers of workers together in factories and workshops, and the subsequent extension of organization, cooperation and interdependence between those so employed.

While Marx, writing in the nineteenth century, had stressed the dialectical process by which bringing workers together in factories would create the conditions of possibility for the emergence of class consciousness – as workers would begin to realize both the social nature of their work and their shared interests in opposition to the capital that employs them – Guéry, writing in the aftermath of 1968, is instead preoccupied with the failure of modern capitalism to produce a revolutionary working-class movement. Rather than creating solidarity between workers, he argues, the vast socialization of the labour process under capitalism had instead been associated with their progressive individuation and isolation. Far from harmonizing the biological with the social, the consolidation of the productive body had entailed a traumatic split between the worker and the social nature of their work.

At the heart of this process, Guéry argues, is capitalism's separation of intellectual from physical work – the body from the head – and the related phenomenon of the growth of management expertise. While at the stage of handicraft production, it was common for one worker to conceive of and execute an entire product from the start to finish, with the expansion of the scale of production and division of labour the task of each individual becomes increasingly specialized and discrete. Where once a single worker could understand each operation that went into the completion of a product, now the overall scheme of production in which the worker is embedded becomes increasingly distant and obscure. At this stage, the figure of the manager or engineer – the avatar of capital in the labour process, or its 'mediator' – appears as 'the intellectual element of production', giving direction, purpose and unity to the fragmented labour process.[16] From the perspective of the workers, as Marx puts it, 'the interconnection between their various labours confronts them, in the realm of ideas, as a plan drawn up by the capitalist'.[17] As capital – through these mediators – takes greater control in the organization and planning of production, the body of the worker is correspondingly reduced to the status of a physical tool, carrying out a specialized, mechanical function, while capital has 'appropriated the intellectual and technical forces of work for itself'.[18] The accumulated technical knowledge evidenced in work as a whole now appears not as a shared human endeavour but as the exclusive private property of the manager, the supervisor, the technocrat, 'the person who exercises surveillance'.[19]

As production becomes increasingly dominated by machinery in the era of large-scale industry, the disintegration of the labour process and the separation of manual from mental labour are further intensified, as the function of the individual worker is reduced to supervising the work of machines whose complex functioning is a matter of highly technical expertise. Crucially now, the productive body is no longer simply an extension of the collective worker – an organism whose parts are human beings – but a cyborg assemblage of body and machine. Boundaries between living and non-living labour are collapsed, as capital moves to take 'the worker out of the process of production'.[20] Machinery, rather than workers, now appears to be performing the important tasks of production, as well as fulfilling the functions of coordination and supervision, setting the pace of work and forcing the worker to adapt their movements to its own. Technology – rather than enabling or enhancing human capacities – is experienced as further weakening and fragmenting them, as the human worker is reduced to a passive 'accessory' in an increasingly mechanized process.[21] 'The productive body ceases to be a biological metaphor', and the biological body, as Deleule develops in his section of the book, is reduced to a 'body-machine'.[22]

If the 'privatization of social functions' which characterizes the composition of the productive body is an outcome of the capitalist division of labour, its effects can be seen well beyond the factory.[23] In the fully developed capitalist *system* which is inaugurated by the era of large-scale industry, the appropriation of knowledge from the labourer, and the insertion of various mediators and managers in between workers and owners, comes to structure not simply the organization of work but our wider understandings of the world, our relationships to ourselves, to our bodies and to each other. What Guéry and Deleule call the productive body, then, should be understood not only as a material facet of the capitalist mode of production but as an ideological ideal which is sustained, normalized and reproduced through a range of political, economic and scientific discourses, which themselves in turn feed back into the process of value extraction and exploitation of resource.

Both Guéry and Deleule are concerned with how logics of productivity come to inform not just the organization of work but the development of wider systems of knowledge. In particular, they are concerned with the development of scientific knowledge as a manifestation of capital's drive to dominate the natural environment, and to appropriate the productive forces of organic nature for itself. In Marx's account, the emergence of a specifically capitalist form of production brings with it 'the conscious use of the sciences, of mechanics, chemistry, etc., for specific ends'.[24] In other words, the pursuit of these sciences not in their own right, but as means to greater profit, for example, through the development and application of machinery within the production process. As such, Guéry argues in his section of *The Productive Body*, over the course of the nineteenth century the natural sciences had themselves taken on 'the role of eminent productive forces, presupposed by production'.[25] Just as technology enters the factory on the terms of the capitalist, scientific *knowledge* as a whole takes its place as 'the delegated presence of capital in the process of production'.[26] These arguments remain applicable in the context of ecological crisis, where the 'productive' application of science in the name of resource extraction and profit proceeds at phenomenal cost. But what is true of the physical sciences, as Deleule goes on to develop, is also true of the human sciences. While medical, biological, psychological, anthropological and sociological discourses of definition, classification and categorization increasingly shape our understanding of what it means to be human, they do so not in the interests of an integrated social body but as technologies of the productive body. Scientific models of the human body are therefore made in the image of capital, reifying and legitimating 'a representation of living beings in which work's production is constitutive of the perceived being'.[27]

In Deleule's section of *The Productive Body*, the history of psychology is presented as one case study in the development of scientific knowledge as it aligns with the emergence of capitalist interests. Tracing the systematic study of psychology back to Descartes' division of mind and body and *cogito ergo sum*, Deleule argues that it is capitalism's unique scission of intellectual from physical labour – and of the individual set apart from the social body – which makes possible the isolation of the 'psychical object' as a discrete entity for analysis.[28] The Cartesian split produces the human mind as something self-evident, objectively knowable and open to scientific investigation, and entails the divorce of the psyche, as an object of knowledge, from both bodily existence and subjective experience. Instead of an understanding of human beings as fundamentally interconnected and embedded in the natural world, 'what is now promoted is the identity of a being that can be represented and therefore mastered.'[29] With the rise of machinery in the nineteenth century, it becomes possible for scientific psychology to reimagine the human body and mind in mechanistic terms, and to investigate them through mechanical means, subordinating them to this machinery and the wider social machinery of capitalism. The 'task of modern psychology' becomes 'to adapt the living machine to the dead one'; 'to proceed in such a manner that the living machine, in its ordinary functioning, becomes as adapted as possible to the social mechanism into which it is in fact integrated, so that its productive act develops in optimal conditions and its gears don't grind too loudly.'[30]

For Deleule, psychology performs a dual role in the construction of the productive body. On the one hand, the increasingly sophisticated techniques which psychological science develops for understanding, measuring and categorizing individuals make possible the scientific enhancement of the body's productive capacities. Psychological screenings, personality tests, time and motion studies and other psychological interventions assist in fine-tuning individuals and groups to a point of maximum efficiency. At the same time, psychology also takes on a palliative function, serving to ameliorate the potentially disruptive consequences of capitalism's destruction of pre-existing social bonds. As human relations become incorporated within 'the overall system of cogs that make up the social mechanism' – as the machine comes to dominate the labour process and the human element is reduced to the 'role of a slave dependent on a "lifeless mechanism"' – so the 'intervention of Psychology will... be based on the inevitable need to manage this circuit'.[31] As capitalist work becomes ever more alienating, psychological intervention functions 'to restore the subject to an alien awareness of his condition', centred on the artificial supplements of 'belonging', 'group identity', 'personality' or 'well-being'.[32] This second function of psychology feeds productively into the first, reducing the potential for resistance and allowing workers to be more efficiently integrated into the productive body as both workers and consumers.

While the picture of capitalism Guéry and Deleule present in *The Productive Body* can at times appear to be that of a totalizing, all-encompassing hegemon, they also offer glimpses of resistance. If the productive body of capitalism is managed and maintained through the privatization of social knowledge, Guéry argues, then the 'corresponding thesis is the idea that socialism is basically the affirmation of the appropriation of the productive sciences by manual workers', 'short-circuiting' capital's networks of power, knowledge and control, and reappropriating the productive body of collective labour 'so that it can do the bidding of a renewed social body'.[33] Rather than nostalgically mourning a period in which a more 'natural' integrated and communal social body existed, or imagining a future in which the development of technology will by itself liberate workers, he proposes adopting a 'perspective of non-history' – the perspective of that 'cohort of the dispossessed' that is excluded from the traditional narratives of historical progress belonging both to bourgeois liberalism and to orthodox Marxism. Suspending teleological certainties which assume the inevitability of a final victory over capitalism, he instead urges us to prepare for a long and uncertain struggle; to be 'like a paradoxical weed that springs furiously from the ground after every attack', forcing its opponents 'to attack and attack again'.[34] Capital's drive to machinify living labour, Deleule argues – to 'tidy up the body's proper meaning by scouring away all of its unmanageable and stubborn subjectivity, and replacing it with the marvellous intelligibility of finely-tuned gears' – will always come up against the resistance of bodies which refuse to be incorporated. 'Behind the beautiful homogeneity of the machine lies the threatening heterogeneity of subjects.'[35] The productive body,

> constrained as it is to tear life away from living beings in order to reduce them to desirable, machine-like acts, encounters at every step and in all its diverse forms the resistance of life – whether in class struggle, in the form of a resurgence of aspirations for living work, or, in everyday life, as demands for the recognition of alterity – and must, in consequence, and in the strongest sense, take account of it.[36]

*

Returning to *The Productive Body* four decades after its initial publication, its insights into the intertwining relationships between capitalism, work and the body still seem strikingly relevant. The accelerated progress of mechanization and automation since the 1970s, far from freeing us from the drudgery of work, has only intensified the control of capital, and our own dependence on the productive body, in all areas of life.[37] New technologies of communication and surveillance are mobilized to keep us 'at' work 24/7, while discourses of leisure and recreation, psychology and 'wellness', even unemployment and welfare, have become progressively more infected by the language and imperatives of working life, to the extent that we are increasingly unable to draw distinctions between them.[38] Employers, insurance companies and private healthcare providers collect data about our health and well-being, while online algorithms, smartphones and wearable technology target precisely our physiological and emotional responses, plugging our bodies directly into the web of global capitalism.[39] Meanwhile, the physical body is itself assaulted by the environmental consequences of this same productive drive and industry, from the impact of air pollution to the migration forced on a global scale by climate crisis. Technological advances, far from the serene promise of a disembodied, digital future, have only brought the body more violently into view.

In a contemporary global context of continuing wars and dispossession, ongoing racist police brutality and growing levels of incarceration, increasingly precarious and exploitative conditions of labour, extreme inequality of access to health care and welfare, and environmental destruction, understanding and rethinking the interlinking matrices of capital, labour and bodies start to look less like a theoretical abstraction, and more like an existential emergency. Several major tendencies of capitalism either unaddressed or only briefly gestured at by Guéry and Deleule have continued to develop and grow in significance in the intervening years, and the chapters in this collection – including one from Guéry himself – take on in various ways the challenge of developing, complicating, and extending *The Productive Body*'s analysis, and of presenting new methods and approaches through which to understand the body under contemporary capitalism, contributing to a broad and growing field of related work within and outside of the academy.

Empire and colonialism for example, which, as Dan Taylor's chapter points out, are only fleetingly touched upon in *The Productive Body*, continue

to determine global flows of capital and labour, while the strategies of
racialization and racism which are their historical legacy continue to structure
embodiment under capitalism. Among those theorizing racial capitalism
today, Jodi Melamed has reckoned with the ways in which accumulation is
interlinked with violent methods of neo/colonialism, war and dispossession.[40]
Kalindi Vora understands colonial labour extraction as based not only on the
extraction of economic sources of value,[41] raw materials and labour-power but
on life itself, while Gargi Bhattacharyya has drawn attention to how histories
of slavery and colonialism continue to shape the global allocation of resources
under capitalism at present.[42] In developing Guéry and Deleule's insights to
make sense of our contemporary world, much more work will need to be
done to link the historical story they tell about the emergence of capitalism
in the West with the simultaneous and intertwined expansion of European
imperialism, and to show how histories of race and racism complicate or
reinforce the complex processes of individuation, surveillance and control
described in *The Productive Body*.

Another determination of capital notably absent from Guéry and Deleule's
analysis is the gendered division of labour and the work of social reproduction.
This has since been brought into focus by generations of socialist feminists,
who have shown that it must be at the heart of any understanding of the body
and capitalism in the twenty-first century. Recent work by Tithi Bhattacharya,
Cinzia Arruzza and Susan Ferguson, for example, positions human labour
and its reproduction as essential to capital accumulation, and examines
questions of oppression – gendered, racialized or otherwise – in this context.[43]
Marxist-feminist interrogations of gender under capitalism are expanded
from the perspective of transgender experience in a recent collection edited
by Jules Joanne Gleeson and Elle O'Rourke, which analyses the relationship
between gender and labour, intersecting with and extending some of the
claims of this collection by examining the ways in which capital shapes, but
is not able to appropriate entirely, the physical form of the body.[44] Recent and
ongoing sex worker activism raises crucial questions around the recognition
of socially reproductive labour *as* labour, the relationship of labour activism
to socially devalued forms of work and the ways in which these forms of
work interact with interpersonal and state violence. These questions have
been theorized by authors such as Melissa Gira Grant, and Juno Mac and

Molly Smith.[45] In this collection, contributions from Grace Tillyard, and Helen Charman and Christopher Law, examine the productive body in its gendered composition. Tillyard's chapter analyses how anti-abortion groups employ digital surveillance technologies to disseminate targeted anti-abortion messaging, intertwining issues of privacy and profit (i.e. production) which ultimately shore up the imbrication of reproductive futurity with capitalism's grammars of whiteness, heteronormativity and the nation state. Charman and Law explore the reproductive body in relation to a 'poetics of miscarriage', turning to contemporary lyric poetry to consider the intertwinement of (the language of) life and reproduction and the needs of capital.

Over the last half-century, capitalism has developed and expanded in ways which Guéry and Deleule were, by definition, unable to address. For their analysis to remain relevant, and to comprehend the status of work, the worker and conditions of labour today, it must be adapted and re-applied in light of new developments. Chapters by Phil Jones and by Philip Barnard and Stephen Shapiro take up this challenge, examining some of the most significant transformations in the nature of capitalism and the regulation of work. Jones examines the increasing precarity of labour within an increasingly financialized and speculative global capitalism, with workers – far from the self-valorizing 'entrepreneurs of the self' posited by some theorists – under constant pressure to offer capital the promise of future value within an increasingly competitive labour market. Barnard and Shapiro see an extension of the tendencies identified by Guéry and Deleule for capitalism to separate knowledge from embodied labourers in the emergence of new forms of 'algorithmic capitalism', where the intensified fragmentation of the social body under the conditions of neoliberalism is increasingly managed by automated systems.

The speed and scale with which capitalism has appropriated technology to its own ends testify to its single-minded drive to dominate and to instrumentalize any resource for its own purposes. This drive, identified by Guéry and Deleule in relation to scientific knowledge and the mechanization of living labour, now seems brutally apparent in relation to ever-intensifying global crises of climate change and environmental destruction. Capital's extraction of labour-power from bodies parallels, bolsters and undergirds its extraction of resources from the earth. In turn, ongoing and increasingly extreme environmental destruction and pollution condition and delimit populations, impacting upon bodies differentially in ways that entrench existing inequalities.[46] Implicitly challenging Guéry and Deleule's critique of scientific knowledge as *inherently* bound up with capitalist interests, Graham Jones makes a provocative case for Marxists to re-engage with contemporary natural science, arguing that a lack of scientific literacy has left socialists ill-equipped to respond to emerging ethical and political issues, of which climate change is the most urgent. In his own contribution, François Guéry both looks back to the original context in which he and Deleule wrote *The Productive Body*, and contends with the new challenges presented by a global capitalism which has not only outgrown the material constraints of the human body, but which also now threatens to surpass the limits of environmental equilibrium, putting itself and the planet as a whole at risk. Guéry posits a return to the body and a political ethics of care, responsibility and solidarity as the only possible way to check the uncontrolled destruction of capital.[47]

The picture of capital's permeation of the body and of life as a whole painted here is a daunting one and a bleak one. But it is not a hopeless one, and several of the chapters take up the critically important theme of resistance. Marina Vishmidt challenges the status of the 'body' as an unproblematic site of resistance, arguing that a transformative politics is possible only if we reject the tendency, frequently manifested in left theory and activism, towards substantialized concepts of the body – concepts which only reproduce a substantialist concept of value, and lead to a moralistic, rather than revolutionary, politics. Other chapters look at how *un*productive bodies challenge normative logics of capitalism, and how this can be mobilized politically. Dan Taylor, developing a dialogue between Spinoza and Marx which emerges from a reading of *The Productive Body*, takes up the problem of bodies breaking down, wearing out or self-destructing – instances of the productive body in crisis – to ask what kinds of powers of resistance are available today. Dawn Woolley examines the body as both an object of discipline and a potential site of dissent, looking at the Quantified Self 'health' movement which simultaneously promotes normative ideas about what a body should be and seeks to optimize bodies' productive capabilities. For Woolley, the fat body might, in its refusal of this 'control' and embrace of eating for pleasure, materially undermine the value system of 'health' and its correlation to productivity. Arianna Introna develops an 'autonomist cripistemology' of the productive body, taking disability as a lens through which to examine how non-normative bodies and minds function as 'faulty springs' of production, and arguing that their non-productive qualities might be key to stalling the (re)production of the productive body, and therefore the reproduction of capitalism.

We believe that the chapters brought together here demonstrate both the ongoing relevance of Guéry and Deleule's original insight, and the wealth of new directions in which this can be taken. This collection is not intended to offer a totalizing account of how bodies work and are worked under capitalism today, nor it is intended to provide a blueprint for resistance. It is, however, intended to offer an opening onto questions of work, the body and capitalism: a snapshot of the breadth and depth with which such questions may be treated, and an indication of the critical importance of such questions to better understanding, and therefore, we hope, better resisting capitalism today.

Notes

1   François Guéry and Didier Deleule, *The Productive Body*, trans. Philip Barnard and Stephen Shapiro (Winchester: Zero Books, 2014), 67. Hereafter *TPB*.

2   It is worth recognizing that the terms Global North and Global South have a contested usage. See for example: Nour Dados and Raewyn Connell, 'The Global South', *Contexts* 11, no. 1 (2012): 12–13; Shangrila Joshi, 'Postcoloniality and the North–South Binary Revisited: The Case of India's Climate Politics', in *The International Handbook of Political Ecology*, ed. R. L. Bryant (Cheltenham: Edward Elgar Publishing, 2015), 117–30.

3   Franco 'Bifo' Berardi, *The Soul at Work: From Alienation to Autonomy* (Los Angeles: Semiotext(e), 2009), 21.

4   The cheap, de-ruralized human labour that in large part constitutes artificial intelligence further erodes the myth of contemporary capitalism's 'immateriality'. In China, for example, a burgeoning industry of start-up 'data factories' employ high numbers of low-wage workers to do the work of labelling tens of thousands of images a day, in order to 'teach' AI how to differentiate between different objects such as vehicles, humans, obstacles and animals. See Li Yuan, 'How Cheap Labor Drives China's A.I. Ambitions', *The New York Times*, November 2018, https://www.nytimes.com/2018/11/25/business/china-artificial-intelligence-labeling.html; Jeanne Whalen and Yuan Wang, 'Hottest Jobs in

China's Hinterlands: Teaching AI to Tell a Truck from a Turtle', *The Washington Post*, September 2019, https://www.washingtonpost.com/business/2019/09/26/hottest-job-chinas-hinterlands-teaching-ai-tell-truck-turtle/.

5   See Brian Merchant, 'Life and Death in Apple's Forbidden City', *The Observer*, 18 June 2017, http://www.theguardian.com/technology/2017/jun/18/foxconn-life-death-forbidden-city-longhua-suicide-apple-iphone-brian-merchant-one-device-extract; Jamie Condliffe, 'Foxconn Is under Scrutiny for Worker Conditions. It's Not the First Time', *The New York Times*, 11 June 2018, https://www.nytimes.com/2018/06/11/business/dealbook/foxconn-worker-conditions.html.

6   Julie Bort, 'Amazon's Warehouse-Worker Tracking System Can Automatically Pick People to Fire without a Human Supervisor's Involvement', *Business Insider*, August 2019, https://www.businessinsider.com/amazon-system-automatically-fires-warehouse-workers-time-off-task-2019-4; Shona Ghosh, 'Undercover Author Finds Amazon Warehouse Workers in UK "peed in bottles" over Fears of Being Punished for Taking a Break', *Business Insider*, April 2018, https://www.businessinsider.com/amazon-warehouse-workers-have-to-pee-into-bottles-2018-4?r=US&IR=T.

7   Jamie Woodcock, 'The Algorithmic Panopticon at Deliveroo: Measurement, Precarity, and the Illusion of Control', *Ephemera* 20, no. 3 (2020): 67–95; Robbie Warin and Duncan McCann, 'Who Watches the Workers? Power and Accountability in the Digital Economy' (New Economics Foundation, 2018).

8   See for example Byung-Chul Han, *The Burnout Society* (Stanford: Stanford University Press, 2015); and on the blurring between life and work see for example, Carl Cederström and Peter Fleming, *Dead Man Working* (Winchester: Zero Books, 2012); Sarah Jaffe, *Work Won't Love You Back: How Devotion to Our Jobs Keeps Us Exhausted, Frustrated, and Alone* (London: Hurst Publishers, 2021).

9   Guéry and Deleule's influence on Foucault, and in particular the potential of *TPB* to act as a link between Foucauldian and Marxist traditions, has been a central focus of much of the early reception of the English translation. See for example Philip Barnard and Stephen Shapiro, 'Editors' Introduction to the English Edition', in *TPB*, 1–45; Jason Read, 'Missed Connections', *Radical Philosophy* 188 (November/December 2014): 63–4.

10   For more details on the intellectual and political context into which *TPB* was published see Barnard and Shapiro, 'Editors' Introduction'; Ed Cohen, 'Capitalizing on "The Body,"' *The Los Angeles Review of Books*, 25 July 2014, https://lareviewofbooks.org/review/capitalizing-body/.

11 Karl Marx, *Capital: A Critique of Political Economy*, trans. Ben Fowkes, vol. 1 (London: Penguin, 1990), 448. Emphasis added.

12 Marx, *Capital*, 1:449. Emphasis added.

13 *TPB*, 51.

14 Marx, *Capital*, 1:644.

15 *TPB*, 52.

16 *TPB*, 89.

17 Marx, *Capital*, 1:450.

18 *TPB*, 88.

19 *TPB*, 77.

20 *TPB*, 85.

21 *TPB*, 90.

22 *TPB*, 84, 97.

23 *TPB*, 51.

24 Karl Marx, 'Appendix: Results of the Immediate Process of Production', in *Capital: A Critique of Political Economy*, trans. Ben Fowkes, vol. 1 (London: Penguin, 1990), 1024.

25 Marx, *Capital*, 1:508.

26 *TPB*, 89.

27 *TPB*, 106.

28 *TPB*, 98.

29 *TPB*, 99.

30 *TPB*, 118, 102.

31 *TPB*, 129.

32 *TPB*, 131.

33 *TPB*, 92.

34 *TPB*, 94–5.

35 *TPB*, 99, 117.

36 *TPB*, 133.

37 See Kathi Weeks, *The Problem with Work: Feminism, Marxism, Antiwork Politics and Postwork Imaginaries* (Durham: Duke University Press, 2011); David Frayne, *The Refusal of Work: The Theory and Practice of Resistance to Work* (London: Zed Books, 2015); Peter Fleming, *The Mythology of Work* (London: Pluto, 2015); David Graeber, *Bullshit Jobs: A Theory* (London: Penguin, 2019); Helen Hester and Nick Srnicek, *After Work: The Fight for Free Time* (London: Verso Books, 2020); Amelia Horgan, *Lost in Work* (London: Pluto, 2021).

38 See for example Carl Cederström and Peter Fleming, *Dead Man Working* (Arlesford: Zero Books, 2012); Ivor Southwood, *Non-Stop Inertia*

(Winchester: Zero Books, 2013); Jonathan Crary, *24/7: Late Capitalism and the Ends of Sleep* (London: Verso, 2014); Weeks, *Problem with Work*; Frayne, *The Refusal of Work*; Lynne Friedli and Robert Stearn, 'Positive Affect as Coercive Strategy: Conditionality, Activation and the Role of Psychology in UK Government Workfare Programmes', *Medical Humanities* 41, no. 1 (June 2015): 40–7; Jaffe, *Work Won't Love You Back.*

39   See for example Carl Cederström and André Spicer, *The Wellness Syndrome* (New Jersey: Wiley Books, 2015); William Davies, *The Happiness Industry: How the Government and Big Business Sold Us Well-Being* (London: Verso, 2016); Richard Seymour, *The Twittering Machine* (London: Indigo, 2019).

40   Jodi Melamed, *Represent and Destroy: Rationalizing Violence in the New Racial Capitalism* (Minneapolis: University of Minnesota Press, 2011) and 'Racial Capitalism', *Critical Ethnic Studies* 1, no. 1 (Spring 2015): 76–85. Work by theorists such as Jackie Wang and Ruth Wilson Gilmore develops detailed critiques of carcerality and policing as key mechanisms of racial capitalist dispossession and accumulation, and Adam Elliott-Cooper has recently examined contemporary and historic Black British resistance to policing, illuminating the work of Black British activists who situate state racism as intrinsically connected to capitalism through colonialism. See Ruth Wilson Gilmore, *Golden Gulag: Prisons, Surplus, Crisis, and Opposition in Globalizing California* (Berkeley: University of California Press, 2007); Jackie Wang, *Carceral Capitalism* (Cambridge and London: MIT Press, 2018); Adam Elliott-Cooper, *Black Resistance to British Policing: Racism, Resistance and Social Change* (Manchester: Manchester University Press, 2021).

41   Kalindi Vora, *Life Support: Biocapital and the New History of Outsourced Labor* (Minnesota: University of Minnesota Press, 2015).

42   Gargi Bhattacharyya, *Rethinking Racial Capitalism: Questions of Reproduction and Survival* (London: Rowman and Littlefield, 2018).

43   Tithi Bhattacharya (ed.), *Social Reproduction Theory: Remapping Class, Recentring Oppression* (London: Pluto, 2017); Susan Ferguson, *Women and Work: Feminism, Labour and Social Reproduction* (London: Pluto, 2020); Cinzia Arruzza, 'Remarks on Gender', *Viewpoint Magazine*, 2014, https://viewpointmag. com/2014/09/02/remarks-on-gender/; and 'Logic or History? The Political Stakes of Marxist-Feminist Theory', *Viewpoint Magazine*, 2015, https://viewpointmag. com/2015/06/23/logic-or-history-the-political-stakes-of-marxist-feminist-theory/.

44   See Jules Joanne Gleeson and Elle O'Rourke (eds.), *Transgender Marxism* (London: Pluto Press, 2021).

45 Melissa Gira Grant, *Paying the Whore: The Work of Sex Work* (London and New York: Verso, 2014); Juno Mac and Molly Smith, *Revolting Prostitutes: The Fight for Sex Workers' Rights* (London and New York: Verso, 2018). In the UK, these questions have also been central to the activism of groups such as the English Collective of Prostitutes and SWARM (Sex Worker Advocacy and Resistance Movement).

46 See Hiroko Tabuchi and Nadja Popovich, 'People of Color Breathe More Hazardous Air. The Sources Are Everywhere', *The New York Times*, 28 April 2021, https://www.nytimes.com/2021/04/28/climate/air-pollution-minorities.html; Niamh McIntyre and Damien Gayle, 'Poorest Areas of England Have Less Than Third of Garden Space Enjoyed by Richest', 26 February 2022 https://www.theguardian.com/inequality/2022/feb/26/poorest-areas-of-england-have-less-than-third-of-garden-space-enjoyed-by-richest.

47 For recent work on capitalism and the environment see for example Jason Moore, *Capitalism in the Web of Life: Ecology and the Accumulation of Capital* (London: Verso Books, 2015); Andreas Malm, *The Rise of Steam Power and the Roots of Global Warming* (London: Verso, 2016); Matthew Lawrence and Laurie Laybourn-Langton, *A Manifesto for the Age of Environmental Breakdown* (London: Verso, 2021).

2

The Productive Body revisited

François Guéry Translated by Philip Barnard

'The productive body': this expression was first formulated by Marx, then adopted and transformed into a title by Didier Deleule and myself, in another time, during the last third of the twentieth century! To dust it off in 2019 and reconsider what still merits or will merit our attention in the near or distant future, several points need to be considered. Additionally, the text's contemporary relevance depends on that of Marx, and the texts that Marx himself read, used and sometimes falsified in a sense that suited him.

Marx sought to foretell a future that both did and did not turn out as he envisioned, and we, his interpreters one century later, did the same. We followed false prophecies and neglected more truthful ones. Now, in the third millennium, things may be a bit clearer: this future that was once seen, once foreseen, has become our present, and threats that Marx warned about have or have not materialized, whence the idea of evaluating his vision retrospectively by comparing it to our present. Thus the question, 'What is Marx still good for?' begins to become answerable. But the answer that begins to take shape is not 'the dictatorship of the proletariat' as a desired or undesired future. This is due not only to history's contingency but also to Marx's mistaken evaluation of the consequences of his discovery.

The Productive Body offers a response to the question of this future that has materialized into our present. This response is not obvious, so much so that, even as author of the book's first part, I was forced to do some serious labour, fifty years later, to reread and grasp my own propositions. I had to retrace the paths indicated by this dense and allusive text, which is uneven and too often imitative of other writers I then admired – for example, Deleuze, as the author of *Nietzsche and Philosophy*. But Marx's thinking dominates the whole and, fortunately, the book's mimicry is limited to its style and the particular turn given to certain concepts.

My part of the book, the first part, consists of an explication of *Capital* volume 1's historical chapters in Part 4, which retrace the history or genesis of capitalist industry. My reading of the text extrapolates from its analyses without betraying them. My basic goal was to demonstrate that rising relative surplus-value, the object of the critique of political economy, exacts a high price on a different valence, one that is neither economic nor political. By this, I mean that the human body's anthropological status, thought to have been transhistorical, now undergoes a delayed metamorphosis with catastrophic consequences. Marx indicates the disproportionate, overwhelming nature of the change: 'Manufacture ... converts the worker into a crippled monstrosity by furthering the false development of this specialized dexterity and sacrificing a whole world of productive drives and inclinations, just as in the states of La Plata they butcher a whole beast for the sake of his hide or tallow.'[1] Thus eternal man is 'butchered' [*immolé*] to increase surplus-value, and this small gain is paid for by the loss, not of man himself, but of what was previously the body's healthy limit on production's uncontrolled and unlimited expansion.

This resulting loss is, in fact, far greater than that of man alone, who had fixed the limits of his productive powers by the finite dimensions of his own body. For what is also lost is humanity's former environment or scope of activity [*rayon d'action*], both life and the planet itself, as the basis for this life. It is this view of the future in Marx's work, now greatly amplified, that today remains as a vision of our own future and of the threats that weigh upon all of human history.

My part of *The Productive Body* ends with an aporia, or, in other words, an impasse. Neither class struggle, nor the newly liberated production of capital open onto a future. Thus, history itself, which was supposed to be endowed with a 'meaning' thanks to eternal class struggle, loses that meaning in this process. This part of the book ends by evoking a universal negation of history – a *non-history* that I did not define, but which gives the lie to a resolution of working-class struggle in victory. In the meantime, both *altermondialistes* and the advocates of 'an other destiny', to use the

Heideggerian phrase, were trying to rethink this 'end of history' and give it new meaning in renewed hope or even a new *Renaissance*.[2]

An *other destiny*, other than the 'meaning of history', also presupposes an *other* point of view and an *other* mode of thinking. As opposed to universal commodification – a form of the culture of utility and all the shortsightedness and limitations this 'utility' may have – what is required is taking care of, being attentive to, and preserving *that which is*, in its own being, and thus adopting the perspective of what was previously the 'object' of commodified market exchange, destined to consume the world in all its elements. Marxian analyses of capital's growth and circulation are based on the market's expansion and reabsorption as more market capital. This is the course of things that has to be reversed or overturned.

Industrial capital threatens the planet and its peoples with an extreme crisis of commodification, and therefore of 'progress', understood as ever-increasing human power over a nature that freely supplies 'goods'. Reversing this perspective necessarily means to break with the ideology of progress. Hans Jonas has presented such an approach in *The Imperative of Responsibility*, a treatise on care or concern for the object of responsibility.[3] Jonas develops an ethics of the other that partly breaks with Heidegger's philosophy of 'care' or 'concern' (*Sorge*), as Jonas acknowledges technology's blind, irresponsible control [*emprise*] over all that exists. According to Jonas, an *other destiny* is still undefined, but we must refuse the concept of humanity's absolute sovereignty over the totality of being, its 'will' to power, as a modern imperative. I now consider that my essay in *The Productive Body* did, indeed, present capital's control over labour as 'will' and not only as selfish exploitation and calculating 'interest'.[4]

To go a step further, the ongoing threat to the planet is what matters most: an all-powerful capitalism threatens life, and thus living humanity, and thus that which humanity, as a unique living being, possesses. Effectively, both Jonas and Heidegger attribute to humanity an openness onto Being [*être*] that no other being [*étant*] possesses. Humanity responds to the call of Being [*être*]; it knows and can attest to Being, and can name it for what it is [*qu'il y a de l'être et quel il est*], which no other being on earth can do. A testimony or witnessing of Being is therefore at stake in the loss of the living world which, at this moment, is becoming a visible horizon.

To return to the theses of Marx, which are the sole object of *The Productive Body*, the starting point of this enormous threat is in the struggle of capital against 'corporation', or in other words against the human body as the boundary and limit of all production. Limit here means measure, harmony and moderated scale; transgression of this limit means excess, cacophony and uncontrollable scale. This question of the size or scale of human works [*oeuvres*] is discussed by Hannah Arendt in *The Human Condition*, which I read with great interest.[5] In 'Work' [*l'oeuvre*], the fourth part of her book, distinct from the third part on 'Labour' [*travail humain*], she develops an analysis of long-lasting works which are larger than the humanity that constructed them (buildings, above all), but also more durable – which resist the wear of time. But the instruments of industrial production are different, since they are freed from all size limitations and thus develop a limitless scope of action. They have neither longevity nor any relation to anything besides the global, and thus gigantic, market. Arendt relates this kind of work or *œuvre* to art and to thought, more so than to her third category of 'Action'. Giant productive installations such as nuclear power plants, oil-drilling rigs or oil and gas pipelines are no doubt on the scale of the Egyptian pyramids that decimated thousands of slaves during their construction, but the pyramids were not limitless. They symbolized the divine and the cosmos, relating to a non-human scale out of respect for that which surpasses humanity.

In Marx, the disproportionateness and limitlessness of the era of high capitalism is curiously, in some ways admiringly, defined, with images such as the modern 'Briareus' or 'Moloch'.[6] This is because Marx still accepts the ideology of 'technological progress' that was commonplace in his era. Likewise, the extraction and concentration of intelligence in a 'head', the true name of capitalism (from the Latin *capitulum* or *caput*), still summons us to a social reunification, a reconfiguration of the collective labourer around engineers, in a form of solidarity that may regain strength [*reprendrait ses forces*] after the onslaught of capital.[7] These perspectives nourished three generations of Soviet socialism and produced an ecological crisis equal to that of the capitalist world. This capitalist–socialist mixture must be rejected by a humanity that has threatened its own existence by serving capitalism, defined in this manner as the 'power of a head without its body', without its heart and *without* an understanding [sans *le sens*] of its responsibilities.

One final feature I want to emphasize is that this limitless, uncontrollable gigantism is also a response or reaction to a demand, and thus also a mediation, and that this contradicts capitalism's appearance of absolute autonomy and autocracy. Industrial production 'responds' to consumer demand, on a scale that corresponds to that of the consuming population, in whose service this production is developed. With the once foreseen and now achieved global expansion of the market, gigantism is achieved de facto, and, therefore, the very size of a global population driving consumption becomes a threat both to itself and to the entire ecosystem. Thus only a thorough transformation of consumerist behaviours may offer a last chance at salvation, a last chance to control a machine gone mad. The generations following mine have understood and realized this!

*

Having taken a brief and panoramic look at *The Productive Body*'s future from the perspective of a present that has exacerbated the contradictions and threats already perceived by Marx and by us as his readers, we need to examine its genesis or initial development, which contains the proofs of its relative pertinence today. How was the text composed – on the basis of what sorts of facts, ideas and actions? Testing out the points we have developed thus far can allow us to clarify arguments that may otherwise have appeared hasty, as if we had prescribed a social critique without supplying it with sufficient grounds.

The first part of *The Productive Body* reviews the chapters of *Capital* that are concerned with the historical rise of industrial capitalism – what historians call the 'industrial revolution' and its *take-off*[8] or development. It is on the basis of this American term that 'under-development' has been defined and struggled against. Historically, the industrial revolution is an English affair; more specifically, it occurred in Manchester. Friedrich Engels was a step ahead of Marx in 1843, when his *The Condition of the Working Class in England* documented and indicted this economic take-off's excesses and negative consequences for a range of social actors, who were drawn to industrial centres by the offer of wage-work, and became servants of innovative machines.[9]

Following Engels's example, Marx re-reads reports published by labour inspectors who, right from the start, had enquired into the conditions of these then-novel types of labourers. He likewise reads writers like Andrew Ure and Charles Babbage, who developed apologias for industrial development and advocated innovative social and technological measures. Marx judges and condemns this economic literature as 'bourgeois', as written from the perspective of bourgeois class interests, developing in sync with the revolution in manufacture. The readings that Marx prepared for Chapters 12 to 15 of *Capital*, volume I, trace out an extremely valuable pathway for reconstructing this crucial history of modernity. Indeed, the alphabetical 'Index of Authorities Quoted' for the volume runs to thirty-three pages (pages 1739–1772 in the *Pléiade* edition) [twenty-four pages in the English Penguin edition, 1095–1119].[10] This French edition, edited and annotated by Maximilien Rubel, is particularly valuable in that it retraces an itinerary of readings often absent from Marxist and militant publications, which tend to minimize footnotes.[11]

In this manner, Marx examines this 'productive body' as it is being born, and characterizes it in a work that is intended for a general readership and oriented to a particular point of view, partisan and critical. His account is extremely well documented on the basis of first-hand reports prepared by actors – the classical political economists up to Marx – who are a part of the industrialization process, who are equally partisan and oriented to their own points of view, but also equally solicitous about verifying, in detail, how this revolution, initially of manufacture and subsequently of large-scale industry, has managed to succeed. The paradox is that Marx can criticize only their bourgeois 'point of view', and not the concrete understanding of the terrain that they have accumulated and communicated. He depends on them for the basics, while opposing them for their point of view, angle of perception, sensibilities and 'bias'. The history he retraces is thus that of the emergence of a remarkable phenomenon, with momentous consequences: the appearance of mechanisms capable of relaying artisanal knowhow [*savoir-faire*] by recopying, on a larger scale, technical gestures inherited from tradition.

Localized in space in Manchester, this mechanical revolution likewise revolutionizes other branches of production, as it affects all the conjoined operations that result in the market for cotton fabrics, for example, the printed or plain fabrics that are first spun and then woven on now-gigantic mechanisms, initially powered by water with a system of water-wheels transmitting the motion of streams or rivers, such as the Mersey. Engels's *Condition of the*

Working Class in England opens with an evocation of this specific locale and process, but Marx, curiously, does not place such local episodes at the centre of his historical reconstruction. He offers a wider vision, always following the thread of social consequences, and examines the entire sphere or system of artisanal production that is invaded by capital, that is mechanized and industrialized as soon as motor power [*puissance motrice*] unleashes its productivity. He does not follow the precise historical genesis of mechanized industry, another name for what we describe in *The Productive Body*, but rather retrospectively reconstitutes, on the basis of the results outlined in *Capital*, the phases through which he passed in order to reach them. In other words, he presents the reader with a teleological and completed productive process, as if a premeditated intention had taken shape in a struggle to the death with the formerly productive class.

The 'class perspective' always foregrounded by Marx – for example in his early thesis on *The Difference between the Democritean and Epicurean Philosophy of Nature* (1841), where Epicurus is devalued because of his 'bourgeois point of view' – thus leads him to emphasize the class-based premeditation that guides large industrial transformations, because the dominant class obtains greater surplus-value by raising productivity and lowering the value of labour-power [*force du travail*]. *The Productive Body* is not fully wedded to this problematic because of a historical distancing related to the events of the 1960s and 1970s, which modified our perceptions of what was 'revolutionary'.

In this historical part of the text, Marx undertook a reflection on a question that the well-known 'GPCR', or Great Proletarian Cultural Revolution, tried to deal with in practice: that is, the question of an enormous and profound split between two social 'classes', one can almost say two different humanities. The British prime minister Benjamin Disraeli took up this question in his novel *Sybil; or, the Two Nations* (1845), which cuts the British nation in two: the rich on one side and the poor on the other. In the nineteenth century, this opposition between the rich and the poor is only an observation [*n'est qu'un constat*], a description of a society that is enriching itself, but in an unequal manner, in the sense that poverty appears to be an emerging injustice, a pathology linked to development, and not an eternal inequality. To struggle against this inequality is to accept development as a natural or inevitable framework for understanding history and society, even as one denounces its negative effects.

The Cultural Revolution takes on a different problem, which Marx helped to define. The Chinese Maoists aimed to extend the social, egalitarian revolution into a so-called cultural revolution in order to get to the basis of this eternal inequality and root it out. For them, the division between the rich and the poor was not rooted in the economic or social realms, but in the productive order: it is inherent to production itself. It is likewise deeper than 'technology', for it makes the latter possible.

The same goes for intelligence and its status. I mean human intelligence, which is implicated in the practice of production, in any form it takes. There is always a repetitive, mechanical element in labour – here I refer to manual labour such as spinning or weaving – but at its origin there is also, necessarily, an element of creative, shaping [*fabricatrice*] intelligence, with a view to, or vision of, an entire process spread out over time. Production is a teleology: it aims at an end and arranges means to it. It thus has an initial vision of a sequence that moves towards an end through stages, even if the men or women who execute them have no need to share in this *insight*[12] and, indeed, are often denied it.

A 'division' therefore takes place from the very start, between the initiators of the process, of the finished sequence, and those who execute it, because the process cannot do without it: it may be a division in time (with initiators preceding executors) or in hierarchy, with the initiators forcing or constraining the executors to this repetitive labour. The economic question is a supplement that is grafted onto this fundamental inequality.

This presupposes that we go beyond economism, or economic determinism. For 1968's Parisian Maoists, this path led beyond mere revisionism vis-à-vis the period's Soviet version of Marx and the binary economic rivalry of the Cold War era (the pacific coexistence of countries with different social systems), and likewise brought them into conflict with the PCF [*Parti Communiste Français*] which affirmed this same division of power.

The Productive Body was born of this question: it searches in Marx for the origin of the Great Proletarian Cultural Revolution, which was a typically 'Marxist-Leninist' concern only very partially shared by my collaborator and friend Didier Deleule, then a colleague on the faculty at Besançon, who had a contract with the publisher Mâme for a work of his choosing. Nevertheless, he agreed to address my problematic, to the point of adding references to Marx in his part of the book – references that were not originally part of his arguments.

The Great Helmsman (Mao Tse-tung, Mao Zedong) was then somewhat of a cult figure for us, and this cult lasted longer than that of Benny Lévy, the founder of the UJC-ml (*Union des jeunesses communistes marxistes-léninistes*), founded in 1966 and dissolved in 1968, for whom I confess to have retained eternal affection, but not admiration. His reversals were credible, in the end, except that the return to Sartre, and then to absolute Zionism, were the very things that, as a leader, he fiercely prohibited to all who followed the Marxist-Leninist line. I gradually lost my confidence in his decrees.[13]

Hence, *The Productive Body* is not a reflection on Marx per se but on the opportunity to use the name 'division' to address this split, gap or gulf identified by Maoist critiques. Is it correct to speak only of a 'division' between the intellectual and manual dimensions of labour [*travail*], as if we were 'dividing the work [*travail*]' between equals? If one writes, in bad French, 'the division of manual and intellectual labour' or even 'the division between … ', is that enough to obscure the gulf or canyon that industrial production hollows out between these two levels, a gap that cries out for attention as capitalism becomes industrial? I proposed to use the phrase 'productive body' to name that which is born with this application of capital to industry. When I later met Foucault, he told me that *The Productive Body* had both interested and irritated him because he would have liked to have thought of it first, and to have linked discipline and technology, schooling [*dressage*] and production, as we did.

The link with the 'cultural revolution' was quite present to my mind, because of the type of work that had been undertaken as part of the UJC-ml on the Marxist sources of the movement against the division of (or between) manual and intellectual labour. Today, with distance, I see this idea – which the Red Guard used to persecute those who had culture, knowledge, or expertise, in the name of a quasi-nihilist principle, which persists later, and even today, in the notion that whatever is not possessed by all should be possessed by none – as a superficial egalitarianism that masks deep-seated envy, rancour, resentment and hatred of qualified privileges. The Khmer Rouge, the militant political communist movement inspired by Maoism that ruled Cambodia from 1975 to 1979, tortured and massacred those who possessed knowledge and expertise in the name of this regressive 'revolution'.

Interpreted through the filter of the text of *Capital*, which examines the birth of mechanized large-scale industry, the phenomenon of this revolution became a means to combat one of the fundamentals of this gigantic development: the manner in which automation, in the form of a vast apparatus of energy-transmission and machinified execution, recuperates the entirety of prior knowhow [*savoir-faire*] that was concentrated in traditional artisanry, and that was manual in both the proper and figurative senses, because, before the advent of machinism, all domestic tools (looms, spinning wheels, etc.) were on a human scale [*taille*].

When I speak of 'human scale', I mean that these apparatuses could not exceed a body's grasp, or, at the limit, the grasp of several bodies united to operate them, and in no case could they exceed the scale [*l'ordre de grandeur*] of the energies and skills contained in human bodies, whether these be the span of its extended arms, the size and speed of its fingers, etc. The unleashing of large-scale automation [*du grande automate*] – let's say of the factory or of manufacturing – relative to human scale, has enormous meaning and consequences, which Marx attempted to clarify, and is revolutionary in more ways than one (I am thinking of the consequences for the planet). It takes on a superhuman, apocalyptic dimension, and it is here that Marx evokes 'Moloch' and 'Prometheus'.[14]

Cleary, in all this, I sought neither to resuscitate any metaphysics, nor to invent concepts 'as big and empty as abandoned lots in the city' ['*aussi gros que des dents creuses*'] – an expression Deleuze used against the 'nouveaux philosophes' who wanted to discredit him – but to keep close to, to describe, a historical reality.[15] It may falsely seem that this sort of intervention into historical affairs [*les affaires du siècle*] involves disdain for 'pure philosophy', but, classically [*au grand siècle*], to proceed in this manner is the philosopher's duty.

These views about the 'division' between intellectual-managerial and manual-productive functions are, in fact, so radical that the outcome seems blocked, for how can a revolution – a revolution that would remain productive and technological – give back to labourers what they have lost, as a result of this vast migration of their former powers? Maoist China tried an experiment that was both ridiculous and catastrophic, reducing the size of enterprises, localizing small factories and establishing the power of large numbers over a miniaturized productive apparatus: this was the 'great leap forward' that brought on famines and failed so memorably.

At the same moment, another fraud reigned in the West, with the same motives: 'overcoming Taylorism' with the development of participatory managerial methods that would create new space for individual initiative, and a long parade of 'group dynamics' that were supposed to empower labourers while retaining the structure of industry itself. Conclusive results were sought in Japan and Sweden; dreams were chased. And what remains of it all?

Thus there is a play between, on the one hand, capitalist industry as an emerging superpower and, on the other, dominated and exhausted forces whose chances of victory are vanishing. The real phenomenon of modern times is that capital sucks up the vital forces of everything, not only those of old-fashioned or so-called manual labour, and that it empties the entire earth of its forces and resources. If I had been reading Heidegger in 1972, I would have formulated my hypotheses differently, as they are corroborated by the overall critique of the destiny of the modern that he developed in the post-war period.

Heidegger offers not a 'solution' but a path, a clearing towards a certain truth of the situation: that the earth is being devastated, dispossessed of itself and placed under a form of supervision [*tutelle*] that does not protect it, but threatens it in its entirety. Intelligence is a name for what he refers to as 'seeing what is in its being' ['*voir l'étant dans son être*'], the *logos* in antiquity or 'calculation' in modernity, which reduces all beings to the 'calculable' and thus to their capacity to be potentially mastered, to the masterable. The 'division' between the manual and the intellectual, the split that *The Productive Body* brings into view, is a symptom of the vast caesura between what exists and its being [*l'étant et son être*] as it is conceived, perceived and calculated.

Therefore we should, at present, return to the root of what seems to me a philosophical error on the part of Marx and the Marxisms that followed: he should have opened his eyes onto the world and the earth, and drawn them away from 'inequalities' that sometimes produce benefits for humanity and everything that lives on the earth. To understand and appreciate better than the average person is not a curse, but a benefit for all!

*

With the benefit of hindsight, and knowing the course of events since the book appeared, we can emphasize what *The Productive Body* had to say. Condemning capitalism is a given in left political thought of the 1960s and 1970s, in France and elsewhere, and naturally the book makes its contribution by returning to Marx himself as source of the critique of modern political economy. But the historical emergence of a Maoist China in upheaval, of a people unchained against a privileged managerial [*dirigeante*] class, raised new questions about revolutionary thought that reached beyond anti-capitalism and proletarian internationalism.

Can social inequalities as such be abolished, whether capitalist or socialist? Here, the question of an *ancien régime* as opponent, whose inequalities are the foundation of political life, becomes obsolete, given that two emergent regimes have supplanted it. The revolutionary Chinese, the Red Guard, aimed to prevent a return, not to an older feudal regime, but to capitalism, which, however, had no Chinese history. The idea [*motif*] was that the managers [*cadres*] who were not sufficiently revolutionary were effectively accomplices of capitalism, which was a prophetic vision, figuratively speaking, given that China is now a great capitalist nation. They sought, therefore, a socialism that would be rigorously non-capitalist; not in the sense that the ownership of the means of production risked being privatized, but in the sense that, within socialism itself, an intellectual and organizational elite had emerged, that was capable of directing the masses and distinguishing itself from them. Here capitalism is reinterpreted, and this is *The Productive Body*'s point [*sens*]. Even if the Red Guards analysed neither words nor things,[16] they put their finger squarely, if heavily, on a key aspect of capitalism as they returned to the origin of the term in *the power of the head*. Capital is precisely the head, the *caput*, and thus also that which commands and directs, that which counts the most, an *arké* or origin, a principle. There is a power of the head, a power that is exercised on its members, on its internal and external organs, a head that both emerges from and belongs to them. The true split is here, in denying that this head belongs to the body, in the way one part exerts command [*emprise*] over the whole, and plays the role of a controlling and directing whole.

Mao lost his place as head of the Party after the disaster of his utopian politics in the 'Great Leap Forward'. He aimed at the head in order to replace it without saying so, and the militant crowds of the Cultural Revolution decapitated the accomplices of central power on the public squares. Denouncing the head was a rallying cry of the dissident Surrealists who founded the review *Acéphale* or 'Headless'.[17] And Pierre Klossowski, in his *Nietzsche and the Vicious Circle*, showed how Nietzsche, in his illness, suffering from violent headaches and vomiting, hated the head on behalf of the body and organs it dominated.[18] He condemned the head and, with it, all of culture, as by-product of the cerebral, the reign of the brain. All of these quasi-psychotic phantasms live within and haunt revolutionary thinking; anti-capitalism picked up the baton after the founding episode of the Terror and its frenzied decapitation of all that reigned since the Middle Ages.

In *The Productive Body*, following Marx, we sought in technology the root of a properly capitalist power of the head. Technology launches a migration of the power of labourers' bodies towards a head that serves capital – a head composed of engineers and their scientific knowledge [*connaissance*] of the productive process – and thereby inaugurates a new reign of the brain over the social body. The 'Vast Automaton' of productive machinery concretizes and materializes this power.[19] This is the capitalist version of the hated power. But as history moves on, in the twentieth century, technology and industry liberated from [*délivrée du*] capital, in socialist countries and even in a society that wanted to be socialist and was governed by guardians of 'historical knowledge' [*savoir*], became the targets of new radical revolts in the name of the 'social body'. We referred to the Chinese Cultural Revolution, and likewise the Khmer Rouge, that decimated urban society and the intellectual bourgeoisie in the name of a 'proletariat' which was not industrialized, but represented the fantasy of a body without a head and against the head, a body that could auto-decapitate.

Is this history finished? That seems doubtful, given the 'Arab Spring' of the early 2010s and ongoing uprisings in Europe against 'powers' that are in crisis in the early twenty-first century. New and more genuine leadership [*élites*], greater intellectual efforts [*efforts de tête*], more sober and genuinely shared reflection is needed to find our way out of the ecological rut of a planet made sick by the consumerist orgies that followed the industrial revolution of the eighteenth century. Can we replace the call to murder with calls to the calm of self-consciousness?

Notes

1 Tr. note: Karl Marx, *Capital: A Critique of Political Economy*, vol. 1, trans. Ben Fowkes (London: Penguin, 1990), 481. The German here gives *Talg*, i.e., fat or suet; tallow is made from suet, but Marx is not referring to something that has already undergone processing.

2 Tr. note: *Altermondialisme*, sometimes called alternative globalization in English, was a 1970s–80s social movement that sought alternatives to neoliberal globalization. Figures like Norwegian Gro Harlem Bruntland were leaders in this tendency. French writers and philosophers pursuing Heideggerian critiques of technology and globalization include Michel Haar, Didier Franck or Kostas Axelos.

3 Tr. note: Hans Jonas, *The Imperative of Responsibility: In Search of an Ethics for the Technological Age* (Chicago: University of Chicago Press, 1984).

4 Guéry note: See for example Heidegger's 'The Age of the World Picture' ['*Die Zeit des Weltbildes*'. (1938)], in *The Question Concerning Technology and Other Essays*, trans. with an Introduction by William Lovitt (New York: Harper Colophon, 1977), 115–54; and the discussion of European Nihilism in his *Nietzsche, volume IV: Nihilism* [1961], trans. David A Capuzzi, ed. and annotation David Farrell Krell (San Francisco: Harper & Row, 1987), 1–196.

5 Tr. note: Hannah Arendt, *The Human Condition* (New York: Doubleday Anchor Books, 1959).

6 Tr. note: The reference to the hundred-handed giant Briareus, son of Uranus and Gaia, is absent in the standard English and German texts, but appears in the French 1875 Paris edition, the Roy translation, which was overseen and approved with additions by Marx ('Traduction de M.J. Roy, entièrement revisée par l'auteur'). Where Roy & Marx give '*Le travailleur collectif, Briarée, dont les milles mains sont armée d'outils divers … .*', the standard English translation gives 'The collective worker, formed from the combination of the many specialised workers … ' (chapter 14, p. 464 in the Fowkes Penguin edition). The 1880 German edition gives, '*Mit einem Teil seiner vielen instrumentwaffneten Hände zieht der aus den Detailarbeiten kombinierte Gesamtarbeiter den Draht… .*' The oft-cited line in which interest-bearing capital 'appears as a Moloch, demanding the whole world as a sacrifice belonging to it of right … ' appears in 'Theories of Surplus-Value', in Karl Marx and Friedrich Engels, *Collected Works* digital edition, volume 32 (London: Lawrence & Wishart, 2010), 433.

7   Tr. note: Here the reference is to *The Productive Body*'s emphasis on the separation of managerial and labouring forces in capitalism, summed in the etymological derivation of capital: 'Capital is still driving the migration of productive energies into the capital or *capitulum* of the body, the head, and thereby fully living up to its name.' Francois Guéry and Didier Deleule, *The Productive Body*, trans. Philip Barnard and Stephen Shapiro (Winchester: Zero Books, 2014), 51. Hereafter *TPB*.

8   Tr. note: In English in the original.

9   Tr. note: Friedrich Engels, *The Condition of the Working Class in England* [1845] (London: Penguin, 1987).

10 Tr. note: The French *Pléiade* edition referred to here is Karl Marx, *Oeuvres I: Economie*, Préface par François Perroux, Edition établie et annotée par Maximilien Rubel (Paris: Gallimard, Bibliothèque de la Pléiade, 1965). This edition brings Rubel's commentary together with the 1875 French text of *Capital* I by M. J. Roy and Marx himself, previously mentioned here in footnote 4. In this *Pléiade* edition, Rubel has slightly revised the Roy–Marx translation. For an up-to-date summary of information about and commentary on the 1875 French edition, along with a review of the history of French-language translations and editions, see *Le Capital, livre I: Présentation, commentaires, et documents* (Paris: Editions sociales, 2018).

11 Guéry note: One should note that Althusser, author of *For Marx* and co-author of *Reading Capital*, condemned this edition on the grounds that it divided Marx's work into slices: economy, philosophy, journalism, etc. He did not acknowledge the sum of erudition it offers, which was generally absent wherever Marxism was cultivating, in that era's parlance, 'dialectical materialism' and 'historical materialism', i.e. in the Eastern countries, where knowledge of Marx remained, for this reason, incomplete and decontextualized.

12 Tr. note: In English and emphasized in the original.

13 Tr. note: Benny Lévy (1945–2003) was an influential student leader during the 1968 uprisings, above all as a member of the UEC (Union des étudiants communistes) and then as a founder and leader of the Maoist UEC UJC-ml mentioned in this paragraph, as well as the Maoist GP or Gauche prolétarienne (Proletarian Left). He was a fellow student at the Ecole Normale Supérieure with Guéry and played a key role in the particular Parisian-Maoist orientation evoked in this passage. Always a controversial figure, he went on successively to renounce Maoism, co-found the newspaper *Libération*, become a protégé and then the final secretary of Sartre, and convert to a form of Orthodox

Judaism. Thus Lévy is proverbially known in French circles as having turned 'from Mao to Moses'.

14   Tr. note: For 'Moloch', see note 4. Prometheus is evoked in *Capital* volume 1, chapter 25: 'The General Law of Capitalist Accumulation', where Marx writes that 'the law which always holds the relative surplus population or industrial reserve in equilibrium with the extent and energy of accumulation rivets the worker to capital more firmly than the wedges of Hephaestus held Prometheus to the rock' (799).

15   Tr. note: When asked, in 1977, 'What do you think of the nouveaux philosophes?' Deleuze replied, 'Nothing. Their thinking is useless [*nulle*] .... First, they proceed through big concepts, as big and empty as abandoned lots in the city [*aussi gros que des dents creuses*]. THE law, THE power, THE master, THE world, THE rebellion, THE faith, etc ....' The interview was originally published as a supplement to the journal *Minuit* 24 (May 1977) and distributed as a broadside. Now available online at http://www.generation-online.org/p/fpdeleuze9.htm.

16   Tr. note: ' ... *ni les mots ni les choses* ... ' alludes to *Les mots et les choses*, 'words and things', the original title of Foucault's *The Order of Things* (1966).

17   Guéry note: *Acéphale* – literally, *Headless* – is the title of a review that was founded and directed by Georges Bataille, along with the physician Georges Ambrosino and Pierre Klossowski. It appeared publicly in five issues from 1936 to 1939 and was accompanied by a secret society whose history is still mysterious. Klossowski later discussed the secret society, notably in *La monnaie vivante* (1970), in English *Living Currency; followed by Sade and Fourier*, trans. Vernon W. Cisney, Nicolae Morar and Daniel W. Smith (London: Bloomsbury, 2017). A facsimile edition of *Acéphale*'s full run is available as *Acéphale: religion, sociologie, philosophie, 1936–1939* (Paris: Jean-Michel Place, 1980). See also Georges Bataille, et al., *The Sacred Conspiracy: The Internal Papers of the Secret Society of Acéphale and Lectures to the College of Sociology*, ed. Marina Galletti and Alastair Brotchie (London: Atlas Press, 2018).

18   Tr. note: See Pierre Klossowski, *Nietzsche and the Vicious Circle* [1969], trans. Daniel W. Smith (Chicago: University of Chicago Press, 1997).

19   Tr. note: For 'the vast automaton', see *Capital* vol. 1 (Fowkes translation, Penguin edition), 502 and 544. Marx takes the term from Ure's *The Philosophy of Manufactures* (London: C. Knight, 1835). See also *TPB*, 88–90, 131–2.

3

Do we still not know what a body can do?
Spinoza, Arendt and *The Productive Body*

Dan Taylor

'We live, as we dream – alone.'[1] Joseph Conrad writes in *Heart of Darkness* (1899) of the debilitating individualism of the human condition. But this sense of isolation is discovered not through some aloof moment of solitude, but in being among others – the fellow opportunists, adventurers and crooks narrated in Conrad's imperialist voyage down the River Congo. Despite the esteem it's sometimes given as revealing deeper psychological truths of human existence, *Heart of Darkness* is primarily a critique of European imperialism and racism, and the destructive psychological and physical changes it wrought on its proponents. The characters find themselves increasingly alienated not just from each other but also from a certain experience of being human, of feeling passions, of being corporeal. The Europeans become disembodied, ghost-like, separated from the earth. Confronted by 'prehistoric man' – Conrad shared at least some of the racist triumphalism of his British readers – he writes that

> we glided past like phantoms ... We could not understand because we were too far and could not remember ... The earth seemed unearthly ... and the men ... No, they were not inhuman ... what thrilled you was just the thought of their humanity –; like yours – the thought of your remote kinship with this wild and passionate uproar.[2]

In *The Origins of Totalitarianism*, Hannah Arendt dedicates the second of her three-part analysis to late-nineteenth-century European imperialism and the 'Scramble for Africa'. In particular, she identifies a new ambition for unlimited expansion, as the European bourgeoisie dreamt of 'the unlimited accumulation of capital'.[3] 'Expansion is everything,' she quotes Cecil Rhodes. '[T]hese stars ... these vast worlds which we can never reach. I would annex the planets if I could.'[4] This was the 'moving principle' of the new imperialist era, a unique combination of rapacious capitalism, scientific racism and the rise of modern bureaucracy.

For Arendt, the Industrial Revolution had generated surplus capital (from increased production and decreased labour costs) and surplus people, expropriated by land enclosures and rising rents, or unemployed by cyclical economic crises and the disappearance of old forms of work. They were exiled, 'spat out' from bourgeois European society. These 'superfluous men' came from many different European states to join the various commercial expeditions like that in Conrad's tale. 'The mob', as Arendt called them, were the 'shadows of events'; they existed without necessarily being alive. They were '"hollow to the core," "reckless without hardihood, greedy without audacity and cruel without courage"', she writes, quoting Conrad's character Marlow. 'They believed in nothing and "could get (themselves) to believe anything – anything."'[5] They were a peculiarly modern person, a by-product of a new kind of productive capitalism.

The mob, dispossessed from society by the extraordinary developments in industrial production analysed in Marx's *Capital*, had coalesced around a new kind of human association, one premised on isolation and individual subsumption into wider political mass movements, like Nazism. But Arendt's point about imperialism, whose consequences for British history remain inadequately confronted, is that its concepts, processes and effects were all consequential to the rapid development of industrial capitalism. Moreover, this logic of unlimited accumulation would inevitably continue, thought Arendt, warning readers in the revised 1960s edition of the continued spectre of economically and socially superfluous men, dispossessed refugees and a collective state of 'organized loneliness' among many in the West.[6]

*

It may seem strange to begin an essay on François Guéry and Didier Deleule's *The Productive Body* (*Le corps productif*, 1972) with an excursus on imperialism, which is mentioned only once in this short, elliptical polemic.

'Since Lenin, we know that the maximum spatial extension of the productive body may be that of the planet itself, since imperialism has effectively covered its entire surface.'[7] Guéry's brief remark contains more of Arendt than Lenin's theory of imperialism, whose *Origins* were beginning to be published in French from 1972. *The Productive Body*'s demarcation of the biological, social and productive bodies (more on this shortly) also bears more than a passing resemblance to Arendt's categorization of labour and work in *The Human Condition*.[8] But imperialism gives one historical outline for thinking about the economic and political causes of the isolation and fragmentation of societal bonds (or decline of the 'social body', in its lexicon) produced by capitalism. To live as one dreams – alone – is, in Conrad's context and via Guéry and Deleule's analysis, to exist to produce economic value for the capitalist. Or, as the book formulates, to be merely a productive body and a biological body, while also alienated from the social body. Like Arendt, Guéry and Deleule seek to rediscover some kind of human agency from what Walter Benjamin called 'the rags, the refuse' of modernity, the damaged bodies and minds created by industrial capitalism.[9]

But whereas Arendt will make a case for the value of spontaneity, creativity and democratic deliberation to energize political life, Guéry and Deleule take a more difficult, circumlocutory route. One immersed in the Spinozist vitalism of Gilles Deleuze and the Althusserian conceptual framework of ideology, but which also offers an insightful and original series of responses to what we might call *the problem of June 1968*. That is, after several weeks of spectacular student and worker occupations involving up to ten million across France over May, General Charles de Gaulle was re-elected on a landslide on 23rd June with the promise of restoring civic order amid a 'communist plot'.[10] Given that, for many, France had been on the cusp of a new kind of socialist revolution, why had so many workers gone back to work and so many students given up on the occupations? 'Retour à la normale,' joked one iconic poster from May, bitterly. But had they?

New intellectual and political energies were brewing in the years immediately after, as young intellectuals came increasingly to blame the French Communist Party for apparently conspiring to subdue the demonstrations. They instead drew on the wider influence of a New Left that was more internationalist, feminist and attuned to personal and embodied forms of political oppression.

An older intellectual generation of the 1940s–1950s that had venerated Hegel, Heidegger and then the Structuralism of Merleau-Ponty and Levi-Strauss was being supplanted by ambitious new theoretical work that drew on Nietzsche, Freud and the young Marx – whom Paul Ricoeur called the 'three masters of suspicion' – alongside Spinoza.[11] Important figures within this tradition included Althusser, Foucault and Deleuze, the latter two of which were associated with a new kind of revolutionary leftism, as much pitched against existing large-scale left-wing political parties and unions as against the 'silent majority' that had supported De Gaulle.

In particular, Deleuze had recently published two incisive studies of Spinoza – *Spinoza et le problème de l'expression* (Expressionism in Philosophy: Spinoza) in 1968 and *Spinoza: Philosophie pratique* (Spinoza: Practical Philosophy) in 1970.[12] In 1969, Deleuze had moved to Paris to teach at Paris-VIII Vincennes, alongside other radical luminaries like Alain Badiou, Jacques Rancière, Jacques Lacan, Luce Irigaray and Judith Miller.[13] That same year, he met and began collaborating with the radical psychoanalyst Félix Guattari, the first fruits of which appeared as *Capitalisme et schizophrénie: L'anti-Œdipe* (Capitalism and Schizophrenia: Anti-Oedipus) in 1972. Remembering this period, François Guéry recalls seeing Deleuze lecture at Vincennes, while preparing this new material. The effect was like having a 'mental bath', becoming immersed – or even baptized – in a new kind of conceptual universe.[14]

One of the foundational questions of *Anti-Oedipus* is what Étienne de la Boétie had called, four centuries earlier, the problem of 'voluntary servitude'.[15] Why do the oppressed and exploited masses support and defend undemocratic regimes? Deleuze and Guattari write:

> Even the most repressive and the most deadly forms of social reproduction are produced by desire. … That is why the fundamental problem of political philosophy is still precisely the one that Spinoza saw so clearly, and that Wilhelm Reich rediscovered: 'Why do men fight *for* their servitude as stubbornly as though it were their salvation?' How can people possibly reach the point of shouting: 'More taxes! Less bread!'?[16]

For Deleuze and Guattari, the question had to be approached via the rubric of desire. Desire 'produces reality', and social relations are bound up by investments of desire.[17] Desire is at the foundation of everything, and can express wonderful, formidable and revolutionary power, 'calling into question the established order of a society'.[18] Hence the lengths the authorities will go to repress or redirect ('reterritorialize') these desires into more conventional, socially reproductive forms.[19] Lacan would later wryly describe this as the moral imperative of the 'service of goods' of consumer ideology: 'Carry on working, work must go on.' Which, of course, means: 'Let it be clear to everyone that this is on no account the moment to express the least surge of desire.'[20] Desire finds itself again pitched against the utilitarian, *boring* morality of the authorities.

But one problem with Deleuze and Guattari's Spinozist concept of desire is its sub-idealist, transcendental treatment. Desire seems to have a life of its own, one that predates and interrupts all forms of social inscription. If one accommodates oneself to life under a violent regime and refuses on pragmatic grounds (like the survival of one's family) to oppose it, does that therefore entail that one desires it? This may be a step too far. The question for progressive and revolutionary thinkers remains how to speak of political agency or revolutionary consciousness amid passivity and disempowerment.

Marx's solution to this question was to turn it on its head. 'It is not the consciousness of men that determines their existence,' he writes, 'but their social existence that determines their consciousness.'[21] This problem was articulated forthrightly (if less clearly) by Althusser, whose theoretical work and seminars at the École Normale Supérieure over the 1960s used Marx to explore how this social existence ideologically conditions subjects. They come to accept their own place within these wider structures as natural, realistic even, a condition achieved through the family, education system and the church. For Althusser, in his famous 1970 essay 'Ideology and Ideological State Apparatuses', 'ideology interpellates individuals as subjects'.[22] One experiences and recognizes oneself as a subject when one is hailed, for instance by a policeman in the street. Guéry has this in mind in his hyperbolic attack on the 'guards' that are said to police 'all public or private property'.[23] But Althusser still rests a great deal on the linguistic and symbolic structures within the heads of subjects to achieve this interpellation. What if passivity and disempowerment was inscribed in oneself long before one was addressed and subjected by a figure of authority – what if this passivity was not only inscribed but embodied, felt, lived through, lived alone?

It is to these questions that Deleule and Guéry's *The Productive Body* offers a fruitful contribution, with its turn to the body under capitalism, rather than the mind – and indeed, the mind's separation from the body. It presents a threefold distinction in bodies and their relation to capital: the biological, the social and the productive. The biological body concerns what sustains life. The social body corresponds to the division of labour which predates capitalism, and associated in their discussion with the guilds.[24] But the productive body relates to a peculiar separation of minds from bodies, associated with the mind-body dualism of Descartes, which has led to specializations in psychology and a growing machinification of the body. This becoming productive, becoming what is variously called a 'body-machine' and 'living machine', is to be put to use and integrated into the functional processes of capital. The power and agency of the body take on decisive significance.

It is through the power (or, indeed, weakness) of bodies under capitalism that the work makes its most startling and original contributions, taking a separate route to desire and ideology to account for a new kind of alienation of workers under modern capitalism. This is one in which, as the co-written foreword sets out, the body has become an instrument of capital, subject to a 'conversion into a means of production' which is also a 'privatization' of the body's social functions.[25] Yet from the outset, this contribution is indebted to the thought of Spinoza.

Guéry begins his half of the book with a question of the body in Spinoza. 'Spinoza said: we don't know what a body can do.'[26] The line is not an obvious place to begin with Spinoza, but bears the influence of Deleuze, who emphasized what he called this 'war-cry' found in the *Ethics*, Part 3, Proposition 2.[27] What is meant by it? The argument comes in the context of a radical turn to Spinoza in France during the 1960s, which often placed him antagonistically against the Christian mind-body dualism of Descartes. For Deleuze, Spinoza is a philosopher of immanence, the body, desire and joy. 'The *Ethics* is necessarily an ethics of joy,' he writes, 'only joy is worthwhile, joy remains, bringing us near to action, and to the bliss of action.'[28] In Deleuze's explanation of Spinoza's metaphysics, the power of substance depends on the modes which constitute it – not a top-down but a bottom-up power, a power understood and expressed through material structures and relations.[29] For Guéry, this leads to the question of a given body's power: 'We need to know what it can do, before we can worry about what it is.'[30] The body is identified early on by its power or range of activity, which effectively constitutes its essence (what it *is*). This political interest in metaphysical power is one of the central tenets of the French materialist revival of Spinoza over the late 1960s, associated with the seminars of Althusser and major publications by Martial Gueroult, Deleuze and Alexandre Matheron over 1968–1969.[31] It would lead Antonio Negri to later emphasize the productive power or *potentia* of the multitude.[32]

But what makes such a body powerful or weak? For Guéry, the 'question about power refers to an experience of perception about intensity, an experience of knowledge'. Beyond the Deleuzian framework ('intensity', 'perception'), this definition raises more questions than answers. What is an intensity? What is the nature of this perception or knowledge? Are these not the mental, psychological categories the book is attempting to think its way around? This problem is reminiscent of the earlier critique of Deleuze and Guattari on desire – how can we speak of the revolutionary or insurrectionary power of a given desire, intensity or 'experience of knowledge' when it remains embedded in the material structures that the authors are supposedly deploying it against? Indeed, throughout the work, both Guéry and Deleule struggle to articulate in what way bodies might become more powerful, that is to say, less productive, and in Deleule's latter half of the book, part of 'the resistance of life'.[33]

But we can reconstruct an account through how the pair describe a given body's weakness. This occurs principally in two ways – by an identification with and internalization of the machinic nature of modern work, or becoming a productive body; and by a 'privatization' of the individual who becomes disconnected or alienated from the social nature (or body) of this work, and so separated from others.[34] These two ways are accomplished by a more general conceptual separation or 'scission' of minds from bodies, associated with Cartesian dualism, which Deleule associates with the development of the discipline of psychology.[35] Let's consider each in turn, before exploring how a kind of Spinozan monism is brought against this duality.

The becoming-productive of the body forms the bulk of the argument. Early on, productivity is distinguished from a more general condition of production. 'We call it the *productive* body, not the *producer*', as Guéry writes, as it 'exists for and by the consumer's products. To be the proprietor of products is to dominate production'.[36] This dense, unclear formulation – characteristic of the text – implies that productivity involves a more direct integration of the individual's body (their biological body) into the reproductive processes of industrial capitalism. Guéry's analysis explores this through Marx's *Capital* Volume I, Part 4, through the concept of relative surplus-value, achieved in Marx's analysis by a specialization in production through machinery, which reduces the cost of labour and increases the surplus-value to the capitalist of the completed product. For Guéry, this is also achieved by a profound identification with the new machinery of production, and of conceiving oneself as mere 'accessories or substitutes for [its] mechanical organs'.[37] What it reveals is that 'capital was obliged to incorporate these elements all over again, to integrate them into a new body, which is the productive body'.[38] But how precisely were these elements incorporated?

Deleule offers more detail on this count. Once more, there's an implicitly Spinozan framework of bodily power used, wittingly or not. 'For what this metamorphosis brings about is first and foremost an increase in power'.[39] Without understanding this 'fundamental point', everything else remains mysterious:

> In effect, the idea is not that the machine should be able to replace living things in a project of conquest that is impossible for them, but rather that in its essence life is conquest and that the machine, to accomplish its function, must be inscribed in a motion that prolongs that of the living organism.[40]

In other words, the emergence of bourgeois capitalism involves a new philosophical perspective of life, one in which life is conceived in Promethean terms as a 'conquest' and 'mastery' over nature.[41] While it goes unremarked, this view could be reinforced with C. B. Macpherson's thesis of a tradition of 'possessive individualism' in early modern philosophy, contemporaneous with the rise of this mode of production, particularly in Hobbes and Locke, which had been translated into French in 1971.[42] 'The body-machine is both life affirmed in all the exuberance of its dominating movement', Deleule writes, and 'the machine required for the development of effective potentialities, required as the guarantee of functional movement'.[43] The biological body becomes 'a tool' of the new machinic processes of capital, and increasingly comes to be experienced as mere machinery ('machinified'), or what Guéry called the mechanical organs, under the direction of a foreman, manager or more distant and magical economic forces.[44]

The second key contribution of their argument theorizes how this tighter integration of the body into the productivity of capitalism also results in a decline of the individual's social relations and make-up. In their co-written foreword, the pair offer a useful corrective to Althusser and indeed to Foucault's later concept of disciplinary power. All the sites of disciplinary power – the family, church, school, prison, hospital, factory – which imply an 'intended socialization' are 'replaced by a privatization of social functions'.[45] Productivity involves a tendency 'toward the privatization of these organs, toward their integration within the productive body as elements of production'.[46] The old sites of disciplinary socialization serve to produce pliable and productive bodies, no longer slowed down by solidarity, friendship or workplace militancy. Industrial specialization involves a de-skilling of the old 'work' (in the Arendtian sense) of the artisan and the guilds, and a new world in which creative genius belongs not to the worker but to the tool. Workers become expendable, superfluous, a 'perfected tool',[47] like that of the Fordist conveyor belt and the rise of piecework.

Some of the most convincing material in demonstration of this comes via Marx's discussion of the modern factory. 'Their unification into one single productive body, and the establishment of a connection between their individual functions, lies outside them,' Marx writes of the modern workforce.[48] 'These things are not their own act, but the act of the capital that brings them together and maintains them in that situation.' Workers experience what might be called a double alienation: alienated not just from their own social bodies and into the machines, but also from any sense of agency or participation in the production process. As Guéry notes, quoting Marx, 'the interconnection between their various labours (those of the wage labourers) confronts them, in the realm of ideas, as a plan drawn up by the capitalist, and (that) the unity of their collective body appears to them, practically, as his authority, as the powerful will of a being outside them, who subjects their activity to his purpose.'[49] They are like the lonely men of 'the mob' in Arendt, disempowered, de-skilled, hollowed out, no longer quite believing in anything except their individual survival.

Whereas Deleuze's Spinozism emphasizes joy and becoming, Guéry and Deleule focus more on how bodies are restricted, subjugated and disempowered.

This extends to what they call the 'illusion' of Trotskyism, that the body possesses a natural productivity that is then expropriated by parasitical capital. While Deleule's later analysis will unwittingly make a fairly similar claim for the body's living power against dead capital, it's the peculiar Spinozism of what happens next that's interesting. 'From a Spinozan perspective that has been adopted in the Althusserian exegesis,' Guéry writes, 'this is a simplistic conception of the illusion. Attacking the illusion will accomplish nothing unless we do away with its real basis.' But what was the Althusserian exegesis?

Althusser didn't publish anything substantial on Spinoza over this period – one rumour has it that his plans were shelved after reading Matheron's *Individu et communauté chez Spinoza* (1969), which had apparently made his own argument better than he could have done.[50] But Spinoza had been a vital interlocutor in Althusser's seminars and research on ideology. What Althusser saw as demonstrated in Spinoza's analysis of the religious customs, ceremonies, historical narratives and societal rules of the Jewish people in the *Theological-Political Treatise* was 'the materiality of ideology'.[51] For Althusser, this provides 'perhaps the first historical form of a theory of ideology', in establishing how bodies were conditioned into collective obedience through cultural rites and shared imaginaries.[52] As Althusser writes elsewhere, 'ideology' exists both as a real (i.e. economic) and as an 'imaginary' or 'lived' relation.[53] The two are mutually reinforcing: to function effectively in the former, our desires and identifications must be bound up with the latter.

Again, to think from a Spinozan perspective is to think from one of bodies and their power, but one that also recognizes that their power is established and conditioned by formidable social structures. But for Spinoza, one can only overcome a state of slavery (*servitudo*) by learning to understand what causes harmful ideas or passive thinking, like false representations of nature and the world, or powerful sad passions like hatred and fear, which often compel us to obey tyrants.[54] It requires something along the lines of what second-wave feminists of this period would call 'consciousness-raising' – meeting with others and sharing one's experiences of disempowerment, in order to better understand their causes and how to challenge them. A form of bodily power that is necessarily social and interrelational then. But in Spinoza's argument it also requires a return to the state, to capturing and reorganizing the political state as a democratic, liberal republic. The purpose or 'end of the republic is really freedom', he says in the *Theological-Political Treatise*.[55] His arguments for the state and the political were often overlooked by his Marxist readers over this period. One finds few similar sources of enthusiasm for the state during this time, with the exception perhaps of Arendt, and her emphasis on establishing political spaces of deliberation and democratic decision-making.

Spinoza's thought also challenges Descartes's dualism, an important point for *The Productive Body*. Whereas Spinoza's monism is metaphysical – there is one substance, of which a body and a mind are two different attributes of one being that exist in parallel, sometimes called 'parallelism' – Guéry and Deleule historicize dualism as reflecting a separation or scission between minds and bodies that reflected the intensification of capital into European society. For Guéry, this scission is also one of 'the body from its powers' – while the body is reduced to mere machinery, the mind is elevated to the origin and force of production.[56] In the combination of the two, he writes, the 'body-machine thesis is supplanted by the humanist thesis that makes *knowledge* (in contrast to the more practical, social and less aloof *know-how*) the weapon with which man makes himself "master and possessor of nature," *and … of the machine-like nature* of the body in general'.[57] In other words, the mind (or 'capital', riffing on the etymology of the latter as relating to the head or top) becomes the place of knowledge and management over passive, mechanical, desocialized bodies. This point is continued in Deleule's account of Descartes, who had famously considered bodies as like mechanical things, operated (in humanity) by the soul through the animal spirits. In response, Deleule pitches up a certain parallelism. Quoting André Godfernaux ('The goal of parallelism is precisely this: to put what is called the mind, this imaginary edifice constructed through the centuries, back into its real home, the body'), Deleule provides a rare instance of clarity around the book's intentions: 'The goal of our work will be precisely to determine what sort of body this is, how it is put together, and how it sustains itself.'[58]

As readers will know, this concludes a section that had begun with a delightful, unexpectedly light-hearted phenomenology of touch, as a 'pair of iron calipers with cork tips at the ends' explore what a given body can do.[59] Indeed, before turning to some of the lingering problems of the account, it's worth contextualizing this within a wider *secret history of bodies*, as opposed to the rather tired canonical history of ideas. A form of active enquiry that explores how bodies are constituted by, communicate, imitate, inscribe, reinscribe, subvert or actively resist societal norms, rules and 'acceptable' pastimes and occupations, from work to sex to definitions of leisure. One in which transmission occurs not through the intellectual influence of a printed *magnum opus* say, or a family tree of conceptual development led by Great Men, but through places and spaces of relationality;[60] through encounters with others, be they public or private, marked as much by affects of love, care, solidarity or humour as of hatred, anger or loneliness – the latter characterizing the private retreat of the 'productive body' so usefully outlined by Guéry and Deleule.

The secret history of bodies draws on Foucault's method of genealogy – 'a historical investigation into the events that have led us to constitute ourselves and to recognize ourselves as subjects of what we are doing, thinking, saying'.[61] It serves as a counterpoint to the prevailing phenomenology of Husserl and Merleau-Ponty, with its supposition of a raw, unmediated, transparent experience of the mind or the body. Such an experience, which Derrida dismissed as a 'metaphysics of presence',[62] would be also economically conditioned, if we keep in mind Marx's claim that it is our social existence that determines our consciousness, and not vice-versa. A secret history of bodies then is alert to how social and economic forces suffuse, empower or restrict the very range of what our bodies can do, feel, act or act on, reciprocate, exchange. Yet it remains secret by eluding or being overlooked, remaining hidden in plain sight, by histories whose focus is predominantly on cultural texts and ideas.

What would be the standpoint of the body on industrial production? Guéry suggests this question later in the work, in asking us to consider Marx as a physician who studies the 'physiology of manufacture' and finds everywhere 'sickness, torture and enfeeblement'.[63] What does the doctor prescribe? While Marx often invoked monstrous imagery, Guéry and Deleule suggest images of physical decay – 'contagion', 'parasitic', the 'sick patient'.[64] But both seem overwhelmed by what they conceive as the power of capital's *will* – one which has the power to animate and control the undead productive bodies of the workers under its management. Against the gruelling onslaught of modern capital, Guéry recommends only a war of attrition, as unemployed intellectuals attempt to forge transient alliances with proletarians and the wider 'forces of non-history', like a 'paradoxical weed that springs furiously from the ground after every attack'.[65] Meanwhile, Deleule appeals not to any existing social or political forces, but to a distant, eschatological principle of life itself, in opposition to death. While hinting tantalizingly at the possibilities of the standpoint of the body, both writers ultimately row back to vague divinations that cannot empower bodies to collectively become forces of history, or at least their own history. In this they might have drawn on developments in other parts of the post-1968 New Left, like processes of 'consciousness-raising' mentioned earlier, vital to a new wave of feminist activism in this period, outlined in the Anglophone work of Carol Hanisch, Kathie Sarachild and others, or in France, in organizations like *La Mouvement de libération des femmes* (MLF).[66] Or, among wider industrial struggles, in practices of mutual aid and worker self-management that had shown fleeting possibilities in the May 1968 occupations, like of Rhône-Poulenc (Vitry) or Renault Cléon and Billancourt – forms of collective organization by which individuals become more powerful, collectively.[67]

On one level, this position justifiably concedes to the continued expansion of capital's power over everyday life, which grew over this period and has subsequently intensified with the shift to post-Fordist or neoliberal capitalism and decline of unionized labour (presaged here with references to 'surveillance', 'software' and the rise of 'temp work').[68] *The Productive Body* can be fruitfully read alongside Deleuze's 1990 'Postscript on the Societies of Control' in this respect.[69] Both respond in different ways to the problem of June 1968, in a fusion of the economic, the cultural and the psychological. But the argument is too fatalistic: a secret history of bodies would richly incorporate the many instances of the subjects of capital not merely preferring not to – as per Herman Melville's Bartleby, an important resource for this period – but actively disrupting, protesting or refusing, as bodies occupying streets, workplaces and public places. And, sometimes, succeeding.

*

In Part 8 of *Capital*, Volume I, Marx gives an historical outline of the emergence of capitalism. 'Primitive accumulation' is marked by violence and terror, as powerful and ambitious figures expropriate common land and impose forced labour on the poor. In characteristically grotesque imagery, 'capital comes dripping from head to toe, from every pore, with blood and dirt'.[70] While focusing on early modern Europe, Marx was aware of an accelerated form of primitive accumulation taking place in the imperialist race for Africa. But whereas Marx believed capitalism would inevitably collapse through its own internal economic conditions, Arendt's analysis of late-nineteenth-century capitalism identified two additional features key to its adaptation and survival: the development of an extensive and powerful state bureaucracy, with which it became interlinked, and the creation of a new kind of human nature: one not merely befuddled by the opiates and false consciousness of the capitalist superstructure, but affectively conditioned to fear and distrust others and to uncritically obey authority.

Addressing this loneliness in the third part of Arendt's *Origins*, Claude Lefort argues that Arendt 'underestimates' what he considers 'one of the most characteristic features of fascism and communism, namely the attempt to create in the social sphere a species of bodies in which individuals are united'.[71] But this overlooks one of Arendt's more startling points: the loss of reliable social bonds (being 'deserted by all human companionship') is conditional to the isolated individual identifying not with peers but wider mass movements of global, historical ambition.[72] In other words, individualism is conditional to mass conformity and obedience. But in the phrasing of Deleule, this individualism is, if not dead, then half-alive. It describes the miserable persistence of individual minds, whose scission is not just from other minds, but also from their own body's power of acting, its joyous passions and electrifying desires.

By the Spinozist stakes of Guéry and Deleule, we still do not know what a body can do. Our own era is shaped by increasing automation, while work itself becomes more precarious, 'self-employed', subject to surveillance and management. Can we speak of an agency that belongs only to the body, and not the mind? This would involve a shift away from exploring workers' ideas about their subjection, something necessarily limited and difficult to accomplish given the decline of the social body, towards the behaviours and breakdowns of bodies. Just as, in recent years, mental illness has been politicized as an effect of living under the insecurity of late capitalism, could we also politicize bodily disorders and breakdowns, like off-work sickness, anxiety disorders or stress? Nic Murray suggests that with the decline of trade union power, the 'experience of distress' that can give rise to longer illness constitutes 'a form of embodied resistance to the current nature of work'.[73] Might we speak then of some bodily agency, even resistance, however desperate, in the ways that say physical tics and catatonic states effect non-compliance? In a recent reading of Freud's essay 'Mourning and Melancholia', Judith Butler has written of 'mania' as an insurrectionary force that effects a 'dis-identification' from the status quo in response to a lost-loved object.[74] Whereas melancholia involves a process of self-beratement and self-destruction, as the self refuses to let go of this loss and internalizes it, mania actively renounces this loss, breaks bonds and refuses reality, challenging the internal tyranny of the super-ego. By the terms of Guéry and Deleule, the biological body breaks down, sabotaging the productive body. For Butler, in the unrealism of such a 'refusal' is a struggle for life itself.[75]

If so, it gives little hope for political resistance. In the UK at least, off-work sick days are at their lowest level on record, as people increasingly work when fatigued or ill, reflecting the precarity of employment.[76] Figures also indicate rising rates of mental illness among the most precarious – often young, female, of minority ethnicity;[77] while life expectancy rates between the wealthiest and poorest have significantly widened (one recent measure gives 9.3 years for women, 7.5 for men).[78] This reflects one of the more serious blind-spots of *The Productive Body* – that there is no universally singular experience of embodiment, but that capitalist (and other) ideologies gender, racialize and classify bodies in different ways.

Instead, via Spinoza, we could consider the affects, or ideas of the body's affections, which involve an increase or decrease in our body's power of acting. Affects like hope, fear, anger and love indicate how given bodies experience and persist through capitalism. The recent turn to the affects in critical theory[79] gives a rich domain to think through the question of why the masses seemingly and willingly 'become subjugated', in Guéry's phrase, which *The Productive Body* does not answer.[80] But to focus purely on affective states, like collective joy, radical happiness or anxiety, is to overlook what the affect itself signals: a given body's power of acting, which is conditioned by their relations with others. Joy doesn't beget joy, power does. To know what a body can do, we need to know what makes a body powerful.

In contemporary thought, these questions were explored by the late cultural theorist Mark Fisher, who described 'mandatory individualism' as an effect of living in the miserable, boring, desocialized spaces of capitalism.[81] Drawing on a similar brew of 1960s counterculture and Spinoza in his final, unfinished manuscript *Acid Communism*, he suggested that we need to rediscover 'the spectre of a world which could be free'.[82]

While the form of this spectre remains necessarily elusive, *The Productive Body* suggests a process by which we might approach such a freedom. It would be through collective consciousness-raising of a universal, pluralistic sort. This would not involve the restrictive group identifications of, say, nationalism, nor would it involve what Deleule presciently described as a brand of "'empathy-spontaneity-creativity" … accompanied by its trusty sidekick, "wellbeing"'.[83] The abundance of well-being meditation apps and self-help books that have flooded today's market provide an invaluable function, making the immediate present more tolerable in ways that utopian daydreams do not.[84] But they cannot accomplish more than that. Treatments that focus solely on an individual's self-narrative or neurochemistry continue to perpetuate the productive at the expense of the social. They may increase (or at least reduce what impairs) an individual body's power of acting, but without a lasting collective re-foundation and transformation in making bodies more powerful under neoliberal capitalism – through reductions to enforced work, debt and the creation of places of collective joy and liberating encounters – such bodies are likely to still find themselves distant from others, depressed, alone. What a secret history of bodies might instead call for is bonds of touch, collectivity and solidarity with others, through which bodies affect and are affected by one another, increasing their powers exponentially.

Notes

1   Joesph Conrad, *Heart of Darkness* (London: Penguin, 2007), 33.

2   Conrad, *Heart of Darkness*, 43–4.

3   Hannah Arendt, *The Origins of Totalitarianism* (New York: Harcourt Brace, 1979), 137.

4   Arendt, *Origins*, 124.

5   Arendt, *Origins*, 189.

6   Arendt, *Origins*, 478. Part 3 would continue to be revised until 1966.

7   François Guéry and Didier Deleule, *The Productive Body*, trans. Philip Barnard and Stephen Shapiro (Winchester: Zero Books, 2014), 62. Hereafter *TPB*.

8   Translated into French in 1961.

9   Walter Benjamin, *The Arcades Project*, ed. Rolf Tiedemann, trans. Howard Eiland and Kevin McLaughlin (Cambridge, MA: Belknap, 2002), 860.

10   For a good historical assessment, see Julian Bourg, *From Revolution to Ethics: May 1968 and Contemporary Thought* (Montreal: McGill-Queen's University Press, 2007), 24.

11   Paul Ricoeur, *Freud and Philosophy*, trans. Denis Savage (New Haven: Yale University Press, 1970), 33.

12   Translated into English in 1990 and 1988 respectively.

13   On Vincennes Paris-VIII, see François Dosse, *History of Structuralism. Volume 2*, trans. Deborah Glassman (Minneapolis: University of Minnesota Press, 1997), chapter 14.

14   Guéry said this during his keynote lecture at 'The Body Productive' conference, 8th December 2018 at Birkbeck, University of London.

15   Étienne de La Boétie, *Discourse on Voluntary Servitude*, trans. James B. Atkinson and David Sices (Indianapolis: Hackett, 2012), 17.

16   Gilles Deleuze and Félix Guattari, *Anti-Oedipus*, trans. Robert Hurley, Mark Seem and Helen R. Lane (Minneapolis: University of Minnesota Press, 2003), 29.

17   Deleuze and Guattari, *Anti-Oedipus*, 30.

18   Deleuze and Guattari, *Anti-Oedipus*, 116.

19   Deleuze and Guattari, *Anti-Oedipus*, 257–62.

20   Jacques Lacan, *Seminar VII: The Ethics of Psychoanalysis*, ed. Jacques-Alain Miller, trans. Dennis Porter (New York: W. W. Norton, 1997), 318.

21   Karl Marx, *A Contribution to a Critique of Political Economy*, ed. Maurice Dobb, trans. S. W. Ryazanskaya (New York: International Publishers, 1970), 21.

22   In Louis Althusser, *Lenin and Philosophy and Other Essays*, trans. Ben Brewster (New York: Monthly Review, 1971), 170.

23   *TPB*, 57.

24   Particularly by Guéry, *TPB*, 66–72.

25   *TPB*, 51.

26   *TPB*, 57.

27   Benedict de Spinoza, *Ethics*, trans. Edwin Curley (London: Penguin, 1996), 71; Gilles Deleuze, *Expressionism in Philosophy: Spinoza*, trans. Martin Joughin (New York: Zone, 1992), 255.

28   Gilles Deleuze, *Spinoza: Practical Philosophy*, trans. Robert Hurley (San Francisco: City Lights, 1988), 28.

29   Deleuze, *Expressionism in Philosophy*, 11.

30   *TPB*, 57.

31   For an historical overview, see Knox Peden, *Spinoza Contra Phenomenology* (Stanford: Stanford University Press, 2014).

32   E.g. *The Savage Anomaly* (1981) and *Empire*, with Michael Hardt (2000).

33   *TPB*, 133.

34   *TPB*, 51.

35   Guéry, *TPB*, 65; Deleule, *TPB*, Part 2, Chapter 2.

36   *TPB*, 60.

37   *TPB*, 90.

38   *TPB*, 63.

39   *TPB*, 103.

40   *TPB*, 103.

41   *TPB*, 104.

42   C. B. Macpherson, *La Théorie politique de l'individualisme possessif* (Paris: Gallimard, 1971 [1962]).

43   *TPB*, 103.

44   *TPB*, 105.

45   *TPB*, 51.

46   *TPB*, 52.

47   *TPB*, 83.

48   *TPB*, 74 (and the only instance of 'productive body' in *Capital*).

49   *TPB*, 74, 76.

50   In English, the title would be *The Individual and Community in Spinoza*, though the work has yet to be translated. The Althusser anecdote appears in Ted Stolze, 'Revisiting a Marxist Encounter with Spinoza', *Crisis and Critique*, 2, no. 1 (2015): 153.

51   Louis Althusser, 'The Only Materialist Tradition, Part 1: Spinoza', trans. Ted Stolze, in *The New Spinoza*, ed. Warren Montag and Translator (Minneapolis: University of Minnesota Press, 1997), 3.

52   Althusser, 'The Only Materialist Tradition', 9.

53   Louis Althusser, *For Marx*, trans. Ben Brewster (London: Verso, 2005 [1965]), 233–4.

54   Paraphrasing *Ethics*, Part 5, Proposition 10, in *The Collected Works of Spinoza: Volume I*, trans. Edwin Curley (Princeton: Princeton University Press, 1985).

55   In *Collected Works: Volume II*, trans. Curley (as above, 2016), 346.

56   *TPB*, 65.

57 *TPB*, 80.

58 *TPB*, 118; Godfernaux, 'Le parallélisme psycho-physique et ses conséquences', *Revue Philosophique de la France et de l'Étranger*, 58 (1904): 499.

59 *TPB*, 110.

60 Some theoretical precursors for this approach might include Foucault's later writing on embodiment and power, e.g. *Discipline and Punish: The Birth of the Prison* (1975), as well as in the field of relational autonomy, e.g. Catriona Mackenzie and Natalie Stoljar (eds.), *Relational Autonomy: Feminist Perspectives on Autonomy, Agency, and the Human Self* (New York: Oxford University Press, 2000). It might draw inspiration from practises of workers' enquiry, undertaken in the late 1960s/early 1970s by Italian radical leftists – a form of knowledge-production from below that is embedded in existing social relations while seeking to transform them. (For an introduction, see Marcelo Hoffman, *Militant Acts: The Role of Investigations in Radical Political Struggles* (New York: SUNY, 2019), chapter 3.)

61 Michel Foucault, 'What Is Enlightenment?', in *The Foucault Reader*, ed. and trans. Paul Rabinow (New York: Pantheon, 1984), 46.

62 Jacques Derrida, *Of Grammatology*, trans. Gayatri Chakravorty Spivak (Baltimore: Johns Hopkins University Press, 2016), 24.

63 *TPB*, 64.

64 *TPB*, 62, 65.

65 *TPB*, 95.

66 E.g. Carol Hanisch, 'The Personal Is Political' [1969]; Kathie Sarachild, 'A Program for Feminist Consciousness-Raising' [1968], both in Barbara A. Crow (ed.), *Radical Feminism: A Documentary Reader* (New York: NYU Press, 2000), 113–16; 273–6.

67 These occupations were however short-lived and sometimes only involved a small amount of the workforce. The Citroën strike committee was criticized for being more focused on arranging games of ping-pong and cards than workers' education (are both incompatible?). In the UK, the 1976 Lucas Plan indicates another opportunity for workplace self-management in which workers were actively involved in producing an alternative plan for an aerospace company facing large redundancies and relocation. On 1968 French worker movements, see Michael Seidman, 'Workers in a Repressive Society of Seductions: Parisian Metallurgists in May-June 1968', *French Historical Studies*, 18, no. 1 (Spring 1993): 255–78.

68 *TPB*, 66, 77, 81.

69   This originally appeared as 'Post-scriptum sur les sociétés de contrôle' in *L'autre journal*, 1 (May 1990), and translated into English under the above title in *October*, 59 (1992).

70   Karl Marx, *Capital*, trans. Ben Fowkes, vol. 1 (Harmondsworth: Penguin, 1982), 926.

71   Claude Lefort, interviewed in 'Hannah Arendt et "atomisation de la société"', *France Culture*, dir. Michel Bossuet (1996), https://www.franceculture.fr/philosophie/hannah-arendt-et-atomisation-de-la-societe.

72   Arendt, *Origins*, 474.

73   Nic Murray, 'No Crying in the Breakroom', in *The Work Cure*, ed. David Frayne (Monmouth: PCCS, 2019), 45.

74   Judith Butler, *The Force of Nonviolence* (London; New York: Verso, 2020), 167 [emphasis removed]. While Butler sounds a note of caution, suggesting mania as instead being a possible cipher for insurrection, this desperate position could do more to confront the personal harm such states can cause not just the sufferer, but those around them. Mark Fisher offers another politicization of mental health via anxiety and depression that deals more thoroughly with this issue in 'The Privatisation of Stress', *Soundings* 48 (2011), in which he acknowledges the influence of David Smail, an NHS clinical psychologist, e.g. *The Origins of Unhappiness* (London: HarperCollins, 1993).

75   Cf. Herbert Marcuse's 1964 call for an equally desperate but utopian 'Great Refusal' against 'that which is' – consumer society, positive thinking and the apparent inevitability of capitalism's historical success – *One-Dimensional Man* (Abingdon: Routledge, 2007), 66.

76   ONS, 'Sickness Absence Falls to the Lowest Rate on Record', 2018, www.ons.gov.uk/employmentandlabourmarket/peopleinwork/employmentandemployeetypes/articles/sicknessabsencefallstothelowestratein24years/2018-07-30.

77   NHS, 'Mental Health of Children and Young People in England', 2017, https://digital.nhs.uk/data-and-information/publications/statistical/mental-health-of-children-and-young-people-in-england/2017/2017.

78   Gareth Iacobucci, 'Life Expectancy Gap between Rich and Poor Widens', *BMJ* 2019; 364:l1492.

79   E.g. Brian Massumi's influential 1995 essay 'The Autonomy of Affect', in *Cultural Critique,* 31, 83–109. Massumi also translated Deleuze and Guattari's *A Thousand Plateaus* into English, where the affects (a Spinozan concept) are extensively discussed.

80   *TPB*, 90.

81 Mark Fisher, *k-punk: The Collected and Unpublished Writings*, ed. Darren
    Ambrose (London: Repeater, 2018), 757.

82 Fisher, *k-punk*, 753.

83 *TPB*, 131.

84 One might consider them alongside the rise of individual-orientated exercise
    regimes (running, gyms, cycling, yoga), and the ubiquity of prescribed
    antidepressants.

4

Corporeal and abstract: Is there a 'left biopolitics' of bodies?

Marina Vishmidt

The question of the regulation of bodies and the valences of concepts such as biopolitics and biopower has been emerging with increasing salience and force in global politics, arguably since austerity regimes were widely embraced in the West a decade ago, or since the 'migration crisis' of the mid-2010s which continues in the present. Undoubtedly, it has become a focus with a new kind of urgency during the coronavirus pandemic. This has been a time marked by the vast disproportion between the numbers of those who are exposed to the pandemic's management and the numbers of the direct casualties of the virus itself. The former also breaks down, at least in the more lightly regulated polities, into those who can afford to abide by public health guidelines and those who cannot, due to the 'pre-existing conditions' of racism and poverty that exert effects at least as lethal as diabetes or asthma (with which they are already directly correlated). With various degrees of lockdown as the primary face of this management, state-enforced vs bottom-up approaches to dealing with the threat to health and social reproduction have come to constitute the poles of a debate unfolding in real time, reports detailing an experiment conducted in and on people's lives right now. Marxist critical theorist Panagiotis Sotiris has made one of the most visible contributions here, proposing that a 'democratic biopolitics' can be envisioned as a way of practicing social solidarity in punctual or long-term states of emergency. He opposes this to the sinister authoritarian tint the term 'biopolitics' carries in most critical accounts, as in a series of dubious interventions by Giorgio Agamben.[1] The proposition of a 'biopolitics from

below' or 'from the left' echoes much of the optimism, as well as conceptual
ambiguity, that characterizes social reproduction theory. This echo consists of
an inability to think – as opposed to simply posit – the necessary antagonism
between the social reproduction of the oppressed and the social reproduction
of capitalism.[2] However, in 'left biopolitics' the problem is sharpened by the
attempt to re-appropriate a concept initially developed to talk about capitalist
modernity's management of populations – with the isolated, vulnerable
body as nucleus – in order to develop a theory of emancipatory care, which
is not similarly bound by the biopolitical imperatives of control, extraction
and subjectivation as asset and entrepreneur, but takes dependency and
vulnerability as its compass points.[3] The pedagogy of suffering bodies, however,
is mute, and their needs will never be ameliorated *at scale* by anything but a
state, in abeyance of other consequential social transformation. For this, as
well as other reasons I will go on to enumerate, a 'left biopolitics' that takes
the suffering body as the baseline of a new politics of mutually administered
social solidarity has serious difficulties. At the same time, however, it seems
to make intuitive sense. This reflects the fact that a now-established political
vernacular takes the primacy of 'bodies' as axiomatic to all emancipatory
narratives.

This chapter will thus explore how this discourse of 'bodies' became
ubiquitous and, indeed, productive in recent political vernaculars, and will
attempt to develop a provisional critique of 'left biopolitics' to account for this
phenomenon. 'The body' emerged as a central signifier of much poststructuralist
and post-foundationalist cultural theory and philosophy some decades ago.
However, a more recent terminology of 'bodies' has grown in prevalence, not
only in political theory but in activist idioms and cultural contexts, with the
latter exemplified by the translation of the theme of 'bodies assembling' in
Judith Butler, among related theoretical work such as Leticia Sabsay's, into the
'Parliament of Bodies' at documenta 14 in Athens, as much as by the use of
phrases like 'black and brown bodies' which re-emerged into wide circulation
with the resurgence of the Black Lives Matter/Movement for Black Lives
following the murder of George Floyd at the end of May.[4] Much of the latest
theoretical work has been concerned with a critique of the residual humanisms
of previous generations of 'linguistic' and 'semiotic' critical discourses, even

those of 'the body', which was figured as too abstract, inscribed as it often was into psychoanalytic debates. Instead, recent projects have tried to move beyond this framework by switching focus instead to phenomenological addresses to 'objects', 'actants', 'things', 'affects' – and – 'bodies'. An emphasis on 'bodies', thus, appears to be a move past the residually humanist redoubts of 'subject' and 'people' in figuring political agency. What I will argue in this chapter is that rather than going beyond those redoubts, such an emphasis falls *behind* them. In taking its cue from a type of pseudo-concreteness that often accompanies theoretical projects intolerant of the (real) abstraction that organizes contemporary social life in capitalism, it is in continuity with many of the other tendencies signalled above and their manifest problems.[5] Moreover, the discourse of 'bodies' is pivotal to a 'left biopolitics' insofar as it takes as its object the governance of bodies, life, materiality and affects (often interchangeably) and finds in these both a ground for a collective authenticity and a politics of resistance, within the frame of recognition and representation that is the always slippery conduit to a liberal consensus whose existence could not be less certain at the present time. In keeping with some of the other discussions explored in this volume, it is apposite also to point to the conceptual features of 'vitalism' which may resonate here, particularly in the elision of politics with the unmarked abstraction of 'life as such', without qualities or qualifications, specifically historical and social ones. In accepting the bio-, if not necro-, political, premises of the current dispensation – one that capitalizes on the fragile, isolated and suffering body – this is a discourse, as well as a sensibility, which elides the question of how and why such bodies are *produced* and mediated, and converts this fragility, isolation and suffering into an ethical victory.[6] This can then generate an affective absolutization which paradoxically remains too abstract in its emphasis on direct experience, barring access to an analysis of the brutal effects of social antagonism, always gendered and racialized, to the forming of that experience. Such a stance can seem like an enactment of, rather than a challenge to, a scenario in which 'the reproduction of capitalism and the reproduction of organisms become indistinguishable'.[7] In other words, what form of social relation makes such things as 'bodies' not just legible but also function as the departure point for any political subjectivation within a certain horizon of thought?

Bodies in space

Over the past decade, a range of contexts has seen the reference to 'people' come to be replaced by references to 'bodies', and to a 'person' by a 'body'. It first came to my attention in Judith Butler's 2011 text 'Bodies in Alliance and the Politics of the Street' which was concerned with understanding the occupation of public squares as an emergent shape of resistance. This was on display in the movements in North Africa and in Spain, but also at that time emerging in the United States and elsewhere with Occupy. In this essay, which developed into the book *Notes toward a Theory of Performative Assembly* (2015), Butler drew together her interests in the ontology of precarity and the ethics of vulnerability and exposure to offer an Arendtian argument about public space as the original scene of the political.[8] However, she went beyond and in some ways counter to Hannah Arendt, noting that 'Arendt's view is confounded by its own gender politics, relying as it does on a distinction between the public and private domain that leaves the sphere of politics to men, and reproductive labour to women. If there is a body in the public sphere, it is masculine and unsupported, presumptively free to create, but not itself created'.[9]

If Butler's concept of public space and political visibility is an Arendtian one, her concept of bodies as constituting it is not. Which is to say, she agrees with Arendt that politics creates a public space and happens in that space, and that the political is a performative, and depends upon speech. However, she is interested to expand the concept of the political to include the 'private' or, in Marxist feminist terms, the reproductive, and to substitute bodily performativity for Arendt's prioritization of speech in the enactment of politics, a series of transpositions that culminates with a focus on dependence – on needs – instead of Arendt's prioritization of independent action as the originary mode of the political. The political is generated in the space 'between' bodies, and relies on a recognition of mutual alterity, contingency, and a dependency which can be understood as horizontal (dependency among the assembled) as well as vertical (on the infrastructures of reproduction of life provided, or not provided, by the state and the economy). However, the expansion of the space designated as properly political in a formalist theory of political possibility such as Arendt's, is not sufficient to displace this formalism into a more materialist register. The shift to the salience of the corporeal and the bodily works inversely, namely, to anchor the ahistorical formalism more effectively in the immediacy of a conjured, almost mythical 'lived experience'. As Joan W. Scott has noted, there is a crucial tension between the epistemic politics of experience, which often connotes an individual subject, and the status of the difference this experience is intended to authenticate, which is socially constructed.[10] The register of 'bodies', by grounding experience in the somatic, places it at a yet further remove beyond the enquiry from the social. In effect, the emphasis on corporeality lends Arendt's formalist theory a phenomenological, and, in its gesture to authenticity, a theological cast, one that Butler has acknowledged in discussions of the influence of Maurice Merleau-Ponty, Emmanuel Levinas and Martin Buber on her thinking.[11]

We start to see the ways in which attempts to politically conceptualize 'bodies' exhibit a symptomatic anxiety. It is 'symptomatic' because the mode of communication of this anxiety is expressive. The anxiety longs for concreteness, for real experience, and a desire to bypass the divisive consequences of social abstraction in order to reach the commonality that can be invoked by the suffering body. Though the argument can only be indicated here, this evokes the marginalization of politics by ethics that has been read by philosophers such as Alain Badiou as exemplary of how domination operates in the present.[12] The suggestion I would propose instead is that there is in fact a politics here, the 'left biopolitics' alluded to earlier. 'Left' is perhaps overly schematic, as this is an orientation whose ultimately ethical register leaves it transversal to many points along the political spectrum, from the anarchist left to the communitarian right. Whatever point it occupies, however, the excess of the ethical over the political is constitutive. This emphasis on ethics marks the tendency as an attempt to appropriate the managerial principles of 'biopolitics' as enunciated by Foucault for more socially just or emancipatory goals. In this sense, 'left biopolitics' signals its adherence to liberalism. This is the case because liberalism operates through the preponderance of ethics over the reality of structure (or social abstraction). This is not so much a diagnosis of the privileging of an economy of sentiments over the 'economy itself', as it is of a lack of interest in the systemic connections that imbricate economy and sentiment together.[13] Liberalism evokes a vision of recognition by the state and the market as the fulfilment of its vision of social justice.[14] Hence the salience of terms such as 'marginalization' and 'exclusion' in this narrative, as these are conditions which may be redressed through the expansion of the state and the market to include those pushed into the shadows of the commonwealth. This is the persistent liberalism which evacuates the conflictual 'plans' of movements, formal or everyday, and converts them into the 'strategy' of managing the needs of 'abandoned' or 'underserved' populations, who thus are converted into management's objects, or, conduits for the 'logisticality' of power.[15]

As Butler notes, large groups of people assembling in public space can also provide legitimation to oppressive states, as a testimony to the freedom of assembly in democratic polities.[16] Consequently, it is only the footage of police assault that can undermine assembly as state legitimation. Once again, it is the abused body which performs as the index of political legibility. This is paradoxical, however, since the individual body in pain is, as Elaine Scarry and others have noted, a condition of utmost incommunicability.[17] It is only so far as this pain can be symbolized, that is, translated into a shared set of semantic units, that it can provide a basis for the collective articulation which is the minimum condition of politics. By this point, pain has, admittedly, been translated into a *symptom* or representation of some larger inequity or structural violence. A politics of recognition of the abused body, however, is untranslatable except insofar as its vulnerability already speaks, but of a need that is by definition impossible to grasp in common terms, because it is not translated and thus not available to common praxis. Its communicability is enabled by its bearer's capacity to command authenticity, and thus it takes on a moral rather than a social significance. This creates problems for those who seek a politics that upends the terms of marginalization within a structure of dominance, not simply to exit the position of marginality allocated to them. As Joanne Jules Gleeson writes, '[d]o we really want to boil our lives down into a form that makes them appealing to, and appreciable by, the state?'[18]

Returning to Butler's propositions around a 'politics of vulnerability' as a public exhibition of the radical dependency that constitutes the social, the concern here might be that the vulnerable body is a rather politically ambiguous departure point for an emancipatory politics. The nearness of vulnerability to an experience of suffering and voicelessness divests it of a claim to (collective) political subjectivity, encasing it instead in a symbolic choreography of 'disempowerment'. Vulnerability cannot be argued with; it simply *is* an index of violence which grows in abstraction as it draws further and further into incommunicability. As such, it can be appropriated and mobilized by perspectives which prioritize attenuation of that vulnerability, or, security, as the horizon of their politics. This is in some ways a logical outcome of neoliberal subject formation, where the atomized individual is constantly at threat from competitors in a dog-eat-dog world. Jackie Wang has noted that the 'invocation of personal security and safety presses on our affective and emotional registers and can thus be manipulated to justify everything from racial profiling to war'.[19] These are the discourses of safety and security that traffic in resentment of imposed vulnerability which are habitually, and increasingly, used to obtain consent to violent and divisive social policy. Butler herself has recently distanced herself from the aporias of vulnerability as a basis for solidarity politics, contending that 'neither vulnerability nor care can serve as the basis of a politics'.[20] It is important to note that this is more a warning against idealized visions of human nature with the aggression 'edited' out of them as the basis for such a politics, then it is querying the vulnerable body as the minimal ground of all politics, which is to say, its constitutively *ethical* ground, eliding the uses to which this vulnerability has been put in the hierarchies of life basic to capitalist modernity.

Circling back to the experimental notion of a 'left' biopolitics, it now becomes more possible to understand how a 'body' is made into a talisman of political performativity in an emancipatory key, in a political and existential context marked by individualization and by individualized risk. 'Bodies assemble' and appear as a 'simple aggregate', in Marx's terms, of precarity, exposing their dependency and seeking redress. They are sending distress signals in a vertical channel from the many to the few. As such, the currency of 'bodies' as foregrounded in such propositions is not simply a problem for thought, given its translations into ethical (as well as aesthetic) registers with such equivocal implications. The category of 'left' biopolitics could be used to designate a narrative which prioritizes 'simple abstractions' such as a population and its transhistorical and generic needs as a gesture towards something actually urgent and undeniable, without having to take the detour through socially and historically mediated relations such as subjectivity, antagonism, or the problems of organization. An interesting relation is sketched thereby to Foucault's account of the emergence of biopolitics as population management by the state, and the idea that all management, as a technique of control across sites of power relations in modernity, is ineradicably biopolitical.[21] As such, it would be crucial to attend to the working out of this biopolitical management that Foucault surveys in the lecture course *The Birth of Biopolitics*, namely, to the emergence and traction of the 'human capital' discourse which, to put it succinctly, is the vision of the self-maximizing subject who calculates how to monetize their dependencies precisely as a biological body among others. A vivid elaboration of this Foucauldian–Marxian nexus is provided by the Swiss historian Rudolf Braun's conversion of 'docile bodies' to 'docile capital', albeit at a much earlier moment: the labour discipline promulgated by the Industrial Revolution and its preceding early modern body cultures of disciplinarity.[22]

Bodies at work

And yet, a focus on the (non-) demands of vulnerable bodies standing in abjection before the state in search of the conditions which would allow them to have 'liveable lives' contains an evident kernel of truth. Capitalism composes with isolated bodies, in production, in consumption, in reproduction – this could be termed, following the autonomist grammar, its 'technical' (or, here, technical-ideological) composition. The body as a unit of labour-power, that peculiar commodity which one both has and is, and one which, like all commodities, is in competition with every other commodity to realize value for its seller, now comes into this picture. Biopolitics is an important reference here for another reason; though Foucault has intermittently appeared in this analysis, it is in the combined work of Francois Guéry and Didier Deleule, the still largely under-heralded *The Productive Body* (1972), that the idiom of the body emerges as a naturalizing, symptomatic one – one that is mediated by capitalist social relations such as the division of labour and the competition of capitals. Their ideas are elaborated as a distinctive fusion of Marx and Foucault, in polemical dialogue with Althusser, especially his division between ideology and science and his concept of interpellation. (Rather than focusing on how a cop's interception creates the subject, Guéry is more interested in how the institution of private property creates a cop with the state-given right to intercept.)

Guéry and Deleule's analysis in *The Productive Body* extends commodity fetishism to all of society, and specifically to its concept of the body.[23]

'Mind' and 'body' are both disclosed as reifications of capitalist social and productive relations, separated to create space for management as an agency of subsumption. 'The body' is an artefact of individualizing social relations produced by capitalist competition, which splits the social body into individualized productive bodies, and by real subsumption, which amplifies the division between mental and manual labour:

> As workers become easier to hire and fire, they are increasingly compelled to compete against one another and to consent to work for less money than others. This competition makes it seem to workers that they do not belong to a class or 'social body', but must rely on their individual self or 'biological body'. Hence the 'productive body' that has been created initially in the factory makes the biological body seem more important than the social body. As the work process becomes segmented, structural forces lead workers to begin to see themselves in terms of individual rather than group interests and demands.[24]

This evocation of a social dismemberment functional to domination and exploitation could be read alongside Marx's accounts of the structural as well as literal dismemberment of the worker's body by industrial machines: the body for the capitalist exists as an aggregation of muscles, nerves, and nowadays, an aggregation at a more molecular level: the data that composes the quantified self. The body decomposed into marketable and disciplinary data is of course hardly a new situation, whether historically or theoretically. Aside from Gilles Deleuze's suggestion of a shift from 'individuals' to 'dividuals' precisely owing to the development of the technological means to capture and read such data, Keston Sutherland has recently returned to the Marxian breviary of dismemberment noted above to consider how the valences of Marx's metaphorical language, such as the use of the term 'gallerte' (bone jelly) to figure labour-power abstracted from its bearers, carry political import which has too often gone unnoticed or dismissed in Anglophone critical theory.[25] The rendering and consumption of the body in capitalist labour processes, such as Taylorism, into dismembered parts ('hands' in the nineteenth-century factory, credit scores in the twenty-first-century factory) leaving the worker's living existence a mere husk or 'carcass of time', accentuates Guéry and Deleule's point about how capitalist processes of production – and accumulation – have to be held responsible for generating the bodies we feel must be ours.[26]

Here it is important to dwell on the point that 'production', as in the Deleuze and Guattari register, for Guéry and Deleule falls more on the side of 'social production' rather than the industrial sphere most readily evoked by the term, or the topological sense of a circuit in valorization of capital, as Marx would be using it. However, aside from this more general point on 'production' which concerns 'the body' and 'bodies' as an artefact of a certain mode of production, it ought to be noted that a metric like a credit score marks the point where processes of capitalist valorization lay hold of the body in its attempts to reproduce itself. This can also be read as the sphere of consumption, which includes the self-investment and self-optimization that function as the contemporary guidelines of consumer citizenship and the 'responsibilization' processes it entails. Deleule notes, in the second, single-authored part of the volume that 'the adaptive process incessantly demanded by the system of the productive body [...] affirms the virtues of consumption as a condition of the individual's "biological" survival, while also emphasizing [...] the necessary development of new abilities as the mechanisms on which the subject's "social" survival is predicated'.[27] In light of this thought of consumption as a latter-day extractive scene for the productive body, Butler's precarious assembly can be revisited: deprived of their individual purpose as productive (exploited) bodies, without a social body to fall back on, they are exposed to the harm attendant on being barred from access to the means of consumption. Here, surplus value production can be generatively re-imagined as the uneven consumption of value across more and less socially valorized populations whose relationship to the means of production is more and more cast as the accumulation of human capital.[28] Ann Anagnost has written of 'transfers of value between bodies' from 'low-value' migrant worker populations to the emergent, highly educated bourgeoisie in the cities in early-twenty-first-century China as an upwards redistribution of wealth in terms of human capital, which is known as *suzhi*, the intrinsic value of a person based on the resources invested in them. This echoes the focus of human capital theory from its inception on education as the means of human capital maximization. She observes that to 'track the circuit of value and its accumulation in contemporary China, we must attend to the formative power of *suzhi* as an ideological formation that enables the transfer of economic value from one body to another'. She continues, noting that 'the living labor of the migrant body is derogated in relation to a body whose productive potentiality is fully developed through intensifying standards of middle-class nurture', thus emphasizing that the accumulation of human capital is inscribed in a process of class formation which takes on virtually biological, de-socialized attributes; a process which seems to map 'labour' onto a working or sub-proletarian class and 'human capital' onto the middle classes. The labour of the former enables the production of the 'quality' bodies of the latter.[29] More recently, the discourse of *suzhi* has cropped up again as an aspirational object in the roll-out of social credit systems as part of the panoptic financialization of Chinese society.[30]

Here we can consider that the era of surplus population and 'wageless life'[31] is one where there is a post-labour reification of the body, as vulnerable or threatening in its 'unemployed negativity' (in Read's post-autonomist re-working of Bataille) rather than the power afforded by its skills in or centrality to social production.[32] In this light, bodies gathering in space to become visible to the state as the principal scene of politics today is something like the ultimate 'de-skilling'. From this it is only a short leap to understanding precarity as an ether connecting otherwise purposeless bodies in space. This ether, with its ontological sweep and affective density, is likely to occlude the historical patterns of regularity in capitalist accumulation which ensures the redundancy of ever more people to capitalist accumulation strategies on a cyclical or a secular level, locally as well as globally. Labour is the only source capable of yielding more value for capital than it consumes yet capital must constantly expel workers from the production process as it develops technologically, which is a process that is accelerated but not transformed by contemporary varieties of data-driven automation.

There are counter-tendencies, of course, certainly in the short and medium term, as unorganized and dispossessed labour-power may still be a far cheaper and more efficient force of production than the technologies that may be capable of replacing some of it in specific circumstances.[33] In this way the political pedagogy of 'bodies' in space can be seen as a version of the 'immiseration thesis', which reads off political subjectivity from observable socio-economic tendencies. Just as certain forms of social deprivation are understood to lead to riots which tendentially lead to communism (Clover),[34] the hydraulics of a politics of vulnerable bodies are similarly mechanical, obviating questions of subjectivity and organization in favour of what are offered as self-evident causal chains of deprivation and radicalization. Yet, the 'left' biopolitical content of the proposition is that it sees *power* in this immiseration, and, in common with Foucault's thesis, sees this power as productive. It may be productive in all sorts of ways. It may be productive of the 'value' attendant on all labour revived by some contemporary social reproduction feminists, or it may be productive, as with Butler, of recognition between dependent subject and the forces responsible for inducing this dependency and precarity on them.[35] The unifying thread is the significance of the non-produced, the given and symbolically overdetermined 'body', whatever other historical structures of extraction and valorization may surround it.

This, so to speak, 'pre-critical' promotion of the body and bodies highlights the importance of Guéry and Deleule's arguments on the imbrication of biopolitics, ideology and the subsumption of labour. Further, their appropriation of Deleuze and Guattari's critique of psychoanalysis with the concept of the machinic traces the connections between the notion of the human as a corporeal machine and the maintenance of that machine – the 'productive body' – not just at the sites of production, but the ones of consumption and reproduction, including the academy and the applied social sciences, such as with the behaviourist psychology that flourishes in the present as cognitive behavioural therapy.[36] The industrial machine as an organizing metaphor may have given way to the 'self-organizing system' and now the data algorithm. What has persisted is the mystical idea of the person as a bounded unit that strives for equilibrium, internalizing all social phenomena and processing them either as somatic disorder or neurochemical imbalance. The mind and the body alike emerge as transhistorical, asocial points of departure, the unalterable quanta that stand outside of time. The body becomes as mystical as the basic figure of consciousness in former times, the soul, as does the mind.

Bodies in general

A counter-account of the psychic would engage with the extensive corpus of practice and conceptualization not just associated with the relatively familiar episodes of 'anti-psychiatry' and schizo-analysis, but with Soviet (child) psychology, especially the work of Vigotsky, in whose notion of individuation an ego – or a body – is always the derived outcome of a process of engagement with a social and material reality; a pre-existing constitution of the world discovered, but also formed, by the child.[37] Finally, guarding against the reductive consequences of a biopolitics that stakes its claim on the recognition and emancipation as the flipside of a control and optimization of the weak, suffering body would also mean revisiting the 'machine' side of the problematic traced above. A good reference point would be Gilbert Simondon's theories of the formation of technical objects on the one hand, and his theory of individuation on the other, along with the formidable secondary literature that has grown up around its development of a concept of transindividuation and the transindividual.[38] As Etienne Balibar writes in his book on the subject, transindividuation can be considered 'a generative causality where the whole and the parts function as interconnected productive processes'.[39] The continuity between the individualized body and the state that wields the strategies of neoliberal risk management that determine its conditions of life is set aside by a thinking of transindividuation, as the body is located as an artefact of social, technical and political processes – processes that precede and shape rather than confront a pre-constituted self – rather than a self-evident node of vulnerability awaiting recognition by power. With such a thinking of transindividuation it is no longer possible to take the body, singular or plural, as a point of departure, and even less a replacement for political subjectivity. Read's contribution to this line of enquiry develops it in historical materialist terms that draw on sources in Marx, among others, that locate the biological body as an outcome of historical and social processes, as in his well-known disquisition on the five senses as a product of history.[40]

Here it might be worth returning to the question of vitalism that was raised earlier as a philosophical backdrop to the imperative to isolate 'bodies' as the crux of political and ontological meaning, prior to re-assembling them in a public space constituted by horizontal and vertical dependency. While the history and implications of the category of vitalism, *Lebensphilosophie*, etc. are expansive, its relevance here may be circumscribed by the axiom of the resistance to conceptual determination inherent to vitalism as predicated on the irreducible excess of living force or matter. Contemporary iterations of vitalism, which are often grouped under the generic modifier 'new materialism', and include thinkers such as Jane Bennett, Brian Massumi or Rosi Braidotti,

invoke 'bodies', 'things' and the neuro-scientific shibboleth of 'affect'. These
operate as emblems of concreteness in an approach to theory which claims to
overcome the kinds of hierarchies and exclusions that this current regularly
imputes to earlier forms of critical theory rather than to the social realities
critical theory tries to immanently describe.[41] As Achille Mbembe has recently
noted, such a de-socialized vitalism is a symptom of the impoverishment of
rationality as a social and historical praxis in a historical moment of the global
domination of techno-capital.[42] This unfolds as financialized algorithmic
instrumentality on the one side, and modes of political feeling that draw their
authenticity from the intensity with which they register in an experience both
atomized and synthesized by networked sociality. The vulnerable body and its
excess, of course, have no singular political determination, emerging against
pervasive horizons of common sense and dominant narratives. Affect thus is
the modality (and this has historical echoes) of the surplus – the underside
of the ungovernable excess of affective bodies is the abandonment of bodies
deemed surplus to capital's valorization. In light of present developments, it is
clear that vulnerability can be comprehensively *détourned* by the far right in
the guise of threat to national bodies politic. The promotion of the abstraction
of 'bodies', in common with the specific types of liberal identity claims Asad
Haider has begun to trace in his recent book, is both a consequence and a
pretext for staging a disavowal of this fact.[43]

Conclusion

As noted at the outset, in the context of a global health crisis, political questions
around the governance of the body have been raised to a new pitch of urgency.
Additionally, the implication of the body in the last few years' revolutionary
politics around racism and police violence, as is again massively coming to the
fore at the time of writing – a time when protest in public space had seemed to
be temporarily off the agenda – means that the likewise heightened politics of
the language around 'bodies' and what happens to them is impossible to miss.
The racialization of structural violence reflected in the pandemic's bodycounts
operates as a strange quilting point of the two: 'pre-existing' conditions
like poor health or criminality are sought as an explanation for the impact

of the Covid-19 virus on racialized communities in places like the United States, while emphasis on the structural violence that exacerbates that impact identifies systemic oppression, as well as the state violence that exemplifies it, as that 'pre-existing' condition, illustrated by the popularity of the protest meme 'police are the virus'. And yet the notion of 'bodies' as the object-subjects of this violence doesn't tell us anything; we all 'have' or 'are' bodies, but only specific bodies are exposed to spontaneous executions by the forces of law and order – the ones which power has identified as nothing *but* bodies, thus with the most tenuous claim to both citizenship and life. While these seem like common sense observations, the preceding discussion will have hopefully demonstrated that the commitment to the political vocabulary of 'bodies' obfuscates not only the socio-historical conditions that produce these bodies, but also the selectively determined value of their lives. This is an obfuscation that also affects proximate discourses such as those of 'democratic' or 'left biopolitics', which confounds materialism with a focus on living units over the conditions of their existence and reproduction in a capitalist *socius*. Yet this is not the extent of the problematic of 'bodies', as here there is also the necessity of considering the debate around 'identity politics', as the several passing mentions of Asad Haider's work have noted. 'Identity' happens whenever you have the conversion of a relation into a thing, which may then be occupied, possessed and mobilized. This goes for 'class-first' Marxists as poignantly as for 'race-first' liberals. This likewise mirrors the logic of turning the 'body' into a thing, a thing that can guarantee ethical capital for its defenders, rather than the artefact of a mode of production and a regime of power. If such approaches are asserted in terms of effective concreteness over the esoterica of abstraction, it remains to be emphasized that a hatred of abstraction is a right-wing affect, though it may be expressed in political positions that would locate themselves at quite a distance from the right. This remains the case even if there is a partial truth to accounts that would situate the discourse of 'bodies' firmly in an academic vernacular, implying that this discourse constitutes a certain kind of 'theoreticist' fallacy in its own right. In this case, we would return to the 'use of bodies' (in a non-Agambenian sense)[44] as a 'simple abstraction', which is to say, a reductive story rather than a complexly mediated account.

With those cautionary reflections in mind, it may be worth concluding with a brief elaboration of some original, and perhaps more visceral, objections

I had experienced on encountering what was to me a novel political vocabulary of 'bodies'. 'Bodies' seemed to me to refer to entities that were neither living nor self-determining. Either it referred to an entity that was *no longer* living, or was said in order to draw a boundary: a corporate body, a body of water. This use of bodies could be understood as a grammatical artefact. Certainly, you could also have bodies in a scientific register, tiny ones, such as atoms and molecules. Most importantly, unless subscribing to a certain Lucretian metaphysics that obviously appealed to the matriculating Marx, or later Althusser, Deleuze and different theorists working in the vitalist tradition, 'bodies' could not organize (the caveat about 'self-determination'). Or, more precisely, they could not organize *socially*. This lacuna meant that bodies could only be drawn together by social needs reconceived as natural ones, just as the vocabulary of bodies drew on a 'natural' understanding of what comprised a unit of living matter and extrapolated from there to what comprised a social unit, repressing any account of the social in the process. The valorization of life over its conditions of possibility evoked the totalitarian pragmatism of management; the exclusive focus on means in a situation where ends are placed beyond question. Thus it was not surprising when the common sense of 'bodies' went on to generate the proposition of 'left biopolitics'. We have become accustomed to accepting the management of life as equivalent to its production.

Notes

1   The debate on 'democratic biopolitics' has probably been among the most cogent of the many problematizations of Agamben's Covid-19 piece. Although parts of it have been published elsewhere, the full discussion is at the Critical Legal Thinking website. The pieces are, in order, Panagiotis Sotiris, 'Against Agamben: Is a Democratic Biopolitics Possible?', *Critical Legal Thinking*, 14 March 2020, https://criticallegalthinking.com/2020/03/14/against-agamben-is-a-democratic-biopolitics-possible/; Bryan Doniger, 'Two Problems with Democratic Biopolitics (Critique in times of Coronavirus)', *Critical Legal Thinking*, 28 April 2020, https://criticallegalthinking.com/2020/04/28/two-problems-with-democratic-biopolitics-critique-in-times-of-coronavirus/; Panagiotis Sotiris, 'Democratic Biopolitics Revisited: A Response to a Critique', *Critical Legal Thinking*, 25 May 2020, https://criticallegalthinking.com/2020/05/25/

democratic-biopolitics-revisited-a-response-to-a-critique/. For the Agamben
article, and a series of responses from him to the published discussion, see
the 'Coronavirus and Philosophers' special issue of the *European Journal of
Psychoanalysis*, https://www.journal-psychoanalysis.eu/coronavirus-and-
philosophers/.

2   See Zöe Sutherland and Marina Vishmidt, 'Social Reproduction: New Questions
for the Gender, Affect, and Substance of Value', in *New Feminist Literary Studies*,
ed. Jennifer Cooke (Cambridge: Cambridge University Press, 2020). Sotiris
uses many of the same examples to illustrate 'democratic biopolitics' as many
theorists of social reproduction do, all of which can be summarized as variations
on the Black Panthers slogan for their community endeavours, 'survival pending
revolution'.

3   Michel Foucault, *The Birth of Biopolitics: Lectures at the College de France
1970–79*, trans. Graham Burchell (Basingstoke and New York: Palgrave
Macmillan, 2008).

4   Judith Butler, *Notes Toward a Theory of Performative Assembly* (Cambridge,
MA: Harvard University Press, 2015); Leticia Sabsay, 'Permeable Bodies:
Vulnerability, Affective Powers, Hegemony', in *Vulnerability in Resistance*, ed.
Judith Butler, Zeynep Gambetti and Leticia Sabsay (Durham, NC and London:
Duke University Press, 2016); documenta 14, 'Parliament of Bodies' programme
page, https://www.documenta14.de/en/public-programs/927/the-parliament-
of-bodies; Robin D. G. Kelley, 'Black Study, Black Struggle', *Boston Review*,
7 March 2016, https://bostonreview.net/forum/robin-d-g-kelley-black-study-
black-struggle. Ta-Nehisi Coates was one of the first commentators to bring
the term 'black bodies' into mainstream discourse, but the term was already
prevalent in academic and activist speech, and was prominent in the first wave
of BLM uprising and organizing in the wake of the police murder of Michael
Brown – especially on college campuses, as Kelley notes.

5   The critiques of these tendencies have been manifold and taken up from very
diverse perspectives. For an indicative example, see Thomas Lemke, 'Materialism
without Matter: The Recurrence of Subjectivism in object-Oriented Ontology',
Distinktion: Journal of Social Theory 18, no. 2 (2017); Svenja Bromberg, 'The
Anti-Political Aesthetics of Objects and Worlds Beyond', *Mute*, 25 July 2013,
https://www.metamute.org/editorial/articles/anti-political-aesthetics-objects-
and-worlds-beyond.

6   As Jackie Wang notes, biopolitics and necropolitics are not symmetrical
concepts, insofar as the distinction between the two points to histories of

racialization, coloniality and dehumanization typical of the capitalist mode
of accumulation over centuries. Briefly, Foucault theorized biopolitics as an
administrative but ultimately microphysical and indirect exercise of power in a
society, insofar as it is geared towards an optimization of life; necropolitics is the
underside of this, the direct and blatant violence exercised on the production,
maintenance and elimination of the already 'socially dead'. However, neither
are they mutually exclusive. See *Carceral Capitalism* (New York: semiotext(e),
2018), 339.

7   Elizabeth R. Johnson, 'Reconsidering Mimesis: Freedom and Acquiescence in the
     Anthropocene', *South Atlantic Quarterly* 115, no. 2 (2016): 283.

8   One of the constitutive aspects of the political as a distinct site for Hannah
     Arendt is that the scene of the political is a space of visibility, of acting in public
     and being witnessed. Coming to public expression is the way the new comes into
     the world, making politics the site and source of innovation in human affairs,
     rather than the repetition that belongs to the private scene of biological life, or,
     reproduction and reproductive labour. This birth, or 'natality', plays an important
     role in Arendt's political philosophy as the entrance of a singular human
     subjectivity into a world where it can act and be seen, but that is ontologically
     distinct from 'biological birth', which produces animal being not political being,
     in Arendt's classically Greek paradigm. See *The Human Condition* (Chicago:
     University of Chicago Press, 2018).

9   Judith Butler, 'Bodies in Alliance and the Politics of the Street', first published in
     EIPCP *transversal* web journal September 2011; now available at https://scalar.
     usc.edu/works/bodies/Judith%20Butler:%20Bodies%20in%20Alliance%20
     and%20the%20Politics%20of%20the%20Street%20%7c%20eipcp.net.pdf.

10   Joan W. Scott, 'The Evidence of Experience', *Critical Inquiry* 17, no. 4 (Summer
     1991): 777. This can be seen as an enquiry into historiographic methodology
     with wider implications for the politics of authenticity that continues to inform a
     range of emancipatory movements.

11   *The Other Journal* interview with Judith Butler, 'We Are Wordless without One
     Another', *The Seattle School of Theology & Psychology*, 2 December 2017, https://
     theseattleschool.edu/blog/worldless-without-one-another-interview-judith-
     butler/.

12   'Today, natural belief can be summarized in a single statement: *There are only
     bodies and languages.* […] The individual fashioned by the contemporary
     world recognizes the objective existence of bodies alone.' Alain Badiou,
     'Democratic Materialism and the Materialist Dialectic', *Radical Philosophy*

130 (March/April 2005): 20. For a later version of this idea, see 'Preface', in *Logics of Worlds: Being and Event II*, trans. Alberto Toscano (London: Continuum, 2009).

13 For an early cultural studies approach to get at such an imbrication, see the elaboration of 'structures of feeling', in Raymond Williams, *The Long Revolution* (Harmondsworth: Penguin, 1965), 64.

14 For a critique of recognition as the entry of liberal and colonial logics into radical politics, see Glen Coulthard, *Red Skin, White Masks: Rejecting the Colonial Politics of Recognition* (Minneapolis: University of Minnesota Press, 2014).

15 Stefano Harney and Fred Moten, *The Undercommons: Fugitive Planning & Black Study* (Wivenhoe, NY and Port Watson: Minor Compositions, 2013).

16 Judith Butler, 'Bodily Vulnerability, Coalitions and Street Politics', in *The State of Things*, ed. Marta Kuzma and Peter Osborne (Oslo: Office for Contemporary Art, 2012). It can be noted that this has become particularly acute in the current context of lockdown/protest – the ability to demonstrate is taken to disprove the justification for demonstrating in the first place ('if you're able to protest then surely you can have nothing to protest about!'). Thanks to Joanne Hornsby for bringing my attention to this point.

17 The reason that pain is incommunicable is that it places the subject beyond language; their world is closed off by the experience of being in pain. She suggests that physical pain is language-destroying and, ultimately, cognition-destroying. The analogy is torture; pain kidnaps language. See *The Body in Pain: The Making and Unmaking of the World* (Oxford: Oxford University Press, 1985), 54.

18 Joanne Jules Gleeson, 'Transsexual Solidarity', *Invert*, no. 1 (2020): 88.

19 Wang, *Carceral Capitalism*, 282.

20 'Judith Butler on Rethinking Vulnerability, Violence, Resistance', *Verso blog*, 6 March 2020, https://www.versobooks.com/blogs/4583-judith-butler-on-rethinking-vulnerability-violence-resistance.

21 Macherey's writing on Foucault, and his elaboration of genealogies of productive and docile bodies underlines that it is the labour-power of these bodies that was at issue in Foucault's analysis. See Pierre Macherey, 'The Productive Subject', in *Viewpoint*, trans. Tijana Okić, Patrick King and Cory Knudson, 31 October 2015, https://www.viewpointmag.com/2015/10/31/the-productive-subject/.

22 Rudolf Braun, 'The "Docile" Body as Economic-Industrial Growth Factor', in *Favorites of Fortune: Technology, Growth, and Economic Development since the Industrial Revolution*, ed. Patrice Higonnet, David S. Landes and Henry Rosovsky (Cambridge, MA: Harvard University Press, 1991), 120.

23 François Guéry and Didier Deleule, *The Productive Body*, trans. Philip Barnard and Stephen Shapiro (Winchester: Zero Books, 2014). Hereafter *TPB*.

24 *TPB*, 21.

25 Gilles Deleuze, 'Postscript on the Societies of Control', *October* 59 (Winter 1992); Keston Sutherland, 'Marx in Jargon', *World Picture*, no. 1 (2008), http://www.worldpicturejournal.com/World%20Picture/WP_1.1/KSutherland.pdf, subsequently reworked as 'The Poetics of *Capital*', in *Capitalism: Concept, Idea, Image*, ed. Éric Alliez, Peter Osborne, Eric-John Russell (London: CRMEP Books, 2019).

26 Harry Braverman, *Labor and Monopoly Capital: The Degradation of Work in the Twentieth Century* (New York: Monthly Review Press, 1998); Gerard Hanlon, *The Dark Side of Management: A Secret History of Management Theory* (Abingdon: Routledge, 2016); Deborah Lupton, *The Quantified Self: A Sociology of Self-Tracking* (Cambridge: Polity, 2016); Annie McClanahan, *Dead Pledges: Debt, Crisis, and 21st Century Culture* (Stanford: Stanford University Press, 2016).

27 *TPB*, 124–5.

28 Michel Feher, *Rated Agency: Investee Politics in a Speculative Age*, trans. Gregory Elliott (New York: Zone Books, 2018).

29 Ann Anagnost, 'The Corporeal Politics of Quality (*Suzhi*)', *Public Culture* 16, no. 2 (2004), 189–208.

30 Julian Gruin, 'Financializing Authoritarian Capitalism: Chinese Fintech and the Institutional Foundations of Algorithmic Governance', *Finance and Society* 5, no. 2 (2019), 84–104.

31 Michael Denning, 'Wageless Life', *New Left Review*, no. 66 (2010), 79–97.

32 See Jason Read's long-running blog, *Unemployed Negativity* (http://www.unemployednegativity.com/), which engages with theoretical and pop-cultural instances of thinking around the production of subjectivity in neoliberal capitalism. As Robin D. G. Kelley has recently noted, in Afro-pessimist critical discourse the notion of 'body' and 'bodies' operates to homogenize and de-historicize, even if highlighting some episodes of militancy: the vulnerable (black) body becomes a cipher of sorrow or, alternatively (in the white imagination), a threat, made to 'increasingly stand in for actual people with names, experiences, dreams, and desires' (2016). Sorrow also comes up in Asaid Haider's observation that displacing political agency from the building of collectivities in struggle to the givenness of bodies seeking representation and recognition of their suffering can be seen as an index of political depression: 'Not

only has the idea of universal emancipation come to seem old-fashioned and outmoded, the very possibility of achieving anything beyond the temporary protection of individual comfort seems like a delusion. Hence a call for universally beneficial social change is often heard as a personal affront: instead of an affirmation of my individual demand for security and recognition, I am presented with a goal that lies beyond my powers to achieve.' Asad Haider, *Mistaken Identity: Class and Race in the Age of Trump* (London and New York: Verso, 2018), 101–2.

33   Marx noted capital's preference for rudimentary technology if the labour is cheaper than upgrading tools, as clearly illustrated in nineteenth-century US chattel slavery – see Karl Marx, *Capital: A Critique of Political Economy*, vol. 1, trans. Ben Fowkes (London: Penguin Books, 1990 [1867]). In a similar vein, see Aaron Benanav, 'Automation and the Future of Work – I', *New Left Review*, no. 119 (September–October 2019), 5–38; Aaron Benanav, 'Automation and the Future of Work – II', *New Left Review*, no. 120 (November–December 2019); Jason E. Smith, 'Nowhere to Go: Automation, then and Now, Part One', *Brooklyn Rail*, 1 March 2017; Jason E. Smith, 'Nowhere to Go: Automation, then and Now, Part Two', *Brooklyn Rail*, 1 April 2017.

34   Joshua Clover, *Riot. Strike. Riot. The New Era of Uprisings* (London and New York: Verso, 2016).

35   A recent example is Alessandra Mezzadri, 'On the Value of Social Reproduction: Informal Labour, the Majority World and the Need for Inclusive Theories and Politics', *Radical Philosophy* 2, no. 4 (Spring 2019), 33–41. Butler, op. cit.

36   *TPB*. For a contemporary critique of CBT as the imprint of 'New Public Management' ideology on mental health treatment, see Farhad Dala, *CBT: The Cognitive Behavioural Tsunami: Managerialism, Politics and the Corruptions of Science* (London: Routledge, 2018).

37   Hannah Proctor, *Psychologies in Revolution: Alexander Luria's 'Romantic Science' and Soviet Social History* (London: Palgrave Macmillan, 2020).

38   Jason Read, *The Politics of Transindividuality* (Chicago: Haymarket, 2017).

39   Maria Chehonadskih, 'The Communist Drama of Individuation in Lev Vygotsky', *Stasis* 5, no. 2 (2017): 125.

40   Karl Marx, *Economic and Philosophical Manuscripts of 1844*, trans. Martin Milligan (Moscow: Progress Publishers, 1974), 96.

41   A good example of this, and one which has had much traction also in cultural and artistic discourses, is J. K. Gibson-Graham, *The End of Capitalism*

(As We Knew It): A Feminist Critique of Political Economy (Oxford: Blackwell Publishers, 1996).

42 Torbjørn Tumyr Nilsen, 'Thoughts on the Planetary: An Interview with Achille Mbembe', *New Frame*, 10 September 2019, https://www.newframe.com/thoughts-on-the-planetary-an-interview-with-achille-mbembe/.

43 Haider, *Mistaken Identity.*

44 Giorgio Agamben, *The Use of Bodies*, trans. Adam Kotsko (Stanford: Stanford University Press, 2016).

5

Empty promises: The financialization of labour

Phil Jones

In *Undoing the Demos,* Wendy Brown argues that 'finance capital and financialization bring about a new model of economic conduct' which 'differs significantly from Smithian truck, barter and exchange', one which increasingly organizes its 'strategic decisions and practices' around 'enhancing the self's future value'.[1] Positing the 'neoliberal' or 'financial' subject as self-valorizing, Brown's account is indicative of a position that reimagines value production as an individual activity, as opposed to social one, i.e. one constituted by labour. Her work builds on Michel Feher's influential claim that 'human capital as the successor to the notion of the free labourer' entails a radical change in subjectivity, so that 'our main purpose is ... to constantly value or appreciate ourselves – or at least prevent our own depreciation'.[2]

Both of these writers draw heavily on Michel Foucault's prescient readings of human capital theory in *The Birth of Biopolitics,* a series of lectures that have been of critical significance in developing the theoretical underpinnings of the 'neoliberal subject of value'.[3] In what has now become a grand discursive shift, Foucault critiques the work of the Chicago school economists, Gary Becker and Theodor Schultz, to argue that the liberal subject has been replaced by the neoliberal 'entrepreneur of himself', who no longer receives a wage but an income, is no longer a labourer but an enterprise, and no longer produces a commodity but their own capital.[4] In his work on human capital, Becker extended the traditional economic ground of monetary income to incorporate 'psychic incomes' – the subjective benefits and satisfactions derived from life more generally.[5] Understood so, life becomes a seamless series of investments made to enhance one's present value – each moment an entrepreneurial opportunity to maximize one's worth, and competitively advance one's position in the social order.

Yet, as financial markets have become an increasingly dominant aspect of social reality, Feher claims, Foucault's critique of human capital must be updated, in part because its central focus – income – no longer precisely holds. Miming the fluctuations of stock on a volatile market driven by speculative risk, the 'major preoccupation' of the financialized subject is now 'capital growth or appreciation rather than income, stock value rather than commercial profits'.[6] The notion of 'self-value', a term only implied in Foucault's readings of human capital theory, has since become crucial to framing a so-called new economy of ascendant financial markets and digital platforms.

Now predominantly framed by abstract goals of 'self-appreciation or self-esteem', human capital is defined by the activity of constant valuation in the hope of averting its own 'depreciation'.[7] Continually moving between states of appreciation and depreciation, the 'neoliberal subject of value' moves away from more stable measures such as the wage to contestable metrics such as scores, ranks and ratings, which can then be traded for volatile streams of revenue.[8] 'Likes', 'shares', 'followers' and 'friends', Niels Van Doorn notes, offer a quantitative measure of the subject's fluctuating value 'in a competitive job market whose parameters have become increasingly uncertain'.[9] In this 'neoliberal world of work', Van Doorn further notes, 'secure employment in the present has been replaced by the insecure venture of achieving future "employability", the measure of which is human capital'. According to Van Doorn, 'employability' declines or rises depending on the subject's ability to protect and advance their 'self-brand', a kind of online reputation measured by digital metrics.[10]

From free labourer to human capital, employment to employability and from socially produced value to self-value, the 'neoliberal subject' shifts the ideological stakes of our financialized moment away from social production to the individual – a shift that maps onto a diachronic reading of labour giving way to human capital as the global order transitions from an economy centred around production to finance. Though Feher's and Brown's respective accounts seek, on some basic level, to synthesize insights from the Foucauldian and Marxian traditions, there is a tendency to read the latter's free labourer as a prelude to the former's entrepreneur, as if such categories follow from each other as substitutable equivalents. To reverse this trend, this chapter brings the financialized subject into a Marxian framing, returning the 'productive body' from the realm of the individual to that of the social.[11] I, too, focus on employability, human capital and self-value; however, I argue that far from superseding labour, these categories express its form under conditions of financialization. I wish to argue that such conditions force labour to mime the tension that Marx attributes to finance, termed 'fictitious capital' because it appears as 'self-valorizing value' but is really just the promise of future value.[12] Inflected by this tension, human capital, employability and self-value are not the figures of a new capitalist ontology but express an inherent aspect of labour aggravated into an imperative by finance: the promise of labour-power.[13]

The 'signs of autumn' that began with the collapse of Bretton Woods in 1973 have faded into the cold, barren world of winter that arrived in the wake of the 2008 crisis.[14] As a worker, to endure such conditions at the best of times is hard, not least because financial accumulation discards production, frustrating the worker's ability to sell their sole 'special commodity', labour-power, which is sold under pains of survival.[15] But with no return to profitability forthcoming, our present phase of financialization has pushed the horizon of production into a future that may never arrive, swelling the ranks of the surplus population and intensifying competition to find employment – a process which, I argue, has forced workers to present their 'special commodity' in ever-more promissory and illusory ways. Rethinking the conceptual apparatus of human capital along these lines, I argue that finance remakes the worker, so that promising replaces producing as their guiding imperative.

Financialization and surplus labour

With the effective end of Fordism in the 1970s, and the commencement of the 'long downturn' of overdeveloped capitalist economies, we see an unprecedented expansion of finance capital across the global north, with value becoming an ever-more enigmatic feature of wealth creation.[16] Generated in the production process, value relies on the exploitation of labour, expressed in Marx's general formula for capital, $M\text{-}C\text{-}M^1$, whereby 'M' stands for investment in materials, labour and machines; 'C' expresses labour's employment and the production of the commodity, which, if all goes well, leads to 'M¹', the surplus value realized by the commodity's sale.[17] In the crudest sense, the formula represents the Fordist accumulation regime, characterized by relatively stable labour markets and secure, long-term employment. With the ascendancy of finance, M-C-M¹ is superseded by M-M¹, the circulation of what Marx refers to as 'fictitious capital', under which the employment of labour represented by 'C' is ever-more absent. Now acting 'as a mysterious and self-creating source of interest of its own increase', capital appears to erase the labour and value from which it arises.[18]

As 'profiting without producing' – in the term of Costas Lapavitsas – has become the name of the game, advanced capitalist economies have experienced a decline in real wages, a rise in the rate of unemployment, and increases in 'piece work', 'putting out practices' and 'unpaid labour'.[19] These new insecurities, Dick Bryan and Michael Rafferty suggest, directly result from innovations in financial derivatives, which, by intensifying competition in the market, compel capitalists to 'look to the sphere of production'. A new and urgent race to drive down costs in production has led to a decline in wages, 'flexibility in skills and conditions' and intensified productivity.[20] Perhaps most significantly, productivity gains often require the transfer of productive work from labour to machines. As such, we should see financial innovation as a key driver of automation in our present moment. Alongside derivatives driving this process, Nick Srnicek and Alex Williams note, financialization accelerates automation through its propensity for crises – periods 'when automatable jobs disappear, never to be heard from again'.[21]

Not only, then, does financialization erase the need for labour in general through its pretence to 'self-valorizing value', but also specifically as a driver of automation and new organizational methods. Unable to find employment, a 'disposable industrial reserve army' grows in the shadow of finance, 'always ready', in Marx's term, 'for exploitation by capital'.[22] Rosa Luxembourg claims that this surplus population acts as 'a necessary prerequisite of the sudden expansion of production in times of boom' by driving the new innovations and markets that tend to revive the stagnant industrial sector following a period dominated by finance.[23] Historically, this process soaks up surplus labour and reproduces the system on an expanded scale. Yet, under our present regime, Aaron Benanav claims, this tendency has been entirely disrupted by computers, which, unlike previous innovations that performed a salvational role in restoring employment, 'tend to reduce requirements across all lines by rapidly increasing the level of automation', an ominous suggestion of 'surplus' becoming 'superfluous'.[24]

In *Time, Labour and Domination*, Moishe Postone perhaps best grasps the ambiguous position the worker occupies under such conditions:

> In Marx's account, people are not liberated by, but are subsumed under, the growth in productive capacities that come into being as capital. On the other hand, though, the same development – which signifies a growing disparity between the conditions for the production of material wealth and those for the production of value – makes proletarian labor more superfluous as a source of material wealth. In rendering proletarian labor potentially anachronistic from the standpoint of the production of material wealth, it renders value itself potentially anachronistic.[25]

In raising productivity, financialization accelerates the process by which labour becomes 'superfluous'. It heightens the fundamental contradiction at the heart of the capitalist economy which effectively still requires labour to generate surplus value but at the same time has developed methods of wealth creation that dispose of labour's use-value. Financialization intensifies the dynamic by which capitalism drives its own devaluation, whereby wealth creation is separated from value production, a process that comes to have increasingly negligible significance. At the same time, capitalism continues to posit itself on value-creating labour, the very factor that is being made marginal. Under current conditions of financialization, workers entertain a liminal position, not fully present and useful yet neither entirely absent and redundant; they fall into an ever-expanding surplus reserve, a workforce in-waiting, characterized by their status as underemployed or wholly unemployed, which, due to the processes outlined above, may find their employment postponed indefinitely.

The promise of labour-power

Capital may have no requirement for labour, but the labourer is still dependent on selling their labour-power to survive. Increasingly left to fend for themselves, the worker becomes disproportionately responsible for finding employment. Termed by Brown 'responsibilization', this economic dynamic has become a strategy at the level of governmental and institutional policy in overdeveloped nations, framing problems once considered social as the sole responsibility of the individual.[26] Since the 1990s, governments have largely replaced Keynesian stimulus packages aimed at ensuring labour demand with initiatives such as 'Back to Work' and 'The Work Programme' that make the worker entirely accountable for gaining and presenting the skills necessary for a volatile labour market. As entrenched economic problems are outsourced to individuals, the worker is forced to increasingly 'work-for-labour' – work that, in Guy Standing's words, often 'does not have exchange value but which is necessary or advisable'.[27] 'Working hard *and* hardly working' captures the liminal position of a worker that spends more time crafting their social media presence, updating their CV and undertaking 'internships' than performing the wage labour such activities aim towards.[28]

'Employability' is the name most often attributed to the various responsibilities that comprise 'work-for-labour' – responsibilities that, I would argue, centre around the worker's 'promise'. In their critique of Wolfgang Haug's *Commodity Aesthetics*, Matt Phull and Will Stronge argue that 'employability' represents the *aesthetic* promise of labour-power.[29] Extending Haug's theory of marketing and advertising to Marx's 'special commodity', they consider the aesthetic processes by which the worker markets themselves. Haug locates marketing in a problem inherent to the exchange relation: how to maintain a continual and smooth passage for value between seller and buyer. For value to be realized, the commodity must be sold, which depends on a buyer desiring its use value. A buyer will only purchase a MacBook Pro for instance, if they have some purpose for it. But this raises the question: in a market saturated with laptops, why buy this particular model? Haug asserts that the problem of how to cathect a buyer to a particular product leads to 'a tendency time and again to modify the commodity body', i.e. its 'use form'. Thus, 'the *appearance* of use value', 'the impression of use', not the use-value itself, is what draws the buyer into a purchase. This distinction is important because 'until the sale is effected, the commodity's promise of use-value is all that counts'.[30] Thus, all the semantic and affective connotations evinced in the design and marketing of a MacBook promise the buyer a particular use, which may be as abstract as a particular lifestyle or as concrete as user-friendly software. From the illusion of cosmopolitan cool promised by a MacBook Pro to a billboard depicting a can of Coca-Cola dripping with condensation, the promissory aesthetics of the commodity over its objective form is ultimately what leads to a sale and the realization of value.

Somewhat oddly, Haug does not apply his theory of commodity aesthetics to the labour-power commodity. Elaborating Haug's work, Phull and Stronge argue that the use-value of labour-power similarly transpires as an illusory promise in advance of its sale in the wage relation.[31] In the most fundamental sense, the body of the labour-power commodity itself, that is, the labourer's body, makes a promise to the capitalist buyer. This might be the promise of an able body at the factory gate; the promise of a child's small frame to fit in a narrow chimney; or the promise of the female body to enact reproductive labour.[32] More pertinent to our current purposes, in a moment when the mediation of things and bodies is ubiquitous, the promise of labour-power takes the shape of an '[a]esthetic abstraction', which 'detaches sensuousness and sense from an object and makes them available separately'. This 'second surface', 'incomparably more perfect than the first', might take the form of a CV or social media profile such as LinkedIn, which presents labour-power in an illusory ideal form.[33] Indeed, much as any other commodity, the promise of labour-power comprises a range of promises to solicit a range of buyers, marketing itself through manners, sartorial choices, as well as online media.

But while the theory provides a useful model for investigating the aesthetic quality of labour-power, it does not account for the specific historical dynamics that underpin the rise of this promissory tendency in a moment when an increasingly significant segment of the labour market is falling into the surplus population. Haug, in part, provides an answer here. He argues that moments of increased competition force corporate firms to gain an edge over their competitors by elaborating the aesthetics of their products into ever-more fantastical promises.[34] The same might be said of the promise labour must make in our financialized moment. As already shown, financialization drives the processes of automation and outsourcing that have shrunk the pool of necessary labour, swelling the ranks of the surplus population and intensifying competition for the meagre opportunities available. Following a similar logic to other commodities, competition compels workers to make their labour-power standout on a market featuring identically redundant labour.

Yet Haug only supplies a theoretical lexicon for grasping 'employability', not a precise explanation of its ascendancy; that is, an account sufficiently specific for our present financialized moment. For that, we need a proper analysis of finance's promissory logic. Recall that, for Marx, M-M^1 signals the loss of the production process 'C'; replaced instead by 'promissory note[s]' – loans, futures and exotic derivatives, which in reality only promise the value of future products, but fetishistically act as though they themselves contain value.[35] If labour is the sole source of value, then of course fictitious capital cannot valorize itself; it represents, in Marx's term, 'claims … to future production'; a promise that value *will* be realized; that is, a promise of labour yet to come.[36] Let us take the example of the mortgage: a lump sum of fictitious capital, or credit, is extended to a borrower so long as they promise to repay the sum plus interest at some future date; thus, the promise represents in the present the income from the borrower's future labour. Profits are then generated by interest payments and, more pertinently in our present moment, the repackaging of the loan in derivative form which can be leveraged as risk across a variety of financial markets. Importantly, all of the associated profits index the initial promise made by the borrower, that is, the promise of future labour – a process that has led Joshua Clover to claim 'that the financialized formula M-M^1 is in fact always the formula M-$M^1[C]$. The labour commodity is not truly routed around. It must perforce await in the future, which must be bracketed, but never empty'.[37] That is to say: there is no certainty that labour will later be employed, even though the whole financial circuitry acts *as if* this moment is assured.

The logic of finance, then, does not just apply to the relationship between creditor and debtor, but intensifies the promissory, future-oriented logic of the system as a whole. The promissory role that the labour commodity takes in the financialized circulation M-$M^1[C]$ captures this wider economic logic, which encourages the worker to advance their promise of labour-power. As the 'C' moves from between the two 'M's' to its virtual place at the formula's end, the labourer's role is rerouted away from production in the present to the promise of an uncertain production yet to come; hence, the present epidemic of underemployment and unemployment. Since the 1970s, the coextensive rise of financialization and 'employability' policy bears this speculation out: that a reserve army has been encouraged to work-for-labour in the present for an employment postponed to the future. Such uncertainty encourages the worker to make themselves appear more 'employable', to craft a promise alluring to a system that has deferred its role indefinitely.

To briefly recap, fictitious capital contains a contradiction between its fetishistic appearance as present and 'real' value and its actual form as a promise of future value production, which translates into a promise labour must make. Over the rest of this chapter, I aim to show that it is this contradiction that determines the appearance and form of the financialized subject as they seek to navigate a system in which they must work to survive despite no longer being wholly necessary.

Human capital and the promise of labour-power

As social media has come to provide streams of income for the superfluous mass outside the wage relation, attention has turned to the 'neoliberal subject of value'. Moving away from the conceptual apparatus of 'labour', Van Doorn argues that there has been a paradigmatic shift to 'human capital', creating a subjectivity that installs a whole new system of valuation into the capitalist economy.[38] As earlier noted, valuation and valorization now seem to take place at the level of the individual, who, through speculative investments, appreciates their own value – accumulated, measured and compared through digital metrics such as 'likes', 'shares', 'views' and 'followers'. With the shift from worker to human capital, and from wage to income, accruing such metrics provides a quantitative measure of the individual's 'brand equity', a quality central to this new subject's ability to locate streams of revenue and thus survive.[39]

By framing valorization as an individual as opposed to social process, writers such as Van Doorn, Brown and Feher follow Foucault in positing the emergence of human capital as the waning of labour's ontological status. Feher argues that neoliberalism occasions the 'decline of the type of the free labourer and its gradual replacement by a new form of subjectivity: human capital'.[40] Brown is similarly decisive in her turn away from labour, arguing that 'Commensurate with neoliberal reason's replacement of exchange by competition and equality by inequality, human capital replaces labo.'[41] The culmination of this substitution is Van Doorn's rendition of the financial subject, who has totally abandoned the scene of social production to the solipsistic pursuit of self-valorization. It is worth pointing out that, despite originating in a critique of human capital theory, the Foucauldian heritage has ended up repeating the Chicago school's greatest assault against labour: the categorical refusal of the 'labourer' – without which 'civilizational despair', to use Brown's own term, replaces the strikes and revolts that only remain possible under the 'labourer' rubric.[42]

It makes sense, then, to avoid overstating the ontological status of human capital, if not for this political reason, then at least because financialization does not nullify labour, but postpones it indefinitely. Unable to capture this dynamic, Annie McClanahan suggests, 'human capital' and 'entrepreneurialism' do not really describe 'the experience, or the consciousness, or the actual material status of... the *exemplary* subject of the present: an underemployed part-timer'.[43] Bracketed and deferred, this growing precarious mass is not determined by a new productive ontology, I would argue, but rather takes on the 'self-valorizing' appearance of fictitious capital. Remember, belonging to circulation not production, fictitious capital is unable to generate value, even though, as earlier noted, it appears to automatically produce capital. As such, 'this automatic fetish' is 'elaborated into its pure form, self-valorizing value... and in this form it no longer bears any marks of its origins'.[44] Much as capital under the guidance of financialization appears to become its own source of valorization, so does the worker, as they accumulate the 'likes' 'shares' and 'followers' that provide income; and just as financial capital obliterates any trace of the production process from which it arises, so the 'neoliberal subject of value' erases its originary position as labour – now increasingly a surplus population outside of the conventional workforce, which appears 'entrepreneurial' as it competes for the petty employment available. As the term suggests, fictitious capital acts as capital but without really being capital, much as the worker turned 'entrepreneur' is encouraged to act as a capitalist without actually owning any capital. As Marx notes of this fiction, 'Instead of the actual transformation of money into capital, we have here only the form of this devoid of content'.[45] Human capital further formalizes the void, with the necessary content of labour absent because superfluous, now reimagined in the appearance of the very relation that abolished it: capital itself.

If human capital is a fetishistic mask worn by the social relations of finance capitalism, then it seems prudent to assume that the form it conceals is also generated by those very relations. To reiterate: finance capital appears to valorize itself, but is only the promise of value yet to be generated, an antagonism between appearance and form that holds equally true for human capital. Before proceeding to establish the processes of self-valorization at the centre of human capital as essentially promissory, I must first develop this argument from the original definition of the term as used by Becker to describe investments in education.

The full title of his landmark text *Human Capital: A Theoretical and Empirical Analysis with Special Reference to Education* suggests Becker's primary interest in 'schooling' and 'on-the-job training' as exemplary 'investments in human capital'. In the introductory passages, he notes that 'unemployment tends to be strongly related, usually inversely, to education'; in other words, those who 'invest' in education are more employable than those who do not.[46] Alongside one's formal education, Becker notes that both 'general' and 'on-the-job' 'training' augment the worker's capacity to locate employment. As these experiences and activities translate into a greater range of 'skills', Becker notes, the individual becomes more attractive to potential or current employers.[47] On the surface, at least, human capital appears as a market-oriented synonym for 'labour-power', described by Marx in similar terms to Becker as: 'the aggregate of those mental and physical capabilities existing in the physical form, the living personality, of a human being'.[48] Yet, a fundamental difference prevails: 'labour-power' functions as a commodity, sold by the worker and consumed by the capitalist in the wage relation, while 'human capital' treats the worker like a financial asset, the primary point of which is not to be sold or consumed but to remain in a constant state of valuation. As such, labour-power is interested in *employment*, while human capital is interested in *employability*, a contestable state of valuation that, like a financial asset, may appreciate or depreciate – read here as symptomatic of a financialized system that perpetually postpones labour and its associated arena of struggle. Employment articulates this antagonistic arena of unemployment, the length of the working day and the price of the wage; on the other hand, employability replaces these antagonisms with the labourer's responsibility to find work.

Human capital, then, is neither substitutable for nor synonymous with labour or labour-power, but rather a concept that ideologically refigures a fundamental contradiction between capital and labour – that of employment as the sole responsibility of the labourer. Instead of making this false substitution, I here argue that the great variety of activities subsumed under the heading of 'human capital', from education to Twitter followers, fall under the rubric of the worker's promise. Education makes the worker more employable because it makes a promise to capital that the worker is willing and able to fulfil the requirements of a particular occupation. When a worker 'invests' in a law degree they are enhancing the promise of their labour-power, which, if successful, will solicit the interests of an employer. Looking to hire a new lawyer, a law firm does not *know* in advance whether an applicant is capable; that is, the employer does not know that the worker's labour-power has use-value; rather, an assumption must be made based on the worker's education and experience, presented through their CV, LinkedIn profile or interview conduct. Like a can of Coca-Cola drenched in condensation on a TV advertisement, the labour-power commodity finds a buyer not because its *actual* utility is readily grasped, but because, to take one example, a first-class law degree from Oxford University enhances the promise that draws the employer in to a purchase.

While the promise of labour-power arrives on the scene with the proletariat, who at the factory gate must promise themselves with an able body and a will to work, it has since developed into more 'transparent', 'accountable' and indeed countable forms that suit the needs of an economy organized by auditing processes originating in the finance and accountancy sector.[49] Under this financial regime, 'likes', 'followers', 'shares', 'views' and 'friends' act as the key metrics by which the labour-power promise is measured and articulated. Even in education, university rank and degree mark act as the primary indicators of alumni employability. The same goes for academics, who are measured by REF scores, citations and their number of publications. From her readings of 'digital economy' management texts, Alison Hearn shows that metrics for online scores, ranks and ratings now count to 'human resource professionals' as much if not more than an 'individual employee's skills'.[50] This 'digital reputation' – scored, ranked and rated – translates the illusory qualities of Haug's commodity promise into illusory quantities that appear to offer an objective, that is, impossible measure of labour-power.

Quantified and accumulated, the promise is expressed numerically, as with 'price', the fetish of finance that appears to abolish the labour and value that it nonetheless registers. Considering that, in Haug's argument, the promise the commodity makes to the buyer is not identical with ideology but does frequently act as its carrier, it makes perfect sense that the promise of labour-power takes the quality of 'moneyness'.[51] Originally used by Costas Lapavistas to characterize the peculiar ambiguities and antagonisms of the money form, 'moneyness' can more broadly be used to define the numerical equivalents and 'impossible equation[s]' that comprise the ideological lifeworld of financialization.[52] Take auditing, for example: broken free from the finance and accountancy sector, it now appears in a variety of sublimated forms across the social field, from endless consumer reviews of things and experiences to scores, ranks and ratings of potentially any human activity.[53] What counts in a moment of moneyness is numerical; thus, illusory quantities are promises that count because they are countable and, by extension, accountable.

Surplus promises

'Moneyness' defines the ideological criteria by which scores, ranks and ratings appear to have birthed a new ontology of 'self-value'. Yet, 'self-value' has only gained this position, albeit notionally, due to the space vacated by labour. Precariously poised between the 'Ms' of $M-M^1[C]$, the worker's role drifts ever-more from producing to promising. The reason is intimated in Haug's suggestive claim that as the commodity empties of use it fills with promise, whereby illusions and dreams engulf and, in a certain sense, colonize use-value: 'The imaginary spaces around the commodity are clearly capable of inducing a correspondent meaning activity in their use.'[54] Empty in the present and implied in the future, the voided use of labour-power similarly brims with fantastic impressions, structurally intimated in the labour that we find bracketed in the financial circuitry $M-M^1[C]$, whereby its role is no longer productive but largely promissory.

All of which is to say that, just as marketing, advertising and branding invent illusions that fill the emptied space of product utility, the use-value of labour-power, increasingly voided by financialization, is similarly overwhelmed by the aesthetic illusions that once sustained it. As these illusions have expanded in tandem with the decline of labour-power's use, it is perhaps not surprising that we begin to think of work in terms of 'self-branding'. As many suggest, branding itself ascends as corporate strategy during our financialized period precisely because it conveys the promissory logic of financial profits.[55] Somewhat differently, I would argue, 'self-branding' is best regarded as a discursive strategy for celebrating the 'opportunities' ostensibly afforded labour by its precarious condition, and its subsequent need to promise itself in ever-more elaborate ways. 'The rise of personal branding', as proclaimed by one enthusiastic guru, is nothing more than the promise subsuming the labour-power that it once presented, as the system increasingly makes profits outside of production.[56] Thus, the growth of 'brand equity' through scores, ranks and ratings that Van Doorn regards as the strategic goal of the '*entrepreneurial worker*' is, rather, the morbid symptom of a system that compels a *superfluous worker*, under pains of survival, to competitively measure, maintain and advance their promise.[57] Morbid because 'the rise of personal branding', read here as the replacement of use with excess promise, expresses the abolition of labour-power, the very lifeforce of capital.

To conclude, as use is subjugated to promise, a spectacle of redundant labour pervades the social world, most obviously on platforms such as Facebook, Instagram and Twitter – sites on which, in lieu of their capacity to sell labour-power, users are encouraged to market themselves with anxious zeal. Much like the grand exhibitions of nineteenth-century Europe where, as Walter Benjamin argued, commodities would 'linger on the threshold' of a sale, social media sites act as ostentatious displays of labour-power, where users prime their 'special commodity' to lure a sale through acts of 'branding'.[58] This vast and ceaseless exhibition of solicitous images and opinions, seeking 'likes', 'followers' and 'friends', is the grand spectacle of a workforce attempting to make its presence known to a system that no longer needs it – attempts that only feedback into the system as profits in the form of personal data. Just as the grand exhibitions once curated commodities into fantastic spectacles, digital platforms might be said to organize the dreamworld of superfluous labour, whereby labour-power, divested of use, is taken to 'phantasmagorical' levels of promise and distraction.[59] Understood so, self-brands and self-value are little more than expressions of a promissory logic as old as capitalism itself, a logic aggravated to spectacular proportions by a financial system that is emptying labour of all but its aesthetic illusion.

Notes

1   Wendy Brown, *Undoing the Demos: Neoliberalism's Stealth Revolution* (Cambridge: MIT Press, 2015), 34.

2   Michel Feher, 'Self Appreciation; or, the Aspirations of Human Capital', *Public Culture* 21, no. 1 (2009): 25, 27.

3   Michel Foucault, *The Birth of Biopolitics: Lectures at the Collège de France 1978–1979* (New York: Palgrave Macmillan, 2010); Niels Van Doorn, 'The Neoliberal Subject of Value: Measuring Human Capital in Information Economies', *Cultural Politics* 10, no. 3 (2014), 354–375.

4   Foucault, *The Birth of Biopolitics,* 226

5   Gary Becker, *Human Capital: A Theoretical and Empirical Analysis, with Special Reference to Education* (New York: Columbia University Press, 1975), 9.

6   Feher, 'Self Appreciation', 27.

7   Feher, 'Self Appreciation', 27.

8   Van Doorn, 'The Neoliberal Subject of Value', 354.

9   Van Doorn, 'The Neoliberal Subject of Value', 358. See also, Brown, *Undoing the Demos,* 34. Brown notes that 'through social media "followers", "likes" and "retweets", through rankings and ratings for every activity and domain', the neoliberal subject translates experience into personal value.

10 Van Doorn, 'The Neoliberal Subject of Value', 362.

11 Francois Guéry and Didier Deleule, *The Productive Body* (Winchester: Zero Books, 2014).

12 Karl Marx, *Capital*, vol. 3 (London: Penguin, 1991), 516.

13 Matt Phull and Will Stronge, 'The Promise: A Heuristic for Employability', *Autonomy*, 9 February 2019, https://autonomy.work/portfolio/the-promise-a-heuristic-for-employability/?fbclid=IwAR1uMdq-WPhqXNu85earDOCc0e5Db HSy0FACBxUv9tVwJMD0WlroUyouUZE#_edn2.

14 Fernand Braudel, *Civilization and Capitalism: 15th–18th Century (Volume 3) Perspective of the World* (London: Fontana Press, 1985), 246.

15 Karl Marx, *Capital*, vol. 1 (London: Penguin, 1982), 270, 274–5.

16 Robert Brenner, *The Boom and the Bubble* (London: Verso, 2003), 4.

17 Marx, *Capital* 1, 257

18 Marx, *Capital* 3, 516

19 Costas Lapavitsas, *Profiting without Producing: How Finance Exploits Us All*
    (London: Verso, 2013), 175–7.

20 Dick Bryan and Michael Rafferty, *Capitalism with Derivatives: A Political
    Economy of Financial Derivatives, Capital and Class* (London: Palgrave
    Macmillan, 2005), 176.

21 Nick Srnicek and Alex Williams, *Inventing the Future* (London: Verso, 2016), 94.

22 Marx, *Capital* 1, 784.

23 Rosa Luxemburg, *The Accumulation of Capital* (London: Routledge, 2003), 83.

24 Aaron Benanav, 'Misery and Debt: On the History of Surplus Populations and
    Surplus Capital', *Endnotes* (April 2010), https://endnotes.org.uk/issues/2/en/
    endnotes-misery-and-debt.

25 Moishe Postone, *Time, Labour and Domination* (Cambridge: Cambridge
    University Press, 1993), 359.

26 Brown, *Undoing the Demos,* 132–3.

27 Guy Standing, *The Precariat: The New Dangerous Class* (London: Bloomsbury,
    2016), 141.

28 Leigh Claire La Berge, 'Decommodified Labour: Conceptualizing Work
    after the Wage', *Lateral* 7, no.1 (2018). https://csalateral.org/issue/7-1/
    decommodified-labor-work-after-wage-la-berge/.

29 Phull and Stronge, 'The Promise'.

30 Wolfgang Haug, *Commodity Aesthetics* (Cambridge: Polity Press, 1986), 13–17.

31 Phull and Stronge, 'The Promise'.

32 Sylvia Federici, *Caliban and the Witch* (Brooklyn: Autonomedia, 2004), 11–17.
    In Federici's theory of the female body as reproductive labourer, we can read
    femininity itself as promising a woman's capacity to reproduce the workforce. See
    also Maria Mies, *Patriarchy and Accumulation on a World Scale: Women in the
    International Division of Labour* (London: Zed Books, 2014).

33 Wolfgang Haug, *Commodity Aesthetics, Ideology and Culture* (New York:
    International General, 1987), 115.

34 Haug, *Commodity Aesthetics*, 30–2. Haug here discusses the way that competition
    between firms eventually 'limits itself to the competition between impressions',
    that is, advertising and branding.

35 Marx, *Capital* 3, 597; Marx, *Capital* 1, 163–78. Marx first elaborates the
    idea of 'commodity fetish' in vol. 1 as the perception of social relationships
    as relationships between things. For Marx, under capitalism, things end up

substituting for relations. Promissory notes are doubly, or even trebly, fetishistic in that they stand in for things that stand in for relations.

36 Marx, *Capital* 3, 599.

37 Joshua Clover, 'Autumn of the System: Poetry and Finance Capital', *Journal of Narrative Theory* 41, no. 1 (2011): 45.

38 Van Doorn, 'The Neoliberal Subject of Value', 357–8.

39 Van Doorn, 'The Neoliberal Subject of Value', 362–3.

40 Feher, 'Self Appreciation', 24.

41 Brown, *Undoing the Demos*, 65.

42 Brown, *Undoing the Demos*, 221.

43 Annie McClanahan, 'Becoming Non-Economic: Human Capital Theory and Wendy Brown's *Undoing the Demos*', *Theory and Event* 20, no. 2 (2017): 513

44 Marx, *Capital* 3, 516

45 Marx, *Capital* 3, 516.

46 Becker, *Human Capital*, 9–10.

47 Becker, *Human Capital*, 19–20.

48 Marx, *Capital* 1, 271.

49 Marilyn Strathern, 'Introduction: New Accountabilities', in *Audit Cultures: Anthropological Studies in Accountability, Ethics and the Academy*, ed. Marilyn Strathern (London: Routledge, 2000), 2.

50 Alison Hearn, 'Structuring Feeling: Web 2.0, Online Ranking and Rating, and the Digital "reputation" Economy', *Ephemera* 10, no. 3/4 (2010): 422.

51 Haug, *Commodity Aesthetics, Ideology and Culture*, 156–63. In 'The "Jeans Culture"' essay, Haug shows the way that the commodity promise reciprocates capitalist ideology. The promise is 'opportunistic' of capitalist ideology, Haug notes.

52 Lapavitsas, *Profiting without Producing*, 74–82. Lapavitsas here lays out his original Marxist theory of money. He frames this argument through the term 'moneyness', which describes the strange, contradictory world of finance. Beyond the examples Lapavitsas analyses in the financial industry, I suggest that the term captures the equivalences that organize the social world at large during our present financialized moment.

See also Jacques Rancière, *Dis- agreement: Politics and Philosophy* (London: University of Minnesota Press, 1995), 10. See also Jacques Rancière, 'The Concept of Critique and the Critique of Political Economy; From the *1844 Manuscripts* to *Capital*', in *Reading Capital,* ed. Louis Althusser, Étienne Balibar, Roger Establet, Pierre Macherey and Jacques Rancière (London: Verso, 2015). Rancière uses the

term 'impossible equations' for a variety of purposes across these essays, but I
here use the term to denote the contradictory equivalents that characterize the
money form.

53 Marilyn Strathern, 'Introduction: New Accountabilities', in *Audit Cultures:
Anthropological Studies in Accountability, Ethics and the Academy*, ed. Marilyn
Strathern (London: Routledge, 2000), 2.

54 Haug, *Commodity Aesthetics, Ideology and Culture*, 154.

55 Leigh Claire La Berge, *Scandals and Abstractions* (New York: Oxford University
Press, 2015), 63. See also Richard Godden, 'Fictions of Fictitious Capital:
American Psycho and the Poetics of Deregulation', *Textual Practise* 25, no. 5
(2011): 858.

56 Dan Schawbel, '*Me 2.0: Build a Powerful Brand to Achieve Career Success*' (New
York: Kaplan, 2009). See also Julie Broad, *The New Brand You: Your New Image
Makes the Sale for You* (Los Angeles: Stick Horse Publishing, 2016), xvi.

57 Van Doorn, 'The Neoliberal Subject of Value', 362. Emphasis added.

58 Walter Benjamin, *The Arcades Project* (Cambridge: University of Harvard Press,
2002), 13.

59 Benjamin, *The Arcades Project*, 17.

6

The dialectical body: Bringing science back into socialism

Graham Jones

Marxism in the West today has little or no relation to the natural sciences. Whilst historically – and particularly under Soviet communism – natural scientific enquiry has played a key role in the development of Marxist thought, this connection was severed in the mid-twentieth century, particularly following György Lukács's 1923 book *History and Class Consciousness*, which explicitly restricted dialectical analysis to the social realm.[1] Whilst there may have been sound reasons for a break with such approaches to dialectical materialism – often a tool of totalitarian dogmatism used to justify any action of the party leadership – the division has subsequently hampered natural scientific literacy among the left. The problems with this have become clear with the escalating climate crisis, where until recently Marxists have been on the back foot when it comes to analysing the ecological impacts of capitalism. If the work of ecological Marxists such as John Bellamy Foster has helped to close this gap in recent times, such approaches have been largely aimed solely at that specific terrain, rather than in relation to natural science per se. Without a wider integration of revolutionary theory with contemporary science the left cuts itself off from discourses which could aid it in reflecting upon and renewing its materialism. Further, a lack of technical literacy undermines the left's potential to influence popular discourse involving scientific issues, or science itself. To demonstrate how such a dialogue is possible beyond ecology alone, in subsequent sections this chapter will engage with the broader interdisciplinary framework of complex systems theory, before moving to the related subdiscipline of embodied cognitive science.

In order to enable such an integration however, we have to overcome the scepticism felt by many Marxists towards natural science. Three terms in particular seem to arise in such discussions. First, there is 'mechanical materialism', used by Marx to characterize and dismiss the atomistic and reductionistic science of his time.[2] Second, there is 'bourgeois science', initially used by Marx and Engels to describe the work of political economists like Adam Smith, but in the Soviet Union coming to mean any science undertaken outside of a Marxist framework, and often used to dismiss the findings of Western scientists *tout court*. This can be seen, for example, in the rejection of the study of genetics by the followers of Lysenko, or in the vulgar Marxist attacks on Einstein and Newton.[3] Lastly, there is Marx and Engels's rejection of 'metaphysics', in which they distance themselves from those philosophers who were concerned only with 'beings of thought and heavenly things, at the very time when real beings and earthly things began to be the centre of all interest'.[4]

These three rejections – of mechanical materialism, bourgeois science and metaphysics – whilst derived from Marx and Engels, are themselves today aimed back at Engels. It is now a common belief that Engels's thought represents a Marxism corrupted by idealism and positivism, and thus his contributions are safely extricable from the truly materialist and historicist thought of Marx. But as Helena Sheehan points out, such a dismissal is based on an extremely reductive reading of the relationship between Marx and Engels.[5] Marx certainly never set out any comprehensive philosophy of natural science, unlike Engels, who presented this in *Anti-Dühring* and the unfinished *Dialectics of Nature*. Yet this alone does not demonstrate Marx's disagreement with Engels. Marx read *Anti-Dühring* in its entirety before its publication, and even contributed a chapter himself.[6] He never raised any substantive objections to Engels's dialectics of nature in their decades of correspondence on the subject. Marx confirmed his agreement with Hegel's philosophy of nature, such as the dialectical law of the transformation of quantity into quality, and stated 'that it holds good alike in history and natural science'.[7] And as John Bellamy Foster and Paul Burkett have shown, Marx was deeply influenced by the natural sciences of his time, having drawn from Darwin's theories of evolution and the emerging science of thermodynamics, even in his later political-economic work.[8] Rather than there being a philosophical divide between Marx and Engels, it is more accurate, Sheehan argues, to consider the relationship between Marx and Engels as representing a division of labour within a shared intellectual project, with Marx focusing on the political-economic aspects, and Engels on the philosophical and natural scientific.[9] Thus, if we were to dismiss Engels on the basis of his thought being 'mechanical, bourgeois and metaphysical', then Marx would be equally culpable. In any case, we need not dismiss Engels. It is my contention that all three of these lines of critique can be answered to allow an integration of contemporary science with Marxist analyses.[10]

First, 'mechanical materialism' is a worldview that conceives of the universe as fundamentally machine-like, which Marx and Engels trace back to the influence of Newton and Descartes, although without either necessarily being materialists themselves.[11] It posits that by understanding the motions of parts of the physical universe, we can ultimately come to understand all larger scale phenomena. Thus 'mechanical' also tends to imply reductionism and atomism. This framework was subsequently transposed into the social realm by thinkers such as Thomas Hobbes. In *Leviathan, or The Matter, Forme and Power of a Commonwealth Ecclesiasticall and Civil*, Hobbes develops the principles of matter in motion into a conception of human subjects as atomic, self-interested individuals always on the brink of descending into a conflictual state of nature. Given that this understanding of human nature has formed the backbone of liberalism, it is easy to see why such mechanistic philosophy would be problematic for a Marxist materialism. Whilst this was at one point the ascendant view in the natural sciences, even by Marx and Engels's time it was coming under pressure. Darwinian evolution, with its image of an ever-changing universe, was in tension with this mechanical worldview, as was thermodynamics, which posited the universe as a system which constantly developed towards disorder.[12] These were perspectives which foregrounded processes of change over regularity, and which suggested that complex phenomena may not be fully understandable by a reduction to their atomistic parts. Marx and Engels brought the contours of this new dynamic scientific thought into their political-economic theory – as well as critiquing how others such as Sergei Podolinsky had tried to do likewise – in discussing the evolution of the forces of production, and of labour as a 'metabolic' relationship of energy transfer between society and nature.[13] Since Marx and Engels's time the prominence of such dynamic perspectives in the sciences has expanded massively, with disciplines and theoretical frameworks such as complexity science, chaos theory, quantum mechanics, and general relativity, as well as the further development of evolutionary theory and non-equilibrium thermodynamics.[14] A rejection of mechanical materialism is therefore not – nor ever was – a rejection of natural science itself.

Turning to the second critique mentioned above – the notion that such sciences are 'bourgeois' – this might be interpreted in one of two ways: that the original study was carried out without a revolutionary purpose within bourgeois institutions, or that there is something about the ideas themselves which somehow serve to reproduce bourgeois subjectivity and class society. With regard to the former, to dismiss any natural scientific study not carried out with a proletarian purpose is at odds with Marx and Engels's own work: there was no communist intent in Darwin's writing, and arguably thermodynamics emerged in a specifically capitalist context with the aim of making the blast furnaces powering the industrial revolution more efficient.[15] Clearly, original intent and function do not foreclose later application in unfamiliar contexts, equally in natural science as in Marx's engagement with classical political economists like Smith and Ricardo. We can even affirm this as an ontological principle, drawing on the aforementioned non-reductionist complexity sciences: in contemporary evolutionary theory a 'preadaptation' or 'exaptation' is a previously epiphenomenal feature that comes to fulfil a different purpose *after* it has been created, when new ecological niches emerge.[16]

If on the other hand 'bourgeois science' is implying the reproduction of bourgeois subjectivity and class society through its ideas alone, then this is again challenged by contemporary holistic sciences. In the embodied approach to cognitive science for example – which we will turn to in more detail shortly – the mind is not an atomized individual with essential qualities, but is a dynamic system that emerges in coupling with its environment, which develops historically through its activity, and is culturally and socially situated. We do of course need to maintain a critical eye when studying such work, because academics – tending to come from the middle class – may unwittingly bring liberal ideological tendencies into their work. But this note of caution is very different to arguing for the fundamentally bourgeois character of natural scientific concepts. Indeed, many of the advances in these disciplines are directly relevant to revolutionary organizing: whether in understanding information flow in social networks, the embeddedness of consciousness in the world, the dynamics of chaos in moments of revolutionary rupture or the principles of building resilient organizational ecologies. In short, in drawing from those sciences that resist reductionistic and atomistic approaches we can find a wealth of study around change in systems that leftist analysis can make use of.

In doing so, however, we must acknowledge that systems theories always involve a degree of abstraction across physical, biological and social domains, as well as historical periods. We therefore risk entering an arena which the Marxist tradition has typically rejected as 'metaphysical', arising as early as Marx's comments found in his *Theses on Feuerbach* about 'contemplative materialism'. He uses the term to attack thought which focuses exclusively on the abstract, that misapplies trans-historical ontological status to that which is historically situated, and which demonstrates a lack of concern for practical application. But these criticisms are aimed at a particular approach to philosophy, rather than denying that there are generalities that might arise from natural science and be applicable to the social realm. Around the same time Marx explicitly affirms the importance of natural science, such as in a letter to Arnold Ruge where he comments that Feuerbach 'refers too much to nature and too little to politics. That, however, is the only alliance by which present-day philosophy can become truth'.[17] Later, in the first version of the *German Ideology* – for which the *Theses* were intended as preliminary thoughts – Marx and Engels remarked that '[t]he two sides are, however, inseparable; the history of nature and the history of men are dependent on each other so long as men exist'.[18]

Engels's rejection of metaphysics in his *Socialism: Utopian and Scientific* is similarly misinterpreted. Here he did not intend to dismiss all philosophical speculation on the nature of reality, but used the term specifically to refer to a mode of thinking that was static and rigid, with hard and fast dividing lines, as opposed to the fluidity of dialectical thought.[19] Today this is more likely to be considered as a distinction *within* metaphysics, rather than something *distinct from* metaphysics; as a difference between ontologies[20] focused on categories like 'being' and 'substance', as opposed to 'becoming' and 'event'.[21] Moreover, even if Marx had dismissed metaphysics as an approach to philosophy in its entirety, this does not negate the fact that there is a metaphysical aspect to Marx's writing, in the sense of an underlying understanding of reality that stretches between the natural and social realms. Bertell Ollman has shown that there is a consistent realist ontology underlying Marx's thought, particularly concerned with notions of processes and relations.[22] This can be seen across the Marxist conceptual canon, in terms such as 'relations of production', 'the labour process', 'cycles of accumulation', 'reproduction schemas', 'class relations', 'forces of production' or alienation understood as a severing of our awareness of social relations. This focus on dynamic processes and complex relations is consistent with the non-reductionist, holistic sciences of change previously mentioned.

I argue therefore that we can create a space for articulating Marxism and contemporary natural science through the notion of a *process-relational ontology*. That is, a metaphysical perspective which, rather than foregrounding eternal substances, fixed and clearly individuated objects, and unchanging essences, instead focuses on how things emerge from their histories, develop through their interactions, and remain structurally dynamic. As Anne Fairchild-Pomeroy argues, for such a framework to remain consistent with Marx and Engels's critiques of metaphysics, it must fulfil two further criteria: (1) it must engage with the concrete – that is, experience and practical activity – both in drawing out its concepts and in being oriented towards influencing action; and (2) it must recognize its own historical situatedness and thus fallibility, limitation and incompleteness.[23] Whilst a detailed specification of such an ontology is beyond the scope of this chapter, we can nonetheless progress on the basis of this broad outline. Where a fuller account would attempt to answer such questions as, 'what is a relation?', here I merely suggest that the question is worth asking. In summary, Marxist theory is compatible with non-reductionist approaches to natural science. Contemporary systems sciences can be used for revolutionary ends and – so long as they are approached with a sufficiently critical eye – do not necessitate the reproduction of bourgeois subjectivity. Marxist and natural scientific perspectives can find a framework for interaction through a process-relational ontology. By identifying points of overlap and absence, we can, on the one hand, update Marxist materialism, and, on the other, expand the left's scientific literacy and ability to influence social discourse involving science.

In turning to the contemporary sciences, complexity theory is a particularly appropriate place to begin, because of its little-known history loosely connecting it back to Marxism. The Marxist theorist Alexander Bogdanov – at one point a rival of Lenin's for the leadership of the Bolshevik party – pioneered 'Tektology', which is considered to be the first 'systems theory'.[24] Bogdanov's system became familiar to the circles around both Norbert Weiner and Ludwig von Bertalanffy, who developed cybernetics and general systems theory respectively.[25] These theories have since developed into the modern complex systems science, network theory and embodied cognitive science in use today. So, whilst Marxists themselves may have come to dismiss the natural scientific import of their philosophy, it has continued to have historical influence in spite of them.

Body as system: For a non-mechanistic materialism

Central to any complex systems approach is of course the concept of 'system'. At its most general, a system can be conceived of as an organized whole made out of parts, as it was in the original Greek term *systema*.[26] This is used to refer not just to technological or mechanical systems, as we might tend to imply in casual speech, but can include anything with interrelated parts, including traffic lights, ant colonies, the human body, or even a rock (which can be considered a system at thermodynamic equilibrium). The difference between a simple and a complex system is that where the former may have only one or two different types of parts in one or two types of relations leading to a limited number of output states (as in a set of traffic lights, or a thermostat), in a complex system there are heterogeneous parts involved in heterogeneous relations, leading to a huge variety of output states (such as the complex interlinking of skeletomuscular, respiratory, digestive, neurocognitive and other systems within the human body). One other significant aspect of a system is that it is itself a whole, but can also act as a part within a larger whole, such as a cell being part of a bodily organ which is part of a whole human being. This enables a kind of multi-scalar interrelation of systems, each system emerging out of its substrate systems.[27]

Although Marx does not appear to use the term 'system' in quite such an ontologically specific sense (most uses of 'system' in *Capital* refer to social systems only), he does have an equivalent: body. He uses this term to refer not merely to the concrete human body but to systems more widely, and it is applied to numerous scales and domains. In the 'Commodities' chapter of *Capital*, Marx refers to commodities in their concrete form such as coats, iron and sugar as bodies.[28] Later, and most frequently in the 'Machinery and Modern Industry' chapter, he refers to 'the whole body of capitalists', 'the body of the factory', the 'social body of labour', 'the body of the machine', 'a body of men' and 'their union into one single productive body'.[29] This latter term in particular is taken up by Guéry and Deleule in *The Productive Body*, as part of a threefold distinction of biological, social and productive bodies within capitalism.[30] Within these broad bodies, various subsystems, such as guilds, are themselves described as bodies.[31] Although Guéry and Deleule don't draw attention to this in metaphysical terms, the concept of the body is here functioning to draw parallels between nested series of systems, being applied equally to the human body, to schools, prisons and hospitals, and to the broad organizing principles of the capitalist system.

The Productive Body is presented as an extension of *Capital*, and so we might presume that the concept of 'body' is the same between both works. If an individual commodity, such as a coat, is a body for Marx, then it must be for Guéry and Deleule too. Yet there seems to be a subtle difference in their use of the term. The closest *The Productive Body* comes to defining the body is where Guéry and Deleule state, '[i]t is a body, for it machinifies forces and subjugates them to itself'.[32] This feels appropriate for many of the hugely dynamic bodies they focus on, but it seems odd to include a coat in this definition, or indeed any non-living commodity. Can a coat really be said to machinify forces and subjugate them to itself? The language lends agency to the commodity itself in its own production, as though the coat sleeve was filled with a ghostly arm, stitching its own material. One might argue that, within a complex social totality, the coat could be said to *result* from a subjugation and machinification of forces. But collapsing this distinction between subjugator and subjugated leaves no means of conceptualizing the difference between living and non-living bodies, or between intentional and non-intentional action, and therefore clouds our understanding of *autonomy*, which is a significant concept for Guéry and Deleule. If we were to present an ontology based around a central concept which does not allow these distinctions, we could face problems when coming to apply it to ethical and political matters.

It appears then that Marx's 'body' is a broad equivalent for 'system', including objects, whereas Guéry and Deleule's is a particular type of body, namely a complex system. In particular, these systems that machinify forces and subjugate them to themselves – that is, which extract order from their environments in the process of self-reproduction – could be seen as equivalent to 'autopoietic' bodies. Autopoiesis – derived from *auto* meaning 'self', and *poiesis* meaning 'creation' – is a concept developed by the biologists Humberto Maturana and Francisco Varela, who sought to develop a formal criterion for the notion of life.[33] For Maturana and Varela, self-reproduction is the main characteristic of life, whereby a body through its own internal relations continuously reproduces its internal structure, and its external boundary with its environment.[34] This creation of a boundary enables a certain amount of autonomy from its environment, maintaining the internal structural integrity against external perturbations. However, in order for self-maintenance to be possible, there needs to be an inflow and outflow of matter and information – just as we are constantly taking in food and sense information from our environment, so too does the bacteria cell in different ways. That autonomy is therefore only relative, and indeed this constant relationship with its outside means an autopoietic body must co-evolve with its environment. Such environments are made up of other autopoietic bodies, which through entering into regular relations can become parts of larger-scale autopoietic bodies in a multi-scalar structure. As these bodies interact and co-adapt over time, they maintain their relative autonomy, but their internal constitutions become structurally coupled and thus develop in tandem.[35]

Given the level of abstraction of autopoiesis, it has subsequently been applied beyond the natural scientific realm, to include social and conceptual bodies.[36] Wherever we see a network of forces that autonomously reproduces its own boundary and internal organization, through a material-semiotic inflow and outflow, autopoiesis may be identified. In the case of a social system, this boundary will not necessarily be a physical membrane, but may be a communicative boundary, such as that of, for example, who is or is not considered a member of an organization. (Physical boundaries may, however, be used to help enforce a social boundary, such as with borders or the walls of government buildings.) Corporations, universities, communities and cities can therefore also fulfil this definition of autopoiesis, just as a human body or a single-celled organism can. Although this concept is a relatively modern invention, Marx used a number of his own concepts that cross over with autopoiesis, such as 'metabolism' and 'organism'. As well as using 'organic body' to refer to the autopoietic individual human body, he also referred to 'man's *inorganic* body', that being the wider natural and social metabolisms that sustain human life, connected to us through tool use.[37] This extension of the human beyond its own physical boundaries has interesting parallels with embodied cognitive science, which presumes an autopoietic body as the mind's necessary substrate.

Embodied cognition: For a non-bourgeois science

From its inception, autopoiesis was also a theory of mind, the minimal conditions of life being also the minimal conditions of cognition. Autopoietic approaches to cognition conceive of the mind not as a thing, but as a process, involving sets of internal and external relations.[38] If minds are autopoietic, then what we've said about autopoiesis in general also applies here, such as how minds are on the one hand autonomous, but coupled with others and co-evolving with them. There is no such thing therefore as a completely individual or independent mind, but rather one with relative autonomy.

The way that a nested autopoietic ontology allows for integration of structure and agency into a single language is useful for discussions of ideology. For contemporary left thinkers, ideology is not something that is expressed in clearly defined systems that you can consciously ascribe to (as in 'I am a communist'), but is rather the series of pervasive, unspoken patterns of thought, behaviour, images and institutional processes that make up a particular common sense.[39] Thinking in terms of the coupling and evolution of dynamical systems, we can examine change at different speeds across multiple timescales: the slow physical evolution of the human species and its faculties (phylogenesis), the development of synchronized behaviours across a population over a historical period (sociogenesis), the learning over an individual's lifetime (ontogenesis) and the rapid moment-to-moment cognition of immediate experience (microgenesis), concepts from evolutionary biology that had already been taken up by Marxist psychologist Leo Vygotsky in the 1920s.[40] Those sociogenetic changes create patterns which shape ontogenetic and microgenetic scales in a non-linear, probabilistic manner, creating *tendencies* of subjectivity across a population, rather than rigidly determining all subjects in the same way. Further, ideological apparatuses such as the media, the state and corporate enterprises are themselves autopoietic bodies, and so are open to some measure of change through their structural coupling. As Terrence Deacon has it, interaction in which one body tries to change another in a way which goes against its general tendencies is what produces work (in the thermodynamic sense), or what a Marxist might be more comfortable thinking of in terms of struggle, contradiction or antagonism.[41]

In such a framework, we avoid both an overly subjective focus and a rigid social determinism; the subject is neither an ideological dupe fully and homogenously formed by a shared social environment, but nor is one ever free from being shaped by ideological social forces. One can struggle against or passively accept an ideological background. And on a microgenetic scale one might momentarily think, speak or act in a manner which does not characterize their whole-life ontogenetic trajectory (pointing to a fluidity and multiplicity of mind that is worth considering when it comes to propaganda and persuasion).

The sensing performed by an autopoietic body involves an openness to environmental stimuli, an evaluation of that stimuli, and a reaction of the body based on that valuation.[42] This bears resemblance to what Ollman identifies in Marx as a minimal theory of sensing, involving the three stages of perception, orientation and appropriation.[43] The content of that intermediate moment of orientation or evaluation in the human subject is addressed in cognitive linguistics with the notion of 'schemas' and 'frames'.[44] These are the networks of embodied knowledge – episodic memories, semantic relations, sensorimotor patterns – that are activated alongside a concept. It is common enough to see ideology functioning in the patterns of cognitive schemas that are spread through a population – the particular prejudices around immigrants, benefit claimants or LGBT people, for example, which develop through their constant conjunction with negative frames. As cognitive scientists are fond of saying, 'the neurons that fire together wire together', meaning that repeated exposure to a particular representation is liable to naturalize it over time.[45] We could also see this relating to more abstract schemas like the human, the self and the other, home and safety, nation or reality, ideology thus shaping our very notions of the possible world.[46] We can even consider the impact of ideology on our second-order reflection upon these schemas – that is, whether we are taught to examine our particular prejudices and adapt them, or rather to simply ignore or attack information which does not fit preconceived schemas.[47] And as all of this evaluative work is the basis upon which bodily action is then taken (or not taken), these – often symbolic – patterns have very material effects on the world.

These embodied approaches to cognition are sometimes placed within the broader approach of '4E' cognition: embodied, embedded, extended and enactive cognition (other labels such as affective and distributed are sometimes added).[48] This framework refers to how cognition is: (i) dependent upon characteristics of the whole body, and cannot be reduced to the brain; (ii) always embedded in larger sociocultural contexts, with actions made meaningful through that external history; (iii) extended through tools, whether these are hammers, phones, even language itself, which allows us to externalize memory (such as into shopping lists) or mathematical calculations, and so free up cognitive load; (iv) adaptive in that we are always learning, but that this learning is not simply through sitting and thinking, but through doing and interacting.

We can connect this back to Marx's theory of alienation, which is perhaps the closest he comes to a psychological theory. Marx refers to how capitalism creates alienation from the self, from the products of one's labour, and from the social relations that connect you to others.[49] Reading these in terms of 4E theories of mind, capitalism could therefore be seen as shaping our unconscious information processing, our conscious awareness as directed by those perceptual frames, and our self-consciousness of the mind as such. That is, whilst we always remain broadly '4E' in terms of how our cognition operates and develops (e.g. cognitive processes do not become physically detached from the rest of our bodies), this is not reflected in surrounding social structures, and we thus fail to be consciously aware of that interconnected and processual nature of selfhood. We are alienated in terms of embodied cognition by the mental-manual dichotomy that produces a psychological division within our bodily image. We are alienated in extended cognition by our dispossession of the products of our collective labour (and thus our inability to use and shape the environment with them). And we are alienated in embedded cognition by our social disconnection from those who play vital roles in our daily reproduction. As well as supporting a classical Marxist framework for understanding alienation, this also provides a language for discussing alienation in spheres less commonly explored, such as affective labour, state democracy and educational systems. The way that behaviour is controlled in the workplace, and how this disrupts our emotive reasoning and expression, could be thought of in terms of 'alienation of affective cognition'. A lack of democracy and hierarchical information flow, and how this cuts us off from processes of decision-making in social bodies we are a part of – whether in a workplace, a local community, or our relation to the nation-state – could be seen as 'alienation of distributed cognition'. The containment of education within institutions that you enter into and exit out of at specific points rather than as an ongoing process of enaction and adaptation in all contexts, and how education thereby exists for the purpose of shaping you as a worker rather than for wider self-improvement, might be seen as 'alienation of enactive cognition'. All of this in turn can help us to envisage an alternative to capitalism: rather than asking, 'What does unalienated being look like?' we can ask more specific questions like, 'What personal, intersubjective, institutional and social arrangements best produce and reproduce consciousness of our embodied, embedded, extended and enactive cognition?'

Although this broad notion of 4E cognition arose in a bourgeois scientific context, it explicitly attacks the mind-body and self-other dichotomy that, for Guéry and Deleule, is both produced by, and serves to reproduce, capitalism.[50] But as the 'enactive' strand implies, simply learning about this on paper is not enough to spark revolutionary change. As with the common Marxist view that being involved in active class struggle (such as workplace strikes) is a necessary precursor to class consciousness raising, we can in general say that *one has to learn with the whole body*. And as 'embedded' cognition implies, such revolutionary consciousness raising must be embedded in larger-scale social practices, if it has any hope of becoming permanent and hegemonic. We must therefore move beyond a focus on the individual human body in its relations and transformations, and into wider patterns of social organization and reproduction.

Autopoiesis in social reproduction theory:
For a practical metaphysics

In order to explore some of the ontological implications of complexity and autopoiesis, I turn now to an essay by David McNally entitled 'Intersections and Dialectics'.[51] The piece is an excellent exploration and comparison of the ontologies that guide intersectional and dialectical thought, and is useful in highlighting further points of difference with a complex systems approach. The thrust of McNally's essay is that intersectionality, whilst providing an important discourse for reorienting analyses of capitalism to include different forms of oppression, falls down in relying on a problematic ontology. In particular, intersectional analyses tend to present different systems of oppression as atomized and autonomous from one another, merely *intersecting* at the point of the individual. He argues that a more dialectical approach, seeing individual oppressive systems as each part of a dynamic relational whole, can help us to move beyond the difficulties encountered in theorizing *how* oppressions intersect, by instead seeing them as co-constitutive.

Although towards the end of the piece McNally concedes there is *relative* autonomy between different systems of oppression such as racism and patriarchy, his piece as a whole otherwise relies on a dichotomy between a fully relational and an atomistic conception of oppressions, and it isn't otherwise clear how this relative autonomy is factored in. He identifies for example the importance of seeing how oppressions intersect systematically, beyond their individual systematicities, saying:

> to be *systematically* related involves considerably more than mere intersection. Intersections can be relatively random and haphazard; systems cannot. In a system, all the parts are ordered and integrated in ways that are determined by the other components. For this reason, a system is always more than the sum of its parts. There is an inseparability here in which the whole determines the parts, even as it is reciprocally determined by its subunits in turn.

McNally then goes on to concur with Angela Davis's position whereby 'racial and gender domination are utterly interwoven with capitalist exploitation – so much so that they cannot legitimately be considered separable', and how as a result 'changes in one subset of relations presuppose changes in all the others and in the system as a whole.'[52]

However, this latter statement only follows from the preceding if you understand relations within and between bodies as homogenous and *fully* deterministic, that is, negating any autonomy. For example, human bodies are also 'utterly interwoven' with the global ecosystem, and are 'so much so that they cannot legitimately be considered separable' – yet it does not follow that a change in one subset of relations (such as between various humans) presupposes changes in all the other relations between all other humans, nor in the whole global ecosystem. A key aspect of an emergent whole is that it can maintain global stability whilst going through local instability, meaning that changes in a subset of relations *do not* presuppose changes in the system as a whole. If this were not the case, then the whole would not be 'more than the sum of its parts' – as McNally defines a system – it would merely be an aggregate.

The use of the word 'determines' is worth focusing in on, as this is a concept with a contentious history in Marxist thought, and one which has continued to be debated into recent years.[53] Without entering into those debates per se, it is worth clarifying that in a complex system, interactions are often deterministic (in the sense that everything has a cause) and yet *non-linear*. We do not always have an A → B causality – the billiard ball logic seen in Newtonian mechanics – but a probabilistic relationship, where many simultaneous inputs effect an existing structure and produce an output that may be less than, equal to, or greater than the input, dependent upon the initial system state. Systems where outputs so quickly diverge from their inputs that prediction becomes impossible are referred to as 'chaotic' in the language of non-equilibrium thermodynamics. But the distinction is not a binary one between a chaotic and an ordered system – in fact, the intense complexity and adaptability seen in autopoietic bodies necessitates that they be finely balanced 'on the edge of chaos.'[54] So rather than, as McNally has it, 'changes in one subset of relations presuppos[ing] changes in all the others and in the system as a whole', on the contrary, the maintenance of a complex system's stability in its global functions (and thus its capacity not to change but rather to ward off change) in fact *requires* changeability of relations within its substrate.

If a dialectical ontology is unable to account for how micro relations do not always transform macro properties, it cannot account for stable emergence.

Without emergence one cannot account for the multi-scalar interaction that connects households to communities to cities to the whole global capitalist system – and thus would be inadequate as an ontological ground for social reproduction theory. Whilst dialectical accounts do not always fall into this trap, and indeed McNally's piece generally avoids it, without clarity and consistency on metaphysical notions such as emergence, non-linearity and autonomy, then a dialectical ontology always risks this homogenization of spatiotemporal scale and a corresponding slide into an absolutizing relativism. Integrating complexity and autopoiesis can help to avoid this. It allows us to see that a hugely interconnected dialectical totality is able to reproduce relatively autonomous sub-systems that create their own boundaries and have their own internal systems of reproduction. Due to the non-linearity inherent in these complex systems a change in one subset of relations *does not necessarily* presuppose changes in the others or in the system as a whole, even where each relatively autonomous body is structurally coupled to, and co-evolving with, others.

How does this translate into understanding systems such as racism and patriarchy? To see these systems as autopoietic means that they are complex and adaptive, requiring constant reproduction, and are relatively autonomous in the sense of being interdependent yet still extricable from one another, having their distinct histories even as they are presently co-evolving. The term 'co-constituting' I find misleading, because it can lead us to imagine an originary or essential mutual creation, a lack of any existence prior to the relation. This would be inconsistent with, for example, any theorizing of the differential and pre-capitalist histories of racial and gender oppression. I would argue that the interaction between different oppressive systems is better thought of as *coupling*, analogous to how two autonomous human beings can come together having never known each other beforehand, then begin to evolve together, before eventually moving apart, having been permanently changed by their relationship. The bodies exist prior to, during and after their close relation to one another, and each remains a continuous single body even as their internal constitution is altered. This is consistent with the intersectional idea that it would be possible for, say, patriarchy to be done away with but systemic racial oppression to continue. An autopoietic approach to autonomy shows that the relationality of systems is neither absolute in the way sometimes implied in dialectical accounts, nor atomistic as seen in some approaches to intersectional theory.

Conclusion

Marxism must re-engage with contemporary science on an ontological level in order to update its materialism and have greater weight in contemporary debates, such as those around climate change. However, it must not do this by merely looking back in time. Instead it can do this by understanding Marxism as a process-relational ontology, and then looking to contemporary sciences that match this approach. A reinvigorated scientific Marxism must therefore look more to the complexity sciences than to Engels for its substance, engaging with notions such as non-linear systems, emergence, autopoiesis and embodied cognition. To quote Engels himself: 'just as idealism underwent a series of stages of development, so too does materialism. With each epoch-making discovery even in the sphere of natural science, it has to change its form.'[55] Far from representing a slide into 'idealism' or 'bourgeois science', then, to do so is fully in the spirit of the Marxist tradition.

Notes

1   Helena Sheehan, *Marxism and the Philosophy of Science: A Critical History* (London: Verso, 2017), 53.

2   Erich Fromm, *Marx's Concept of Man* (London: Continuum, 2004), 9.

3   Loren Graham, 'The Socio-political Roots of Boris Hessen: Soviet Marxism and the History of Science', *Social Studies of Science* 15, no. 4 (1985): 705–22; Sheehan, *Marxism and the Philosophy of Science*, 224.

4   Karl Marx and Frederik Engels, *Collected Works Volume 4 (The Holy Family)* (London: Lawrence and Wishart, 1975), 126.

5   Sheehan, *Marxism and the Philosophy of Science*, 25.

6   Sheehan, *Marxism and the Philosophy of Science*, 52.

7   Sheehan, *Marxism and the Philosophy of Science*, 49.

8   John Bellamy Foster and Paul Burkett, 'Classical Marxism and the Second Law of Thermodynamics: Marx/Engels, the Heat Death of the Universe Hypothesis, and the Origins of Ecological Economics', *Organization and Environment* 21, no. 1 (2008): 3–37.

9   Sheehan, *Marxism and the Philosophy of Science*, 49.

10   It is beyond the scope of this essay to engage in any depth with critiques of the notion of scientific truth, such as found in the post-structuralist tradition. In

short however, the author's views on the subject are well represented in the work of Roy Bhaskar, who argues for the compatibility of epistemological relativism and ontological realism. This is in opposition to constructivist philosophies of science for which such relativism forecloses any discussion of shared reality. Such a combination is not only possible but in fact necessary for emancipatory projects, as an absolute relativization of knowledge ultimately inhibits the formation of macro-scale political actors necessary for systemic change. For a summary of his thought see Roy Bhaskar, *Enlightened Common Sense: The Philosophy of Critical Realism* (Oxford: Routledge, 2016), 1–20.

11   Marx and Engels, *The Holy Family*, 125–6.

12   Fritjof Capra and Pier Luigi Luisi, *The Systems View of Life* (Cambridge: Cambridge University Press, 2014), 33.

13   John Bellamy Foster and Paul Burkett, *Marx and the Earth: An Anti-Critique* (Leiden: Brill, 2016), 74; 134–5.

14   Capra and Luisi, *The Systems View of Life*, 63.

15   Philip Mirowski, *More Heat Than Light – Economics as Social Physics: Physics as Nature's Economics* (Cambridge: Cambridge University Press, 1989), 126.

16   Stuart Kauffman, *Humanity in a Creative Universe* (Oxford: Oxford University Press, 2016), 72.

17   Karl Marx, 'Letter from Marx to Arnold Ruge in Dresden', *Marxists Internet Archive* (1843), https://www.marxists.org/archive/marx/works/1843/letters/43_09-alt.htm (accessed 25 May 2020).

18   Karl Marx and Frederick Engels, *Collected Works Volume 5* (London: Lawrence and Wishart, 1976), 28.

19   Sheehan, *Marxism and the Philosophy of Science*, 37–8.

20   For the purposes of this chapter I am treating the terms 'ontology' and 'metaphysics' as broadly interchangeable, to refer to philosophical thought that engages the question, 'what is reality?'

21   Johanna Seibt, 'Process Philosophy', *Stanford Encyclopaedia of Philosophy*, 2017, https://plato.stanford.edu/entries/process-philosophy (accessed 5 September 2019).

22   Bertell Ollman, *Dance of the Dialectic: Steps in Marx's Method* (Chicago: University of Illinois Press, 2003), 4.

23   Anne Fairchild-Pomeroy, *Marx and Whitehead: Process, Dialectics, and the Critique of Capitalism* (New York: State University of New York Press, 2004), 11.

24   Arran Gare, 'Aleksandr Bogdanov and Systems Theory', *Democracy & Nature* 6, no. 3 (2000): 341–59.

25 Capra and Luisi, *The Systems View of Life*, 84.

26 Douglas Harper, 'System', *Etymonline*, https://www.etymonline.com/word/system #etymonline_v_22548.

27 Capra and Luisi, *The Systems View of Life*, 80.

28 Karl Marx, *Capital: A Critique of Political Economy*, vol. 1 (London: Lawrence and Wishart, 1996), 61–8.

29 Marx, *Capital*, 1:324, 420, 421, 376, 332, 336.

30 François Guéry and Didier Deleule, *The Productive Body*, trans. Philip Barnard and Stephen Shapiro (Winchester: Zero Books, 2014), 11. Hereafter *TPB*.

31 *TPB*, 66.

32 *TPB*.

33 Humberto Maturana and Francisco Varela, *Autopoiesis and Cognition: The Realization of the Living* (Dordrecht: D. Reidel Publishing, 1980), xvii.

34 Maturana and Varela, *Autopoiesis and Cognition*, 78.

35 Humberto Maturana and Francisco Varela, *The Tree of Knowledge: The Biological Roots of Human Understanding* (Boston: Shambhala, 1992), 75.

36 Capra and Luisi, *The Systems View of Life*, 136–7.

37 Foster and Burkett, *Marx and the Earth*, 71–3.

38 Capra and Luisi, *The Systems View of Life*, 252.

39 William Lewis, 'Louis Althusser', *Stanford Encyclopaedia of Philosophy*, 2018, https://plato.stanford.edu/entries/althusser/#TheIde (accessed 5 September 2019).

40 Simon Marginson and Thi Kim Anh Dang, 'Vygotsky's Sociocultural Theory in the Context of Globalization', *Asia Pacific Journal of Education* 37, no. 1: 116–29.

41 Terrence Deacon, *Incomplete Nature: How Mind Emerged from Matter* (New York: W. W. Norton & Co., 2011), 327.

42 John Protevi, *Political Affect: Connecting the Social and the Somatic* (Minneapolis: University of Minnesota Press, 2009), 16.

43 Bertell Ollman, *Alienation: Marx's Concept of Man in Capitalist Society* (Cambridge: Cambridge University Press, 1976), 85.

44 George Lakoff, 'Idea Framing, Metaphors, and Your Brain', *FORA.Tv*, 2008, https://www.youtube.com/watch?v=S_CWBjyIERY (accessed 6 September 2019).

45 Manuel Castells, *Communication Power* (Oxford: Oxford University Press, 2009), 142.

46 Mark Bracher, *Literature and Social Justice: Protest Novels, Cognitive Politics and Schema Criticism* (Austin: University of Texas Press, 2014), 7.

47 Bracher, *Literature and Social Justice*, 21.

48   Shaun Gallagher, 'An Introduction to 4E Cognition: Interview with Shaun
     Gallagher', 2018, https://www.youtube.com/watch?v=M7ghXdujfLE (accessed
     5 September 2019).

49   Ollman, *Alienation*, 133–4.

50   *TPB*, 34.

51   Tithi Bhattacharya (ed.), *Social Reproduction Theory: Remapping Class,
     Recentering Oppression* (London: Pluto Press, 2017), 94–111.

52   Bhattacharya, *Social Reproduction Theory*, 111.

53   Stephen Resnick and Richard Wolff, 'On Overdetermination and Althusser: Our
     Response to Silverman and Park', *Rethinking Marxism: A Journal of Economics,
     Culture & Society* 25, no. 3 (2013): 341–9.

54   Stuart Kauffman, *At Home in the Universe: The Search for the Laws of Self-
     Organization and Complexity* (Oxford: Oxford University Press, 1995), 26–30.

55   Karl Marx and Frederik Engels, *Collected Works Volume 26 (Engels 1882–89)*
     (London: Lawrence and Wishart, 1990), 369.

7

Neither appropriated nor expropriated: Notes towards an autonomist cripistemology of the productive body

Arianna Introna

In *The Productive Body* François Guéry and Didier Deleule examine the socialization of the labour-power contained in the biological body, through the mediation of the productive body.[1] The capitalist appropriates in his pursuit of profit not only the means of production but also 'the means of *productivity*, or the inner springs of production'.[2] The productive body is associated with this 'pure power to produce' which is central to the exploitation of labour under capitalism. What happens, then, to the productive body when the biological bodies available for appropriation do not sufficiently contribute to the accumulation of profit, either individually or once their (non-)productive powers are socialized? How can the non-productive qualities that non-normative bodies and minds possess under capitalism stall the (re)production of the productive body, and therefore of capitalism? This chapter will argue that non-normative bodies and minds function as 'faulty springs' of production in ways that speak to, and develop, the perspective of 'non-history' theorized by Guéry and Deleule. Non-normative bodies and minds demonstrate how 'non-history' might pertain to those populations not yet inserted into the productive body, and which refuse to pursue such incorporation.

In order to trace the dynamics generated by these faulty springs of production, my analysis brings together disability studies and autonomist Marxism, developing an 'autonomist cripistemology' of the productive body, where 'cripistemology' indicates an epistemology which takes 'the critical, social, and personal position of disability' as generative ground for critical enquiry.[3]

In *The Productive Body*, the body is dematerialized in the abstractions of the biological, social and productive bodies and framed from the perspective of power rather than of anti-capitalist resistance. An autonomist cripistemology, by contrast, uses insights from different strands of autonomist Marxism to understand the formation of the productive body from the perspective of class struggle. I combine this with a disability studies framework to reflect on the materiality of the encounter that recurs between crip (impaired, disabled or non-normative) bodyminds and the pursuit of productivity under capitalism. Following Margaret Price, I use the term 'bodymind' to indicate 'the imbrication (not just the combination) of the entities usually called "body" and "mind"', and to reference the ways in which non-normative bodies and minds reveal similar dynamics in the capital/labour relation.[4] By bringing together autonomist Marxism and disability studies, we can better understand how the phenomenon of disability weaves together the biological and the social body, ultimately preventing the emergence of the productive body. Outlining the ways in which disability intensifies and incarnates the logic of collective anti-capitalist resistance, based on non-productivity enshrined in Guéry and Deleule's perspective of non-history, I argue that cripping such a perspective is a preliminary step to realizing its potential.

Guéry and Deleule's portrayal of the genesis of the productive body articulates a series of abstract, immaterial bodies. However, an embodied conception of the body and its limits is needed for the concept of non-history to be fully developed as encapsulating the perspective of that which does not experience appropriation, expropriation or property. An autonomist cripistemology of the productive body reveals the ways in which disability as a socio-economic phenomenon, that belongs within the forces of non-history, is key to disrupting the (re)production of the productive body. To show how this plays out, I delineate four theoretical phases through which the interruption of the productive body can become thinkable. First, the development of a transindividual critique of the crip biological body that allows us to engage with the social structures framing processes of individuation for non-normative and able-bodied bodyminds alike, thus challenging the ways in which the sociality of the productive body is obscured under capitalism. Second, a theorization of the revolutionary power the crip biological body possesses as resistant to the demands of capitalism. Third, an appreciation of how by collectivizing the non-productivity of the crip biological body to crip the entire social body, the formation of the productive body can be disrupted. Situating the crip biological body as part of Michael Hardt and Toni Negri's 'multitude' offers a lens through which to appreciate the proliferation of subjectivities produced by processes of failed proletarianization, and ways of connecting these against productivity. Finally, a discussion of how from the perspective of value-form theory it becomes possible to map the ways in which extending the non-productivity of the crip biological body to the entire social body interrupts not only the (re)production of the productive body but also that of the capital/labour relation. In this context, the crip social body may fulfil the function of the means of production but not that of 'the means of *productivity*', and could therefore bring about the end of the productive body.[5]

Theorizing the (able-bodied) productive body

Guéry and Deleule provide an account of proletarianization as unfolding via a series of processes of superimposition that operate 'in two modes, the real mode and the imaginary mode', at a structural, concrete level and at an ideological, abstract one.[6] These two modes respectively conjoin the biological and the social dimensions of the workforce to its productive function and obscure this linkage. At the structural level, this leads to the superimposition of productive and exploitative processes. At the imaginary level, the relationship between 'the productive body and the biological body' is foregrounded, to the exclusion of the social dimension of proletarianization.[7] Guéry and Deleule are concerned with the atomizing impact the socialization of labour exerts on the worker in the development of capitalism. In the real mode, the productive body depends on the 'co-operation of individual workers' to realize a communal task at a scale that can only be achieved through a collective effort.[8] In the imaginary mode, the social body constituted by workers' cooperation becomes unthinkable, obscured by the biological, individualized body of the worker.[9] Significantly, this involves what Ed Cohen has described as the separation of 'the biological body of the laborer from the social body of labor relations'.[10] These dynamics create the 'paradox' whereby, according to Marina Vishmidt, the socialization of labour has 'atomising effects' on the workers.[11]

The genesis of the productive body, and the symbolic and structural superimpositions in which it is grounded, can be read as constantly vulnerable to the risk of non-reproduction if we focus on the corporeality of the workers enveloped by these processes. This is not immediately apparent in *The Productive Body* because Deleule and Guéry deploy a dematerialized concept of 'the body' to explain their model of capitalist development. As Cohen notes, Guéry and Deleule's 'trifecta of embodiment' works with 'abstract bodies': Guéry and Deleule's bodies 'do not represent living organisms entangled in a complex life world, but conceptual persona enmeshed within a Marxist storyline that assumes labor as human history's most decisive factor'.[12] To what extent, then, can the insertion of a crip materiality into Deleule and Guéry's 'trifecta of embodiment' add insights afforded by disability studies and politics into the anti-capitalist analysis of the productive body we can put forward? What does it mean to start from a crip biological body and then trace the disruption it unleashes in any individual or collective pursuit of productivity? What kind of social body and which productive body, if any, does the crip biological body contribute to creating?

Similar questions are prompted by a reading of the metaphors of disability in *The Productive Body*, which infuse its 'abstract bodies' with corporeality. On the one hand, Guéry and Deleule use the language of bodily sickness when discussing how Marx understands the factory as an organism that struggles to function: 'everywhere [Marx] looks he finds sickness, torture, and enfeeblement; everywhere manufacture screeches and groans.'[13] On the other hand, the productive body has a destructive effect on the biological body it appropriates. From Marx's writing, Deleule and Guéry glean a picture of the productive body as, simultaneously, a 'sick patient' and the 'sickness that attacks and tortures the biological body'.[14] Deleule and Guéry thus draw on images of illness to describe the pain caused by unsustainable, exploitative practices. Engaging with the materiality of Guéry and Deleule's biological and social bodies illuminates the ground on which the possibility of interrupting the reproduction of the productive body rests; namely, the economic relations revealed by non-normative bodyminds which are uniquely capable of making the productive body screech, groan and, ultimately, collapse.

Cripping Guéry and Deleule's perspective of non-history

For Guéry and Deleule the non-reproduction of the productive body can only be achieved by those organizing from what they call 'the perspective of non-history', which Philip Barnard and Stephen Shapiro see as pertaining to those excluded from capitalism's 'dominant account of human development'.[15] The perspective of non-history refuses the logic of continuous incorporation of new categories of labour into the capitalist mode of production. For Guéry and Deleule, calling ourselves 'to the attention of capitalism' by making 'vain boasts to the master about the value of [our] services' is tantamount to digging our own grave, as workers are '[n]o sooner appropriated than expropriated'.[16] Indeed, pursuing better worker status on the basis of one's productivity is what constitutes the 'historical parade of structural opponents initially endowed by capital with productive properties, only to be expropriated for the profit of other producers' and cannot attain 'the *radical* [...] power of negation of the forces of non-history'.[17] This radical power derives from the refusal of dispossession, appropriation and expropriation.[18] Disability, I want to suggest, embodies and materializes the perspective of non-history on the basis of the non-productivity that non-normative bodies and minds possess as resistant to capitalist expropriation and dispossession.

In situating non-normative bodyminds within the sphere of non-history, perspectives from critical disability studies can help us unpack the ways in which they are resistant to profit-driven capitalist exploitation. David Mitchell and Sharon Snyder have stressed the historical linkages between disability, labour and the onset of capitalism, noting that '*disability* was first coined in the mid-1800s to designate those incapable of work due to injury'.[19] In a similar spirit, Robert McRuer has connected capitalism to disability by arguing that 'the compulsory nature of able-bodiedness' that underpins the symbolic and material marginalization of disabled people is rooted in the industrial capitalist system.[20] Dan Goodley, Rebecca Lawthom and Katherine Runswick-Cole have theorized our contemporary context of austerity as one dominated by 'neoliberal-ableism', a form of capitalism under which we are all 'subjected to slow death, increased precarity and growing debility'.[21] Mitchell and Snyder likewise present the current moment as one of 'neoliberal inclusivism', which ensures that only 'the abled-disabled' manage to gain 'by paradoxical means … entrance into late capitalist cultures', leaving behind the 'nonlaboring populations' who are 'not merely excluded from, but also resistant to, standardized labor demands of productivity particular to neoliberalism'.[22]

Disability theory has 're-sited disability as an object through which to understand the workings of capitalist society' and, in the process, has developed a critique of labour-normativity which can help us identify and challenge 'the various axes along which labor functions as a disciplinary regime and ontological force under liberal capitalism'.[23] What becomes visible through this work is not only the constructed nature of the organization of life and work under capitalism, but also the considerable extent to which this is inimical to non-normative embodiments and minds. Most importantly, the engagement of disability studies in debates around capitalist pasts, presents and futures draws attention to the possibility for a cripistemology of the productive body to make a significant contribution to anti-capitalist theory. In particular, a cripistemology of the productive body issuing from the perspective of non-history attends to the ways in which the powers of the crip biological body are not easily translatable into means of productivity under capitalist normalcy. Putting disability studies in conversation with autonomist theory allows us to identify points of weakness – constituted by non-normative bodyminds – in the proletarianization process, and to theorize the possibilities these create to disrupt the (re)production of the productive body.

A transindividual critique of the crip biological body under capitalism

The first step in developing an autonomist cripistemology of the productive body is to refigure the biological body to which it is tied, in both the real and the imaginary mode, as a non-normative bodymind. The question that the analysis of these non-normative bodyminds raises for us is: what happens to them once they are plunged into capitalist structures of production, and in which ways can they unsettle the process of proletarianization as articulated by Guéry and Deleule?

By foregrounding the ways in which disability is constituted within society, a disability studies approach counters the de-socialization of labour that occurs at the imaginary level under capitalism. In particular, a disability studies perspective which makes use of the social model of disability is well placed to address the specific ways in which capitalist structures are responsible for disabled people's marginalization within society.[24] The social model of disability, in particular, approaches disability as a phenomenon constituted by the barriers created for non-normative bodyminds within a society organized to suit the needs of nondisabled people. It places the responsibility for disabled people's marginalization 'at the door of a normalising society that has rigidly developed and maintained structures designed to create a docile workforce and to reward those who most closely conform to socially prescribed ideal models of appearance and behaviour'.[25] Both critical disability studies and the social model of disability make thinkable the anti-capitalist intervention disabled people can make as part of the forces of non-history. It is in this way that, as Angharad Beckett and Tom Campbell propose, the social model works as an oppositional device, providing 'a framework for describing practices of invention, collaboration and resistance deployed by people against disciplining practices of subjectivation' and making visible 'a different, nondisabling world in the fabric of the present'.[26]

Using the social model of disability to demystify the de-socialization of labour effected at the imaginary level under capitalism, however, does not involve writing the biological body out of the picture. Rather, identifying what Beckett and Campbell's practices of resistance and subjectivation might look like operates as a form of transindividual critique. A transindividual critique seeks to attend to how individuation occurs in the midst of society; it 'is not just oriented towards dismissing, or even criticizing, individuation, but in situating it as part of a process'.[27] It seeks to put right a situation in which '[i]solated individuals appear, the power of capital appears, but social relations, the way individuals shape and are shaped by their relations, producing themselves and their social conditions, do not appear'.[28] The social model of disability speaks to transindividual critique by theorizing the constitutive effects social structures have on individual experiences, thus confirming that individuation happens in the midst of society. In line with Jason Read's concern to overcome the binary between the individual and the collective via transindividual critique, critical disability studies contests the dualism that the traditional social model of disability originally set up between biological impairment and socially constructed disability (or disablement).[29] It instead seeks to attend to the plurality of lived and embodied experiences of illness and non-normative bodyminds in their socio-economic, cultural and political contexts. Indeed, the main criticisms of the social model of disability focus on the 'impairment/disability dualism' and propose 'an embodied ontology' as 'the best starting point for disability studies'.[30] If the individual emerges as transindividual once 'situated with respect to the relations that constitute and individuate it', a cripistemology of the crip biological body under capitalism addresses both the socially situated experience of non-normative bodyminds and how their transindividuality is obscured.[31] This involves re-centring the biological body in its social formation and examining the possibilities for resistance this opens up.

On not producing the productive body, phase one – the non-productivity of the crip biological body

Re-centring the crip biological body within society, and within practices of proletarianization, illuminates the processes that connect the two – not only as grounds for the marginalization of disabled people from the workforce, but also as dynamics which can hold up the formation of the productive body. The question that analysis of these dynamics opens up is: What impact does the crip biological body have on the emergence of the productive body?

Through substituting a crip biological body for Guéry and Deleule's able-bodied one, an autonomist cripistemology of the productive body identifies limitations in the proletarianization process of the biological body. These limitations centre on capital's need to produce surplus-value from a constant supply of exploitable labour; in other words, labour which is capable of being productive. Marx is clear about what constitutes productive labour: 'Capitalist production is not merely the production of commodities, it is essentially the production of surplus-value. The labourer produces, not for himself, but for capital.'[32] This is why for Guéry and Deleule 'the productive body exists only in a market economy'.[33] Thus, the uneasy fit between non-normative embodiments and minds and the standardized, growth-oriented organization of work under capitalism is inseparable from the uncertainties around the possibility for the crip biological body to contribute to the production of surplus-value. The abolition of the socio-economic exclusion experienced by disabled people 'is ultimately dependent upon and subordinate to the logic of productivity'.[34] If the de-socialization of labour saw the biological body being disconnected from the social body and tied up in 'a productive process from which it is henceforth constrained to derive its subsistence', what happens when crip biological bodyminds do not fit into the organization of the productive process on which they depend for survival?

On the one hand, the exclusion of non-normative bodyminds from the imperatives of productivity generates disabled people's demands for the right of access to work and accommodation in the workplace. These demands are reminiscent of the calls for inclusion within the productive body that are put forward by Guéry and Deleule's 'structural opponents' of capital: they do not escape but in fact perpetuate the dialectic that underpins the capital-labour relation.[35] Disability activism attempts to dismantle the barriers which have both made it difficult for disabled people to take up employment and make a living, and have underwritten the symbolic marginalization of disabled people. As Mike Oliver argues, being 'constantly and consistently denied the opportunity to work, to make a material contribution to the well-being of society ... is the root cause of [disabled people's] being labelled as "other" or "useless"'.[36] This position is problematic when approached through the lens of an autonomist cripistemology of the productive body on two counts. First, it occludes the ways in which non-normative bodyminds create obstacles to the production of surplus-value. Second, it deflects attention away from the undesirability of pursuing insertion within the productive body, as such insertion would only lead to one's productive powers being simultaneously appropriated and expropriated.

In contradistinction to the social model, non-history recognizes impairment as grounding both the impossibility for proletarianization to proceed smoothly, and as a re-connection with the powers of the biological body 'which have been confiscated by industrial civilization'.[37] Disability studies has been increasingly concerned with attending to a 'biological core' that has been occluded or ignored by conventional social models. In an attempt to develop the traditional social model which saw 'disability as an artefact of society rather than something inherent in, or a product of the body', critical disability studies seeks to build models which attend to a plurality of lived experiences.[38]

In this spirit, engaging the socio-economic phenomenon of impairment in our discussion of the crip biological body generates an autonomist cripistemology capable of theorizing the incompatibility between proletarianization, productivity and crip biological bodyminds. The ways in which the crip biological body might become *key* to ending proletarianization can be appreciated when some of the insights yielded by John Holloway's work are considered. For Holloway, the current crisis of capitalism arises from people saying 'no, we are not willing to – or maybe we are just too stupid or backwards – to satisfy the demands of capital'.[39] In these circumstances, thinking about the crisis of capitalism generates two possibilities. One of these possibilities is to accept the terms of capital and declare ourselves 'totally willing to cooperate' to save capitalism through the 'intensification of our subordination to capital'.[40] The other is to say that '[w]e are the crisis of capital and proud of it. We are the crisis of this relation of domination. We are the possibility of another way of living, of another form of social organization'.[41] Disability can spearhead the second response because it highlights both the unsustainability of a model whereby there is a 'constant drive to produce things more quickly', and the problem this model comes up against, namely, our 'incapacity or our refusal to subordinate ourselves sufficiently to the dynamic of capital'.[42] The crip biological body, unable to fulfil the demands of capitalism, threatens the formation of the productive body. However, if the crip biological body remains symbolically disconnected from the social body, its specific interruption of the process of proletarianization will not challenge the overall reproduction of the productive body.

On not producing the productive body, phase two – the non-productivity of the crip social body

A crip social body capable of preventing the reproduction of the productive body can only materialize if the crip biological body's incapacity to produce profit is collectivized to the entire social body. Collectivizing individual non-productivity in both the imaginary and the real mode is the only way to make apparent the ways in which '[f]orces of production and social relations' are not, as they appear from the perspective of capital, 'merely means for [it] to produce on its limited foundation'. Instead, as Marx develops, 'they are the material conditions to blow this foundation sky-high'.[43] This collectivization of individual non-productivity stands in opposition to a pattern in which both the social nature of work and the possibilities for collective resistance on this basis are obscured as 'the biological body no longer recognizes itself as socially engaged with other biological bodies in the productive process'.[44] It brings together individual and collective in the spirit of transindividual critique to build new bases for political practice.[45]

An autonomist and transindividual cripistemology of the productive body tries to think this new practice of politics by extending the non-productive power of the crip biological body to the whole social body. It works to imagine and realize a crip social body as the pivot on which the productive body can be cripped into nonexistence, deprived of any possibility of producing surplus-value. An autonomist cripistemology of the productive body draws lessons from the ways in which the biological body disrupts the capital relation at both the symbolic and the structural level and makes these available for all bodyminds to learn from. As Chris Grover and Linda Piggott suggest, because of its increased vulnerability to non-reproduction under capitalism on the basis of its non-productivity, disability offers a particularly sharp focus through which to 'critically engage with the notion that wage work is an activity that disabled people .... And non-disabled people ... should be forced to engage with on the threat of impoverishment'.[46] If disabled people and capitalism are incompatible in ways that underpin disabled people's marginalization in society, this incompatibility also demonstrates how disability presents an escape from capitalism's modes of oppression and exploitation. It is in this spirit that disability studies rejects a waged work-centred model of society and values instead relational notions of human potentiality.[47]

The collectivization of non-productivity by which the crip biological body is defined can function as the ground on which collective resistance to proletarianization can be built. This however necessitates a shift in society's ways of apprehending disability: in place of '[h]egemonic framings of disability [which] individualise, pathologise, medicalise, psychologise, essentialise and depoliticise', there is a need to re-situate disability as a category through which to 'understand the workings of capitalist society' and to organize around politically.[48] Most importantly, disability provides important and urgent lessons from which anti-capitalist movements can learn.

On not producing the productive body, phase three – a crip multitude of non-productive bodies

The third step in bringing about the impossible materiality of the crip productive body is by creating a crip multitude; namely, it consists in appreciating the place of disabled people within the working class and in building networks informed by practices of resistance specific to the disabled people's movement. Recomposing the social body on the logic of the crip biological body would be grounded in an awareness of how the politics of disability make visible patterns of injustice and inequalities that define society at large. However, as already noted, in the process of this recomposition, the working-class movement would need to shed its able-bodied character and make sure the needs and views of disabled people are acknowledged as belonging within acknowledged as relevant to, and connected with, those of the wider working class.[49]

Hardt and Negri's attempt to move away from the exclusionism that underpins traditional conceptions of the working class through the concept of the multitude goes some way towards relativizing the able-bodied character of the working class. Significantly, Hardt and Negri add the caveat that 'no social line divides productive from unproductive workers', explicitly rejecting the centralization of men as 'the primary producers' within the working class.[50] For Hardt and Negri, a conception of the working class confined to industrial labour does not hold today and needs to be superseded by one which foregrounds how different forms of labour share 'a common potential to resist the domination of capital' in ways that produce an 'equal opportunity of resistance'.[51] Hardt and Negri's concept of the multitude develops into that of the social union and its form of struggle, the social strike, which they develop building on Alberto De Nicola and Biagio Quattrocchi's earlier insights into practices of social unionism.[52] The social union constitutes a departure from the labour union by articulating a mode of resistance and organization in which 'everyone, even the poor, wields in the final instance the threat to withdraw their voluntary servitude and disrupt the social order'.[53]

From a disability studies perspective, Mitchell and Snyder have argued that Hardt and Negri's conceptualization of the working class points to 'forms of creativity that cannot be reduced to an economic exchange value'; not only does it 'expand outward to include those who occupy "nonproductive bodies", but rather takes its lead from those whose capacities make them "unfit" for labor as the baseline of human value.[54] In Hardt and Negri's analysis, Mitchell and Snyder contend, nonproductive bodies have the potential to revolutionize the ways in which we conceive of worker subjectivity by valuing the incapacity to work 'within the narrow standardization efforts of capitalism.'[55] The valorization of this intractability to exploitation is precisely the contribution disability studies and politics can make to anti-capitalist theory and practice.[56]

On not producing the productive body, phase four – cripping value-form theory

The fourth and final step to take in working towards cripping the productive body into non-existence consists in upgrading a crip multitude into that which interrupts the capital–labour dialectic. It speaks to the call coming from the perspective of non-history to evade the dialectical relationship between capital and labour that sustains the reproduction of capitalism and its productive body. It also resonates with the concern of value-form theory to think and effect the ending of the working class as implicated in the capital relation. The negative dialectics that underpins the theories associated with the critical tradition of Open Marxism, a libertarian strand of Marxist theory which positions itself as open in the sense of refusing any deterministic conception of history and form of class struggle. Open Marxism enables us to understand the working class as 'the movement of doing against labor' – thus, as 'a movement against its own existence as working class.'[57] In the same spirit, for the communist discussion group and editorial collective *Endnotes*, 'the history of capitalist society is the history of the reproduction of the capitalist class relation. It is that of the reproduction of capital as capital, and – its necessary concomitant – of the working class as working class'. Therefore, it is by working towards the interruption of its own reproduction that the working class can halt 'the movement of the value form.'[58]

Disability as a socio-economic phenomenon and disability politics are central to the possibility of voicing and practising this refusal. An autonomist cripistemology of the productive body serves to grasp, theorize, and valorize the fact of the impossibility of making all bodies productive for capital, and posits this as the starting point for a more generalized refusal of work and worker status. An autonomist cripistemology of the productive body is key to recognizing what Harry Cleaver calls 'the little internal, capitalist devil urging us to get to work', as well as the 'spirit of autonomy' that urges us to fight it.[59] It foregrounds a rejection of a system in which human worth is defined by one's ability to contribute to capitalist production. Instead, it starts from, and stays with, disability as 'both a signifier of inequity and the promise of something new and affirmative'.[60] Disability struggles as the basis for the anti-capitalist attack on the productive body crucially call for an inclusive and enabling society to be continually pursued.

In practical terms, an autonomist cripistemology of the productive body crips the operaist idea of the refusal of work. In falling outside the labour market, non-normative bodyminds simultaneously function as memento mori for the able-bodied biological body on which the productive body relies. The threat that crip bodyminds pose to capitalism is different from that associated with the working class in general: the working class derives its power from its ability to provide and withdraw its contribution to processes of value creation.[61] Disability forces us to reformulate this threat negatively, as rooted in the crip promise of a permanent 'blockage of the work-process'.[62]

Conclusion

On the face of it, Guéry and Deleule portray the historical and contemporary process of proletarianization as a smooth one, impervious to the possibility of being interrupted and disrupted. This portrayal crucially unfolds within an abstract framework dominated by immaterial bodies: biological, social and productive. However, Guéry and Deleule do theorize the failure of proletarianization through their exposition of a perspective of non-history which is inseparable from the refusal to be subsumed within the productive body. Cripping Guery and Deleule's perspective of non-history opens up ways of achieving its desired outcome of escaping and breaking the dialectic that perpetuates the cycle of proletarianization and struggle. The autonomist cripistemology of the productive body that I have developed here, grounded in the perspective of non-history, demonstrates how the powers of the crip biological body are not easily translatable into productive powers under capitalist normalcy and celebrates the revolutionary potential this unleashes. It calls for a move away from perceiving one's position within the forces of non-history as an undesirable condition to be dreaded and avoided, and towards welcoming this position as the starting point for a different world to be created, outside and against the dictates of the productive body. An autonomist cripistemology of the productive body takes the non-productivity of the crip biological body as a starting point for remaking society in its entirety and works towards its collectivization to imagine a crip social body that renders the emergence and reproduction of the productive body impossible.

Ultimately, it underlines the need for different forms of production and social reproduction to be imagined and established. Introducing an embodied take on the triad of the biological, social and productive bodies that Guéry and Deleule theorize allows us to recognize and work to achieve non-productivity as the basis for non-incorporation into the productive body, and as the basis for defending our lives, as opposed to our productive powers, from appropriation and expropriation. The crip biological body that underpins the crip social body and pre-empts the productive body becomes key to recentring solidarity and vulnerability in reorganizing our collective conditions of existence.

Notes

1   François Guéry and Didier Deleule, *The Productive Body*, trans. Philip Barnard and Stephen Shapiro (Winchester: Zero Books, 2014), 51. Hereafter *TPB*.

2   *TPB*, 61.

3   Merri Lisa Johnson and Robert McRuer, 'Cripistemologies: Introduction', *Journal of Literary & Cultural Disability Studies* 8, no. 2 (2014): 134.

4   Margaret Price, 'The Bodymind Problem and the Possibilities of Pain', *Hypatia* 30, no. 1 (Winter 2015): 270.

5   *TPB*, 61.

6   *TPB*, 74.

7   *TPB*, 74.

8   *TPB*, 75.

9   *TPB*, 75.

10   Ed Cohen, 'Capitalizing on "The Body"', *The Los Angeles Review of Books*, 25 July 2015, https://lareviewofbooks.org/article/capitalizing-body/#.

11   Marina Vishmidt, 'Productive Bodies: A Review Essay', *Australian Feminist Studies* 30, no. 85 (2015): 304.

12   Cohen, 'Capitalizing on "The Body"'.

13   *TPB*, 64.

14   *TPB*, 64.

15   Philip Barnard and Stephen Shapiro, 'Introduction', *TPB*, 31.

16   *TPB*, 94. This resonates with 'Mediocre Dave''s suggestion that although one may be tempted to assert the societal value of workers' contribution as a way of challenging deskilling as a tool of capitalist domination, '[c]elebrating people's aptitude for work that exploits them is a misplaced form of solidarity'. Mediocre Dave, 'Unskilled Work?' *New Socialist*, 25 August 2020, https://newsocialist.org.uk/unskilled-work/.

17   *TPB*, 95.

18   *TPB*, 95.

19   David T. Mitchell and Sharon L. Snyder, *The Biopolitics of Disability: Neoliberalism, Ablenationalism, and Peripheral Embodiment* (Ann Arbor: The University of Michigan Press, 2015), 211.

20   Robert McRuer, *Crip Theory: Cultural Signs of Queerness and Disability* (New York and London: New York University Press, 2006), 9.

21   Dan Goodley, Rebecca Lawthom, Kirsty Liddiard and Katherine Runswick-Cole, 'Dis/ability and Austerity: Beyond Work and Slow Death', *Disability & Society* 29, no. 6 (2014): 980.

22   Mitchell and Snyder, *The Biopolitics of Disability*, 211–12.

23   Dan Goodley, *Disability Studies: An Interdisciplinary Introduction* (London: Sage, 2016), 190–1; Tanja N. Aho, 'Active Citizenship, Liberalism, and Labor-Normativity: Queercrip Resistance, Sanist Anxiety, and Racialized Ableism in Viewer Responses to *Here Comes Honey Boo Boo*', *Journal of Literary & Cultural Disability Studies* 11, no. 3 (2017): 322.

24   Michael Oliver and Colin Barnes, *The New Politics of Disablement* (New York: Palgrave Macmillan, 2012), 12.

25   Claire Tregaskis, 'Social Model Theory: The Story so Far … ', *Disability & Society* 17, no. 4 (2002): 457.

26   Angharad E. Beckett and Tom Campbell, 'The Social Model of Disability as an Oppositional Device', *Disability & Society* 30, no. 2 (2015): 271, 280.

27   Jason Read, *The Politics of Transindividuality* (Chicago: Haymarket Books, 2015), 6.

28   Read, *The Politics of Transindividuality*, 77.

29   Read, *The Politics of Transindividuality*, 2.

30   Tom Shakespeare and Nicholas Watson, 'The Social Model of Disability: An Outdated Ideology?' in *Exploring Theories and Expanding Methodologies: Where We Are and Where We Need to Go Research* (Bingley: Emerald Group Publishing Limited, 2001).

31   Read, *The Politics of Transindividuality*, 6.

32   Karl Marx, *Capital: A Critique of Political Economy* (1867), vol.1, *The Process of Capitalist Production*, trans. Samuel Moore and Edward Aveling (New York: Bennett A. Cerf and Donald S. Klopfer, 1906), 558.

33   *TPB*, 60.

34   Paul Abberley, 'The Concept of Oppression and the Development of a Social Theory of Disability', *Disability, Handicap & Society* 2, no. 1 (1987): 92.

35   See Edward Hall and Robert Wilton, 'Thinking Differently about "Work" and Social Inclusion for Disabled People', in *Disabled People, Work and Welfare: Is Employment Really the Answer*, ed. Chris Grover and Linda Piggott (Bristol: Policy Press, 2015), 241.

36   Mike Oliver, 'Disabled People and the Inclusive Society: Or the Times They Really Are Changing' on IndependentLiving.Org (Public lecture on behalf of Strathclyde Centre for disability research and Glasgow City Council, 1999), http://www.independentliving.org/docs4/oliver.html.

37   Vishmidt, 'Productive Bodies', 304.

38   Janine Owens, 'Exploring the Critiques of the Social Model of Disability: The Transformative Possibility of Arendt's Notion of Power', *Sociology of Health & Illness* 37, no. 3 (March 2015): 385; 388. See also John Swain and Sally French, 'Towards an Affirmation Model of Disability', *Disability & Society* 15, no. 4 (2001); Liz Crow, 'Including All of Our Lives: Renewing the Social Model of Disability' originally published in *Encounters with Strangers: Feminism and Disability*, ed. Jenny Morris (London: Women's Press, 1996), http://www.roaring-girl.com/wp-content/uploads/2013/07/Including-All-of-Our-Lives.pdf.

39   John Holloway, 'Greece: Hope Drowns in the Reality of a Dying World. Or Does It?', lecture delivered at Leeds University, 8 December 2015, https://www.youtube.com/watch?v=k3qc7LrqOs0&feature=youtu.be.

40   John Holloway, *In, Against, and Beyond Capitalism: The San Francisco Lectures* (Oakland: PM Press, 2016), 62.

41   Holloway, *In, Against, and Beyond Capitalism*, 63.

42   Holloway, *In, Against, and Beyond Capitalism*, 57.

43 Karl Marx, *Grundrisse: Foundations of the Critique of Political Economy*, trans. Martin Nicolaus (London: Penguin, 1993), 706.

44 Cohen, 'Capitalizing on "The Body"'.

45 Read, *The Politics of Transindividuality*, 12.

46 Chris Grover and Linda Piggott, 'Disabled People, Work and Welfare', in *Disabled People, Work and Welfare: Is Employment Really the Answer?*, ed. Chris Grover and Linda Piggott (Bristol: Policy Press, 2015), 4.

47 Goodley et al., 'Dis/ability and Austerity', 984.

48 Goodley, *Disability Studies*, 190–1.

49 Vic Finkelstein, 'The Social Model of Disability Repossessed', *Manchester Coalition of Disabled People*, December 2001, https://disability-studies.leeds.ac.uk/wp-content/uploads/sites/40/library/finkelstein-soc-mod-repossessed.pdf.

50 Michael Hardt and Antonio Negri, *Multitude: War and Democracy in the Age of Empire* (London: Penguin, 2004), 135.

51 Hardt and Negri, *Multitude*, 106.

52 Alberto De Nicola and Biagio Quattrocchi, 'Sindacalismo sociale. Appunti per una discussione', 4 June 2014, http://www.dinamopress.it/news/sindacalismo-sociale-appunti-per-una-discussione.

53 Michael Hardt and Antonio Negri, *Assembly* (Oxford: Oxford University Press, 2017), 150.

54 Mitchell and Snyder, *The Biopolitics of Disability*, 211.

55 Mitchell and Snyder, *The Biopolitics of Disability*, 221.

56 For an analysis of how this contribution has played out in times of austerity see Robert McRuer, *Crip Times: Disability, Globalization, and Resistance* (New York: New York University Press, 2018), 4.

57 Holloway, *In, Against, and Beyond Capitalism*, 37.

58 'Crisis in the Class Relation: Yes! There Will Be Growth in the Spring!' *Endnotes* 2 (April 2010), https://endnotes.org.uk/issues/2/en/endnotes-crisis-in-the-class-relation.

59 Harry Cleaver, *Rupturing the Dialectic: The Struggle against Work, Money, and Financialization* (Chico: AK Press, 2015), 8.

60 Goodley et al., 'Dis/ability and Austerity', 972.

61 Mario Tronti, 'The Strategy of Refusal', in *Operai and Capitale* (Turin: Einaudi, 1966), https://libcom.org/library/strategy-refusal-mario-tronti.

62 Tronti, 'The Strategy of Refusal'.

8

The Quantified Self, the ideology of health and fat

Dawn Woolley

This chapter will examine the Quantified Self movement and the ideology of health in relation to *The Productive Body* to consider the body as a site of both discipline and dissent. Robert Crawford describes how the ideology of health, or healthism, supports a neoliberal agenda by situating health and illness as the personal responsibility of the individual.[1] This notion of 'health' enables individuals to make moral and ideological judgements about the bodies of others, masking the sexism, racism, classism and ableism inherent in these judgements.[2] The ideology of health also conceals health's relation to social inequality. In her research examining health inequalities experienced by fat Black lesbian and bisexual women, Bianca D. M. Wilson found that 'major systemic factors [...] such as racism, anti-fat discrimination, sexism, poverty, violence, and heterosexism, are powerful detractors from health (physical, emotional, and mental) and should be considered in a meaningful way as targets for public health intervention'.[3] Stress caused by discrimination and oppression can lead to anxiety, depression, insecurity and low self-esteem, and these, in turn, can lead to chronic health conditions.[4] This process is accelerated and intensified by the absence of the social privileges that enable one to achieve 'good health'.[5]

The achievement of 'good health' is further impeded by neoliberal capitalism's opposing imperatives to work hard and delay gratification, and, what Crawford calls, the consumer dictum of instant pleasure:

On the one hand we must repress desires for immediate gratification and cultivate a work ethic, on the other, as consumers we must display a boundless capacity to capitulate to desire and indulge in impulse; we must hunger for constant and immediate satisfaction. The regulation of desire thus becomes an ongoing problem, constantly besieged by temptation, while socially condemned for over indulgence.[6]

Fitness and working out demonstrate the individual's ability to balance these opposing forces. The 'healthy body' is indicative of success, a strong work ethic and self-control. Shari Dworkin and Faye Wachs write that the 'healthy body' is viewed as a productive resource and medium for creating 'bodily capital'.[7] For people with the financial resources, leisure is transformed into a form of body-labour that complements their economic function and compels them to purchase equipment and services that optimize their 'bodily capital'. They become ideal neoliberal subjects through their pursuit of health.

The Quantified Self movement exemplifies this process. It emerged with the development of wearable devices and apps designed to record detailed measurements relating to the users' physical, psychological and social well-being. Founded in 2007 by Gary Wolf and Kevin Kelly, the movement aims to 'gain knowledge through numbers' and 'support new discoveries about ourselves and our communities that are grounded in accurate observation.'[8] In an article for *The New York Times* Wolf writes: 'We use numbers when we want to tune up a car, analyze a chemical reaction, predict the outcome of an election. We use numbers to optimize an assembly line. Why not use numbers on ourselves?'[9] The body is viewed as a machine-like object that can be monitored and adjusted in order to eliminate weaknesses. The movement is dominated by middle-class white men who have the time and financial resources to purchase and use tracking devices to optimize their bodies and minds.[10]

In contrast to this, fat bodies, that are more likely to be identified as female, working-class, poor or ethnic minorities, are signifiers of lack of self-control and a poor work ethic.[11] Deborah Lupton writes that in the 1990s a lot of scientific and medical research focused on the 'negative health and economic effects of obesity'.[12] Prior to this time, fat tended to be viewed as a symptom of a medical issue, rather than a cause of ill-health. Concurrently, the term 'overweight' became medicalized with the widespread adoption of the Body Mass Index (BMI), a height-to-weight ratio that does not describe or incorporate any other measurements of health. Bodies that might otherwise be healthy are deemed to be ill if their BMI score indicates that they are 'under-' or 'overweight'. A BMI of 18 or below is categorized as 'underweight', while 25 to 29.9 is deemed to be 'overweight' and a BMI of 30 and above signifies obesity. Similar to other aspects of neoliberal culture, the BMI reduces complex health issues to numerical data and erases the social causes of illness.[13] Fat studies scholars and fat acceptance activists argue that the BMI is not a measure of health, and cite research studies that have found that there is no causal relation between being 'overweight' and increased mortality rates.[14]

This intense focus on body weight peaked in the mid-2000s, concurrent with the beginning of the Quantified Self movement in 2007; the technologies used by state and commercial organizations to identify and discipline 'pathological' body weight mirror the apparatus of the Quantified Self.[15] This chapter argues that this quantification creates 'productive' bodies and intensifies ideal neoliberal traits of competitiveness, individualism and self-control. It examines disordered eating behaviours as pathologies of quantification and considers eating for pleasure, rather than health and 'fuel', to be a potential disruption to the neoliberalization of the body and its capacities.

The quantified productive body

The ideology of health developed in the 1970s out of environmental groups that campaigned to raise awareness about toxins in the environment, and the women's health movement that sought greater autonomy for female patients in a healthcare system largely dominated by male doctors and consultants. For example, women's health groups campaigned against the 'norms of non-disclosure' that allowed doctors to withhold information from patients regarding their breast cancer diagnosis and treatment.[16] Fat Underground (FU), a radical feminist group, was formed in the early 1970s to draw attention to the gendered nature of fat discrimination. Members of FU studied medical journal articles about obesity and diet to draw attention to the misleading claims made in the mass media and diet industry advertising.[17]

However, the demands for greater agency for patients and scepticism towards governmental control of healthcare were also taken up by those on the political right, who wanted to reduce state intervention and increase market intervention.[18] The liberal political views of fat activists have been modified to suit this neoliberal agenda by conservative organizations. For example, the US Center for Consumer Freedom, a coalition of food industry businesses, fights to limit the influence of health campaigns that call for individuals to reduce or modify their food consumption in order to improve their health. To protect profits and fight against regulation, the organizations argue that state intervention impedes consumer choice, autonomy and personal responsibility. Deborah Lupton writes that some think tanks even 'represent anti-obesity advocates as "socialists" working against the appropriate forces of capitalism'.[19] The consumption of unhealthy food is presented as a rebellious expression of free will and a protest against the 'nanny state'.

The ideology of personal responsibility aligned healthcare to the cultural values of neoliberal capitalism. Illness came to connote a failure of self-discipline and a sign of poor citizenship. However, this process of disconnecting well-being from structural inequality has been evident from early capitalism. In 'Environments, Bodies, and the Cultural Imaginary: Imagining Ecological Impairment', Steve Kroll-Smith and Joshua Kelly describe a shift in attitudes in relation to an individual's health that took place in the mid-to-late nineteenth century:

> Imagining health as self-regulation rather than the outcome of bodies and their many intersections with industrial environments was truly a win-win for a capital, manufacture-based economy. Not only did a focus on the person and his or her body direct the medical gaze away from increasingly risky industrial environments, it also encouraged a policing of the working class. The habits of this class were surveyed, suggestions were offered, directives were issued, and workplace incentives and punishments were enacted.[20]

Blame for ill health was deflected from unhealthy working conditions and social inequality, and the workers were disciplined to maximize their efficiency; they were transformed into 'productive bodies', to use the terminology coined by François Guéry and Didier Deleule.[21]

A 'productive body' is a body that produces surplus-value for the capitalist. It is optimized to produce surplus-value in the workplace and as a consumer who finds pleasure and stress-relief in the consumption of commodities, thereby continuing the cycle of surplus-value accumulation for the capitalist. The productive body is also a product of alienation that occurs when a division is produced between the body (physical process) and the mind (knowledge of production). Guéry says the intellectual element of the production process is the brain or the 'software', and Deleule names the body a 'body-machine'.[22] The managers are the intellectual part of the production line and the workers are an element of the production machinery. The 'body-machine' is optimized to increase its efficiency, but the production process limits the body's potential by forcing it to perform a specific series of actions. The worker's body is simultaneously optimized and reduced. It is transformed into a 'pure work machine with its blemishes of subjectivity scoured away, with its idleness and laziness denounced and condemned as the incarnation of social evil'.[23]

Concurrently, the development of psychology in the nineteenth century ensured that the worker's mind is 'as adapted as possible to the social mechanism into which it is [...] integrated, so that its productive act develops in optimal conditions and its gears don't grind too loudly'.[24] Like the body-machine, the worker's mind is also optimized and reduced:

> It finds its rightful place in the field of objective knowledge [*savoir*], even though this place deprives it of its unique, multifaceted specificity. What is lost [...] is of course subjective experience. What is now promoted is the identity of a being that can be represented and therefore mastered.[25]

The worker is reduced to quantifiable elements that can be scrutinized, optimized and controlled. To condition them to accept the physical and psychological demands of capitalist production processes, and to submit to such intense scrutiny and control, the worker must feel that survival is a struggle. Deleule argues that psychology functions to promote the conditioning processes that adapt the individual to the machinery and to assert that consumption is necessary for survival.

In their introduction to the English translation of *The Productive Body*, Philip Barnard and Stephen Shapiro write that the text is prescient for contemporary networked, data-driven society. They note that the productive body

> starts with the creation of an 'organology' or knowledge-formation about separable parts or senses of the body [...] As the body becomes conceived as like a machine through new quantifications of sight, touch, and so on,

humans begin to compete against one another in order to do 'better' on these scores, as if achieving higher ratings than others might help us escape death and human demise.[26]

This description of the 'productive body' could also be a description of the Quantified Self movement. The maintenance of the body escalates with tracking devices that map and optimize it, constituting an 'organology', and competitive rivalry is promoted as a motivational tool to enhance the process of optimization. Wolf writes: 'we tolerate the pathologies of quantification [...] because the results are so powerful. Numbering things allows tests, comparisons, experiments. Numbers make problems less resonant emotionally but more tractable intellectually.'[27]

The idea that quantification can reduce the irrational emotions that prevent optimization echoes Deleule's description of the 'body-machine': 'What is radically new [...] is thus the idea that (scientific/technological) production is entirely *rational* in all its parts, i.e. explicable, justifiable, predictable and legitimate, stipulated and therefore efficient, recognizable and therefore manageable.'[28] Quantification makes the body knowable and manageable. According to Martin de Groot, a medical biologist and co-founder of the Quantified Self Institute, self-tracking 'can help you to become more in charge of yourself. Self-awareness is the first step towards self-regulation. And also self-control.'[29] By viewing the self as an object of scientific study, and gathering data on a range of tangible and intangible bodily attributes, the self-tracking devices intensify and multiply modes of surveillance.

Btihaj Ajana writes that in one respect, quantification has 'given the body unprecedented significance over the mind, casting it as a source of "instant truth"'; however, the body is also viewed as 'a passive object of measurement that is amenable to improvement and intervention whether it likes it or not.'[30] To use Deleule's term, the quantified body is treated like a 'pure work machine'.[31] Furthermore, the intense scrutiny and perfectionism that is characteristic of self-tracking can result in 'cyberchondria', in which small fluctuations in data are viewed as signs of illness.[32] This creates an environment in which survival is seen to be a struggle that requires constant vigilance and labour.

The devices increase competitiveness by using 'gamification' techniques such as built-in reward systems. For example, users gain or lose points as a consequence of the quantity of time spent exercising or calories consumed. Because the devices are connected to social platforms that encourage users to share and compare their progress with other users, competition among peers is also encouraged.[33] Rivalry and goal-driven perfectionism is encouraged because neoliberal capitalism, via the ideology of health, assumes that '[t]he physically fit and active person is also a productive, successful worker'.[34] Through the gamification of health technologies, users compete to demonstrate their superior work ethic and ability to succeed.

Self-tracking devices also enable employers to scrutinize the private lives and personal habits of their employees. Reminiscent of the nineteenth-century factory owners who, in the name of health, surveyed their workers' behaviours and offered workplace incentives and punishments in order to increase productivity, a number of American corporations and insurance companies sponsor wellness programmes. They 'encourage their employees to lead healthy lifestyles and become more active, in such a way that leisure time is becoming more and more integrated into the sphere of labour as well'.[35] Because American companies often provide health insurance, there is a financial incentive to compel a healthier workforce, as this will lead to lower premiums as well as greater productivity, and therefore an increase in surplus-value. However, this financial incentive calls into question the idea of engagement with self-tracking practices as a free choice. For example, in 2016 the Equal Employment Opportunity Commission in America implemented new rules that enable employers to offer a 30 per cent reduction in insurance contributions if employees agree to sign up for wellness plans. The American Association of Retired Persons complained that the incentives undermine anti-discrimination laws that make it illegal for employers to collect sensitive health information that is not directly related to work. The wellness programmes are 'voluntary'; therefore, employers are able to 'financially coerc[e] employees into surrendering their personal health information'.[36] Furthermore, if employees are compelled to share the data with their employers, the employee's freedom to undertake 'unhealthy' activities is greatly reduced. Leisure time becomes an unpaid extension of work time, in which the employee's activities are monitored and controlled, and measured against a specific value system.

Additionally, the 'benefits' of self-tracking are not equally enjoyed. For example, a Nielson report states that '[o]wners of wearable devices were more likely to have a high household income', and Lupton writes that the Quantified Self movement is dominated by 'American middle-class white men with high levels of digital technological know-how'.[37] Lower income and lower education levels, older age, existing disabilities and chronic health problems, and being resident in a rural location all reduce an individual's likelihood of using self-tracking equipment and apps.[38] Lupton's study of the use of digital health technologies by women in Australia aimed to find out which apps and devices women used and found most helpful. The female participants were asked a range of questions relating to the use of the internet and social networking sites to gain advice about health, and the use of self-tracking apps and devices. The research found that some women experienced difficulties using self-tracking practices due to

> the demands of pregnancy, breastfeeding, chronic pain or disability or achieving the ideal of the caring mother who devotes most of her health-promoting efforts to her children. Standard health and fitness apps and wearables have not been designed with these bodily states and affordances in mind.[39]

In addition to technological limitations that prefer some types of bodies and social groups, the types of data that are collected and the methods used to categorize them are also 'deeply embedded in cultural, social, political and economic settings that reflect the implicit values and agendas of their contexts'.[40] The devices and apps are predominantly designed by and for white, middle-class, male bodies, and this shapes the way that health is measured. As a result, individuals can experience discrimination when their data is viewed by employers and corporations such as health insurance companies. For example, apps may collect information on exercise and penalize an individual for driving rather than walking, without taking into consideration where the employee lives, and whether they work at night, have a health condition, or have young children.

The introduction of self-tracking technology into the workplace allows surveillance and control to proliferate, leaving no aspect of the worker's body and no moments of leisure time free from scrutiny. Deleule and Guéry describe how the physical and mental optimization of the work-force enables them to work harder and faster, thereby increasing relative surplus-value. When employers track their employee's data, they succeed in maximizing both relative and absolute surplus-value because the compulsion to continual self-optimization means that leisure time is indistinguishable from work time and the working day is extended to its maximum. As Deleule described, when technology liberates the worker's energy for non-productive tasks, it is regained through rest that is only recuperation for work and sport that is 'simply another form of ascetics, a strenuous discipline of self-mutilation.'[41]

For the productive body, discipline and control are experienced as forms of leisure and sources of pleasure. Mike Featherstone observes that fitness and dieting are 'increasingly regarded as vehicles to release the temptations of the flesh' and that '[d]iscipline and hedonism are no longer seen as incompatible.'[42] Byung-Chul Han argues that viewing their body as a 'project' that must be continuously improved provides individuals with a sense of freedom due to the creative potential of the process of reinvention. However, the imperative to perfect and transform the self is a 'form of compulsion and constraint. Indeed, to a *more efficient kind of subjectivation and subjugation*.'[43] It is effective because it 'does not operate by means of forbidding and depriving, but by pleasing and fulfilling [...] It says "yes" more often than "no", it operates seductively, not repressively. It seeks to call forth positive emotions and exploit them.'[44] Consumers are disciplined with the promise of pleasure rather than threat of punishment.

Self-tracking apps and devices further obfuscate the distinction between pleasure and discipline through the gamification of fitness regimes. However, self-tracking devices and body maintenance regimes offer circumscribed forms of pleasure limited in scope and variety. They condition individuals to find pleasure and relief from stress in the consumption of surplus-value producing commodities that further increase the productivity of the body. Quantification also reduces pleasurable bodily sensations to numbers and disregards 'other modes of knowing, recording and understanding the elements of selfhood and embodiment' that may give pleasure.[45]

Quantified consumers

Self-control, attention to detail, perfectionism and competitiveness are traits that are idealized in neoliberal societies and refined through the use of self-tracking devices.[46] Weight-loss apps such as *DropPounds* and *MyFitnessPal* enable the close surveillance of diet in order to optimize health. They employ an income/expense metaphor for calorie counting in which calories are viewed as an 'expense' the consumer must work to pay off. Surplus calories remaining in the budget are 'savings' that also produce the added value of weight-loss. The financial metaphor of tightening one's belt is returned to the body by these apps. In *MyFitnessPal* users log their current body weight and a desired future body weight, and the app determines the quantity of calories that should be consumed in order to produce the desired weight-loss in five weeks. When users log the food they consume, the app states how many calories remain in their daily calorie budget in green coloured text, or informs the user if they have exceeded the budget, with a red negative number, similar to the display of a bank balance. The apps present food as an expense, and as fuel for work and exercise, erasing any notion of the pleasure and conviviality of eating. Foods are reduced to numbers: calorific value, quantity of protein, fat, sugar and fibre, and stripped of sensory qualities such as taste, texture and aroma.

Eating disorders are culture-bound syndromes, in which the symptoms reproduce and exaggerate social ideals.[47] Feminist scholars from disciplines including history, psychology and philosophy theorize eating disorders to be extreme responses to intractable conflicts between traditional and contemporary cultures, sexism and feminism, and unachievable body ideals.[48] In eating disorders socially idealized traits, such as perfectionism and self-control, are presented as expressions of distress.

In research examining the use of diet tracking apps by individuals with eating disorders, self-tracking is reported positively by individuals who are recovering from binge and purge eating disorders. Eating disorder sufferers with a propensity to binge tend to be characterized in current medical and psychological discourse as experiencing high levels of anxiety, impulsivity and lack of control.[49] Within such an emotional state, the ability to record and quantify food intake using the apps may delay the impulse to binge and reduce instances of loss of control. Reducing the anxiety-inducing experience of eating through quantification can, echoing Wolf's statement in praise of the Quantified Self movement, reduce the emotional impact of a problem so it can be more easily overcome.[50] The body and its demands become 'predictable and legitimate, [...] recognizable and therefore manageable'.[51] Users on *DropPounds* discussion forums describe how imagining and expressing food with numbers reduces its emotional value, enabling them to gain perspective and self-control by considering the calorific value of the food they have eaten.[52] Another user writes:

> My usual pattern [of eating] included starving myself and then bingeing, compulsive eating, and sporadic, unsustainable diets. My self-esteem has always been tied to my weight and whether I had a 'good eating day' or a 'bad eating day'. Since I have been on DropPounds, I have finally learned how to eat 3 meals a day (and snacks).[53]

Quantified eating therefore allows this user to manage the anxiety and impulsivity that results in uncontrolled eating, and reduce the negative moral value judgement they attribute to food after a binge.

However, the apps can exacerbate eating disorders for individuals characterized by intense self-scrutiny, perfectionism and the concrete adherence to rigid rules. Current medical texts state that individuals with anorexia tend to be perfectionists, prone to rigidity, high anxiety, 'excessive attention to detail [...], obsessions about food and excessive concerns about weight and shape'.[54] In some respects, attention to detail, obsessive rumination about weight and shape, and the concrete adherence to rigid rules are key methods of the Quantified Self movement's quest to 'gain knowledge through numbers' and make 'new discoveries [...] that are grounded in accurate observation'.[55] Unsurprisingly, apps that foreground concrete numerical data and produce detailed records of consumption habits can produce or intensify restrictive eating habits when used by individuals with these characteristics. One of Eikey and Reddy's participants says:

> [The app] made me more OCD [obsessive compulsive disorder], 'cause I'm like, 'I have to hit this number', basically ... It's made me more, very stringent on what I'm eating and making sure I hit those numbers [...] I feel like eating disorders stem from people trying to be perfect, and with this, you're hitting numbers trying to be perfect.[56]

The apps enable users to view food as quantities of calories, a mode of looking at food that is common in anorexics. In her doctoral research examining how anorexics visualized food and their body, Suzi Doyle found that it was common for anorexics to imagine that food is drained of colour, texture, flavour and aroma to reduce its desirability and make it easier to resist.[57]

Even when self-tracking individuals wish to recover, they tend to return to obsessive thinking patterns when they continue to use the apps because successful self-tracking reproduces some of their eating disorder behaviours.[58] For example, exercise can be entered into *MyFitnessPal* to generate surplus calories that enable the user to eat more food. However, users with restrictive eating disorders manipulate the apps by under-recording exercise and overestimating food intake.[59] Similarly, *DropPounds* gives negative feedback to users when they exceed their calorie limit, and positive feedback if the additional calories are purged with exercise, encouraging compensatory behaviours already familiar to users with restrictive eating disorders.[60] When the calorie budget is overspent, participants report negative feelings of guilt and shame that sometimes lead to vomiting or more severe calorie restriction.[61]

For some individuals the competitive rivalry promoted by self-tracking turns inwards, exacerbating the 'anorexic work ethic'.[62] One participant said that she was 'almost in competition with herself and the app to eat fewer calories each day', and other participants discussed how the apps aggravate their restrictive behaviour 'by making it seem like a game to eat less than the given amount and less than the prior day [...] which fueled their desire to continue and even intensify their restrictive behaviors'.[63]

In an ethnographic study of an eating disorder clinic in America, Helen Gremillion writes that anorexia reproduces and exaggerates the idealized body that efficiently balances consumption with labour so that the signs of consumption cannot be seen on the body.[64] Maude, one of the inpatients, exemplified this work ethic. A week prior to being admitted to hospital Maude had been a high-achieving student, participating in numerous extra-curricular activities. She did not experience body image distortion and was not preoccupied with body fat. Instead her thin body connoted a strong drive to achieve:

> losing weight was no effort at all. But the effort it took to keep up with all her activities at increasingly lower weights balanced out the ease of losing weight. [...] she kept losing weight so that she could continually test her ability to achieve.[65]

Achieving maximum productive output with minimum calorie input connotes a fully optimized and efficient body-machine. However, restrictive eating disorders represent 'the grinding of gears', when self-tracking apparatuses designed to produce optimized productive bodies are subverted by the anorexic work ethic to produce a dangerously emaciated body.

Pleasure without productivity

Self-tracking apps may thus exacerbate or even lead to eating disorders. They also impact on the behaviour and well-being of users more widely. The young mothers that Lupton interviewed said the apps made them feel guilty, ashamed and demotivated because they did not achieve their goals.[66] Some self-trackers 'become too obsessive about self-tracking, losing sight of other aspects of their lives. The intense focus on the body that these devices encourage may place too much pressure on oneself, causing feelings of failure and self-hatred'.[67] In addition to internalized condemnation for failing to achieve 'good health', the assumption that ill-health is caused by an individual's lack of effort also produces discriminatory judgements from others. Moral discourses surrounding self-tracking reproduce the assumption that people who do not or cannot engage with self-tracking methods are 'ignorant, lacking the appropriate drive, or wilfully self-neglecting'.[68]

As previously mentioned, in the United States, healthcare and employment are entwined because employers frequently provide health insurance for workers. This positions health as not just a general and desirable condition of the body and mind, but as specifically related to work. Being healthy is necessary to be productive, and so health care is provided by employers to ensure worker productivity. In dominant health and self-tracking discourses, fat is an emblem of the 'idleness and laziness denounced and condemned as the incarnation of social evil' because body weight is presented as a changeable quality of the body and a personal responsibility.[69] Fat is vilified as a health problem and an economic problem: it is assumed that fat individuals are less productive than their thin counterparts and drain state resources for health and social care. However, Lauren Berlant suggests that work, and the general conditions of life under neoliberal capitalism, are actually making people ill and cause some people to become fat. For exhausted workers, eating too much unhealthy food can be a kind of irresponsibility that's mostly not exuberant (although sometimes 'being bad' is a form of minor triumph) but folds a vitalizing pleasure into the spaces of ordinary living. Obesity is an effect of the intensity with which so many people need more and more mental health vacations from their exhaustion.[70]

Eating is viewed as a form of self-medication that enables workers to 'become absorbed in the present' and 'feel more resilient in the everyday'.[71] Furthermore, when 'absorbed in the present' they are free from the pressure of 'building toward the good life' and the experience of life as a 'projection toward a future' in which gratification is always deferred.[72] Berlant goes on to say that people are not actually becoming more resilient because 'bodies wear out from the pleasures that help them live on'.[73] Physical health is diminished in order to protect mental health, and this form of 'mental health vacation' paradoxically reduces longevity.

However, the assumption that fat causes lower life expectancy is questionable. A study that reviewed research on the health issues experienced by people in the 'overweight' and 'obese' BMI ranges found that high body weight did not increase mortality rates. Furthermore, the risks for moderately underweight women and men were equal to those who were severely overweight, leading Glenn Gaesser to recommend that 'attention to the health risks of [being] underweight is needed, and body weight recommendations for optimum longevity need to be considered in light of these risks'.[74]

Rather than vilifying fat, we might view unrestricted eating as a form of pleasure that reverses some of the conditioning processes that cause stress and alienate the individual from their body. Richard Klein proposes that pleasure, rather than labour and self-restraint, is how good health is produced: 'pleasure improves your health [...], if you inhibit the body's pleasure, you provoke disease'.[75] Klein writes that pleasure and health are personal attributes that cannot be reduced to the standardized norms of contemporary health discourses. In this respect, self-tracking and quantification cannot improve health if they do not produce pleasure. Accounts of competitiveness, obsession, anxiety, guilt and 'cyberchondria' suggest that for many users they do not. Suppressing the tactile qualities and conviviality of eating when tracking and quantifying food may reduce the self-tracker's pleasure further. Klein's Epicurean philosophy of health 'not only absolves of guilt, it says that our guilty pleasures might actually be keeping us healthy – mentally, physically, or both'.[76] Rather than submit to physical and psychological conditioning in order to fit into capitalist society more seamlessly, perhaps contemporary workers require both physical and mental health 'vacations' in which pleasure, rather than productivity, is the goal.

Fat bodies are vilified in contemporary society because they are deemed to be consuming too much, and I would argue, enjoying too much. Le'a Kent looks for examples of representations of fat bodies that do not connote an unhealthy and disgusting body, but instead infer a body marked by its desires. When interpreted this way, the fat body challenges social idealization of the 'good thin body (a body good only because it is marked by the self's repeated discipline)'.[77] Referring to FaT GiRL, a fanzine made for and by fat lesbian women, she says:

> the good body is rewritten as the body that can tell the self its desires, act on its desire, provide pleasures. Suddenly the disciplined body, the dieting body, the subject of 'self-control', seems empty and impoverished.[78]

The fat body represents pleasure, but not the circumscribed pleasure of self-restraint that is championed by self-tracking apps. It destabilizes the productive body ideology of self-denial when it is unapologetic in its display of enjoyment.

Conclusion

The Quantified Self movement embodies and exceeds the conditioning processes described in *The Productive Body*. By reducing health to data, 'laziness' and 'subjectivity' are scoured away, producing a body that is optimized as a productive worker and a productive consumer of technology, apps, fitness equipment and diet supplements. Working-class individuals are turned into productive body-machines via the ideology of health. 'Fine-tuning' their bodies via quantification techniques means that even white-collar workers, considered to be the 'brains' or 'software' of their organizations, also view their bodies as apparatus that must be optimized to increase productivity.

If quantification seeks, as its advocates suggest, to reduce the emotional intensity of our problems, this reduced emotional response is also a reduction of subjective experience: quantified eating presents food as a fuel for labour and not a source of pleasure. It reduces the negative effects of anxiety and impulsivity for some eating disorder sufferers, but the pathologies of quantification are expressed and perfected by those with restrictive eating disorders. The mind overcomes the body, pushing it to work harder with fewer resources, while denying its appetites. The anorexic body is a 'pure work machine, with its blemishes of subjectivity scoured away'.[79] But it is also a sign of the gears grinding and an ironic symbol of the 'living machine' functioning like a 'dead machine', in which all the problems and signs of wasting are painfully apparent.[80] It is consumed by quantified productivity.

The body that eats with enjoyment resists becoming a body-machine. Food indulgences are moments of rest from the experience that life is a struggle that requires continuous self-control. Rejection of the assumed relation between fat and reduced mortality enables fat to signify health and the pleasure of eating. If health and pleasure are unique to each person, standardizing medical and fitness measures such as the BMI and quantification technologies are less credible as indicators of health or illness. Refusal to engage in weight-loss and self-tracking activities is also a refusal to submit to the loss of subjectivity that standardized measures of health produce.

Notes

1   Robert Crawford, 'Healthism and the Medicalization of Everyday Life', *International Journal of Health Services* 10 (1980): 3.
2   Jonathan M. Metzl, 'Introduction: Why "Against Health"?', in *Against Health: How Health Become the New Morality*, ed. Jonathan M. Metzl and Anna Kirkland (New York and London: New York University Press, 2010), 2.
3   Bianca D. M. Wilson, 'Widening the Dialogue to Narrow the Gap in Health Disparities: Approaches to Fat Black Lesbian and Bisexual Women's Health Promotion', in *The Fat Studies Reader*, ed. Esther Rothblum and Sondra Soloway (New York: New York University Press, 2009), 58.
4   Lucy Aphramor and Jacqui Gingras, 'Helping People Change: Promoting Politicised Practice in the Health Care Professions', in *Debating Obesity: Critical Perspectives*, ed. Emma Rich, Lee F. Monaghan and Lucy Aphramor (New York: Palgrave Macmillan, 2011).
5   Deborah Lupton, *The Quantified Self* (Cambridge: Polity, 2017).

6   Robert Crawford, 'A Cultural Account of "Health": Control, Release, and the Social Body', in *Issues in the Political Economy of Health Care*, ed. John McKinley (London: Tavistock Publications, 1984), 99.

7   Shari L. Dworkin and Faye L. Wachs, *Body Panic: Gender, Health and the Selling of Fitness* (New York: NYU Press, 2009), 104.

8   'About the Quantified Self'. Quantified Self: Self Knowledge through Numbers, http://quantifiedself.com/about/ what-is-quantified-self/

9   Gary Wolf, 'The Data-Driven Life', *The New York Times Magazine*, 28 April 2010. http://www.nytimes.com/2010/05/02/magazine/02self-measurement-t.html?_r=0.

10 Lupton, *The Quantified Self*, 32.

11 Paul Ernsberger, 'Does Social Class Explain the Connection between Weight and Health?', in *The Fat Studies Reader*, ed. Esther Rothblum and Sondra Soloway (New York: New York University Press, 2009).

12 Deborah Lupton, *Fat* (London: Routledge Shortcuts, 2013), 4.

13 Emma Rich, Lee F. Monaghan and Lucy Aphramor, 'Introduction: Contesting Obesity Discourse and Presenting an Alternative', in *Debating Obesity: Critical Perspectives* (New York: Palgrave Macmillan, 2011), 1–35.

14 Paul Campos, 'Does Fat Kill? A Critique of the Epidemiological Evidence', in *Debating Obesity: Critical Perspectives*, ed. Emma Rich, Lee F. Monaghan and Lucy Aphramor (New York: Palgrave Macmillan, 2011), 36–59.

15 Lupton, *The Quantified Self*.

16 Maren Klawiter, 'Moving from Settled to Contested: Transformations in the Anatomo-Politics of Breast Cancer, 1970–1990', in *Contesting Illness: Process and Practices*, ed. Pamela Moss and Katherine Teghtsoonian (Toronto: University of Toronto Press, 2008), 289.

17 Charlotte Cooper, 'Fat Lib: How Fat Activism Expands the Obesity Debate', in *Debating Obesity: Critical Perspectives*, ed. Emma Rich, Lee F. Monaghan and Lucy Aphramor (New York: Palgrave Macmillan, 2011).

18 Julie Guthman, *Weighing In: Obesity, Food Justice, and the Limits of Capitalism* (Berkley: University of California Press, 2011).

19 Lupton, *Fat*, 22.

20 Steve Kroll-Smith and Joshua Kelley, 'Environments, Bodies, and the Cultural Imaginary: Imagining Ecological Impairment', in *Contesting Illness: Process and Practices*, ed. Pamela Moss and Katherine Teghtsoonian (Berkley and Los Angeles: University of California Press, 2012), 309.

21 François Guéry and Didier Deleule, *The Productive Body*, trans. Philip Barnard and Stephen Shapiro (Winchester: Zero Books, 2014). Hereafter *TPB*.

22 *TPB*, 81, 102.

23 *TPB*, 106.

24 *TPB*, 118.

25 *TPB*, 99.

26 Philip Barnard and Stephen Shapiro, 'Editors' Introduction to the English Edition', in *TPB*, 36–7.

27 Wolf, 'The Data-Driven Life'.

28 *TPB*, 102.

29 Martin de Groot quoted in *1130 Days: The Quantified Self Institute Three Year Report* (Hanze UAS: Hanze University of Applied Science, 2015).

30 Btihaj Ajana, 'Digital Health and the Biopolitics of the Quantified Self', *Digital Health* 3 (2017): 5.

31 *TPB*, 106.

32 Deborah Lupton, *The Australian Women and Digital Health Project: Comprehensive Report of Findings* (Canberra: News and Media Research Centre, University of Canberra, 2019), 5.

33 Deborah Lupton, preprint version of 'Self-tracking', in *Information: Keywords*, ed. Samuel Frederick, Michele Kennerly and Jonathan Abel (New York: Columbia University Press, forthcoming), 1–2.

34 Lupton, *The Quantified Self*, 68–9.

35 Ajana, 'Digital Health and the Biopolitics of the Quantified Self', 4.

36 David Certner, 'New Rules on Workplace Wellness Programs Make Employees Pay for Privacy', *AARP Where We Stand Blog*, 10 October 2016, http://blog.aarp.org/2016/10/10/new-rules-on-workplace-wellness-programs-make-employees-pay-for-privacy/.

37 Nielson (2014) quoted in Lupton, *The Quantified Self*, 31, 32.

38 Deborah Lupton, 'Self-tracking Cultures: Towards a Sociology of Personal Informatics', paper presented at *OzCHI '14*, 26th Australian Computer-Human Interaction Conference on *Designing Futures: The Future of Design*, 2–5 December 2014, Sydney.

39 Lupton, *The Australian Women and Digital Health Project: Comprehensive Report of Findings*, 48.

40 Ajana, 'Digital Health and the Biopolitics of the Quantified Self', 13.

41 *TPB*, 106.

42 Mike Featherstone, 'The Body in Consumer Culture', in *The Body: Social Process and Cultural Theory*, ed. Mike Featherstone, Mike Hepworth and Bryan S. Turner (London: Sage Publications, 1991), 170–1.

43 Byung-Chul Han, *Psychopolitics: Neoliberalism and New Technologies of Power* (London: Verso, 2017), 1.

44 Han, *Psychopolitics*, 14.

45 Lupton, 'Self-Tracking', 5.

46 Ajana, 'Digital Health and the Biopolitics of the Quantified Self'.

47 Arthur Crisp, *Anorexia: Let Me Be* (London: Plenum Press, 1980).

48 Mervat Nasser, *Culture and Weight Consciousness* (London: Routledge, 1997); Susan Bordo, *Unbearable Weight: Feminism, Western Culture, and the Body*, 2nd edn. (Berkeley and Los Angeles, CA: University of California Press, 2004); Orbach, Susie, *Hunger Strike: The Anorectic's Struggle as a Metaphor for Our Age*, 2nd edn. (London: Penguin, 1993); and Lisa Appignanesi, *Mad, Bad and Sad: A History of Women and the Mind Doctors from 1800 to the Present* (London: Virago, 2009).

49 Samatha Jane Brooks et al., 'A Debate on Current Eating Disorder Diagnoses in Light of Neurobiological Findings: Is It Time for a Spectrum Model?', *BMC Psychiatry* 12 (2012): 76; Janet Treasure, 'The Trauma of Self-Starvation: Eating Disorders and Body Image', in *The Female Body in Mind: The Interface between the Female Body and Mental Health*, ed. Mervat Nasser, Karen Baistow and Janet Treasure (London: Routledge, 2007).

50 Wolf, 'The Data-Driven Life'.

51 *TPB*, 102.

52 E. V. Eikey et al., 'Desire to Be Underweight: Exploratory Study on a Weight Loss App Community and User Perceptions of the Impact on Disordered Eating Behaviors', *JMIR Mhealth Uhealth* 5, no. 10 (2017). https://mhealth.jmir.org/2017/10/e150/.

53 Eikey et al., 'Desire to be Underweight'.

54 Treasure, 'The Trauma of Self-Starvation: Eating Disorders and Body Image'; Brooks et al., 'A Debate on Current Eating Disorder Diagnoses', 2.

55 'About the Quantified Self'.

56 E. V. Eikey and M. C. Reddy, 'It's Definitely Been a Journey: A Qualitative Study on How Women with Eating Disorders Use Weight Loss Apps', Proceedings of the Conference on Human Factors in Computing Systems, Denver. ACM (2017), 642–54.

57 Suzi Doyle, '"Body of Evidence"- The Experience of Patients with Anorexia Nervosa Regarding Imagery Related to Food, Weight and Shape', Unpublished Thesis, Middlesex University and Metanoia Institute, 2013.

58 Eikey and Reddy, 'It's Definitely Been a Journey'.

59   Eikey and Reddy, 'It's Definitely Been a Journey'.

60   Eikey et al., 'Desire to Be Underweight: Exploratory Study on a Weight Loss
     App Community and User Perceptions of the Impact on Disordered Eating
     Behaviors'.

61   Eikey and Reddy, 'It's Definitely Been a Journey'.

62   Helen Gremillion, *Feeding Anorexia: Gender and Power at a Treatment Center*
     (Durham and London: Duke University Press, 2003).

63   Eikey and Reddy, 'It's Definitely Been a Journey'.

64   Gremillion, *Feeding Anorexia*.

65   Gremillion, *Feeding Anorexia*, 49–50.

66   Lupton, *The Australian Women and Digital Health Project: Comprehensive Report
     of Findings*.

67   Lupton, *The Quantified Self*, 80.

68   Lupton, *The Quantified Self*, 74.

69   *TPB*, 106.

70   Lauren Berlant, 'Risky Bigness: On Obesity, Eating, and the Ambiguity of
     "Health"', in *Against Health: How Health Become the New Morality*, ed. Jonathan
     M. Metzl and Anna Kirkland (New York and London: New York University
     Press, 2010), 27.

71   Berlant, *Risky Bigness*, 27.

72   Berlant, *Risky Business*, 35.

73   Berlant, *Risky Bigness*, 27.

74   Glenn A. Gaesser, *Big Fat Lies: The Truth about Your Weight and Your Health*
     (Carlsbad, CA: Gurze Books, 2002), 98.

75   Richard Klein, 'What Is Health and How Do You Get It?', in *Against Health: How
     Health Become the New Morality*, ed. Jonathan M. Metzl and Anna Kirkland
     (New York and London: New York University Press, 2010), 19.

76   Klein, 'What Is Health', 21–2.

77   Le'a Kent, 'Fighting Abjection: Representing Fat Women', in *Bodies out of Bounds*,
     ed. Jana Evans Braziel and Kathleen LeBesco (Berkeley: University of California
     Press, 2001), 131.

78   Kent, 'Fighting Abjection', 142–3.

79   *TPB*, 106.

80   *TPB*, 106.

9

The artefact of losing: The (bio)poetics of miscarriage

Helen Charman and Christopher Law

The productive body, in its most literal sense, is a body that gives birth. The relationship between social reproduction theory, particularly that which is Marxist-feminist in character, and biopolitics is rooted in the intrinsic relevance of the generational renewal of human life to the perpetuation of capitalism. Human reproduction, however, is not a temporally straightforward process, nor is it necessarily *productive*: inscribed within the various realities of pregnancy and childbirth are the possibilities of termination, failure or loss. The role played by miscarriage, stillbirth and abortion in narratives of reproduction is difficult to define, something compounded by the social stigma and political valence of abortion in particular. In the matrix of production, reproduction and the politicized body that constitutes the sphere of the biopolitical, and which achieves one of its most pointed manifestations in Didier Deleule and François Guéry's *The Productive Body*, the termination or incompletion of a pregnancy appears as a potentially insoluble instance of *non*-productivity, an experience of absence that has by and large gone unnoticed, or been expelled, by biopolitical theory. The possibility of gestational non-productivity also illuminates temporalities – maternal time, the time of grief – that have escaped the purview of (bio)political theory and which have (given the irreducibly social and situated nature of pregnancy) generated equally furtive but important experiences of maternal space. In this chapter, we consider the extent to which lyric poetry, and the multiple ways it has been theorized, could be capable of articulating these experiences of absence. In doing so, we propose, lyric has the potential of challenging or reorienting the domain of biopolitics.

Loosely defined as poetry that relies upon the first-person pronoun in order to construct an intersubjective space of address, lyric poetry's relation to politics has always been a complex, arguably dialectical one. As Samuel Solomon's recent work on the relationship between lyric and social reproduction argues, the perceived social irrelevance of poetry in the 1970s catalysed a renewed understanding of the form as a literary mode that could enact political resistance to social, pedagogical and institutional norms.[1] A paradigmatic instance of the politicization of lyric can be found in a now canonical essay, published in 1986, by the theorist and translator Barbara Johnson. In 'Apostrophe, Animation, and Abortion', Johnson leverages contemporaneous debates about abortion in North American civic life in order to query the relationship between the first two terms of her essay's title, a relationship integral to traditional accounts of lyric. In the theory of lyric poetry, a poem's intersubjective effect relies above all on its ability to conjure – or 'apostrophize' – an object of direct address: Johnson notes that apostrophe is a 'rhetorical device that has come to seem almost synonymous with the lyric voice'.[2] This, as lyric theorists have long noted, is no simple matter, for if the poem is to achieve a genuinely intersubjective effect then apostrophe is reliant in turn on the possibility of giving of life to the object of the text's address, an effect referred to as 'animation' by theorists. For Johnson, as for others, the two terms are practically inseparable: apostrophe itself is defined as the 'giving of voice, the throwing of voice, the giving of animation'.[3] The apparently inviolable link between apostrophe and animation thus entangles poetry and 'life' together. Apostrophe involves 'language's capacity to give life and human form to something dead and inanimate'.[4]

This co-constitutive relationship between apostrophe and animation is clearly a condition of possibility of both lyric and lyric theory. As a means of thinking about the relationship between poetry and politics, however – or so it appeared to Johnson in the early 1980s – it is also inadequate. Johnson's essay henceforth turns on the question of what happens to apostrophe and animation when they encounter a third, seemingly heterogeneous term, 'abortion'. The essay, which draws on poetic examples from Percy Bysshe Shelley, Charles Baudelaire, Lucille Clifton, Gwendolyn Brooks, and Adrienne Rich, contends that lyric acts of apostrophe or animation are not always – are indeed rarely – easy matters. After all, if lyric is capable of 'giving life' then it is also capable of saying something about what life is, who has life, and who is worthy of address. 'Rhetoric', then – a term that Johnson borrows from Paul de Man to crystallize this linguistic capacity – is not simply a decorative aspect of a language that is otherwise communicative, but an act of 'figuration', which forms the very contours of what we are capable of recognizing as life. The stakes of this entanglement are unsurprisingly capacious: 'Rhetorical, psychoanalytical, and political structures are profoundly implicated in one another,' Johnson argues.[5]

These problems are not limited to poetry but also determine the public sphere in which abortion is framed as a matter of debate. As Johnson puts it: 'The questions these poems are asking, then, is what happens when the poet is speaking as a mother – a mother whose cry arises out of – and is addressed to – a dead child?'[6] The encounter with abortion staged in Johnson's essay, then, from its title onwards, is presented as an important instance of animation and apostrophe becoming 'literalized'. What happens, Johnson asks, when theoretical problems faced by the lyric speaker intersect with political debates over abortion: 'What happens when the lyric speaker assumes responsibility for producing the death in the first place, but without being sure of the precise degree of human animation that existed in the entity killed?'[7] Like rhetoric itself, this act of literalization is of more than epiphenomenal significance, instead heralding an important recalibration of the relation between poetry and life. Using Gwendolyn Brooks's poem 'The Mother' as a central focus, Johnson offers a reading of lyric address as a space in which questions about the definition of life (and the infliction of violence) can be uniquely posed.

In a recent reading of Johnson's essay – offered in a chapter aptly titled 'The Viability of Poetry' – Sara Guyer distils why the simultaneously poetic and political role of abortion in Johnson's argument holds significance not only for literary studies but also for political theory: 'her reflection on apostrophe, animation, and abortion is an argument for the essentially poetic structure of what we later have come to call biopolitics.'[8] Johnson, as Guyer suggests, understands poetry as integral, even indispensable, to biopolitical theory, because its irreducibly apostrophic-animative character foregrounds the fact that *any* attempt to figure, give, or value 'life' is at bottom (not merely accidentally) political. 'If articulated as a formula,' Guyer surmises, 'it would say that *biopolitics is a biopoetics*.'[9] At least two implications follow from Guyer's insight. First, the paradigms that typically govern our understanding of 'biopolitics' are complicated. Poetry's capacity for animation, insofar as it is effective but by nature ungeneralizable (we are only ever capable of animating singular, 'literalized' lives, never 'life' per se), is uniquely placed to register how the governance of life and death, rather than surfacing as a model for the transformation of political power at a discrete historical juncture, instead emerges in contingent and discontinuous forms *whenever* the question of viability – a term also used to refer to the likely success of a pregnancy – arises.[10] Deleule and Guéry themselves assert that the 'productive body', which serves to mediate between the biological and social body, 'has gone unnoticed until now because it was objectively fetal and indistinct'.[11] Johnson's insight, however, forces us to question such metaphorical conflations between conceptual innovation and bodily generation. The 'birth of biopolitics', heralded by Foucault's famous lecture series, accordingly, is not an epochal occurrence that happens once and for all, either historically or theoretically, but an event that is generated again and again, on singular occasions, without the guarantee of any repeatable framework ever being established.

Second, as both Johnson and Guyer indicate, recognizing that '*biopolitics is a biopoetics*' entails an awareness that the character of the 'debate' about abortion ought to be transformed. Rather than being a question of morals or rights – whether those of the pregnant person or of the foetus – the 'literalized' figure of abortion forces us to interrogate the nature of the debate itself: that is, to question what is at stake in framing such things *as* questions of rights. In our own day as much as in Johnson's, this is a pertinent task. In the lead-up to the 2018 referendum proposing to repeal the eighth amendment to the Irish constitution (which effectively prohibited abortion except in life-threatening circumstances), a considerable number of opinion pieces rallying against the repeal framed their arguments not in the religious terms that had influenced previous legislative outcomes in Ireland, but in a secular language that emphasized the universal human rights of the unborn foetus.[12] Rejecting the very premises of such arguments, the proposal that Johnson offers and Guyer reiterates is that the concept of 'rights' elides or displaces a more fundamental issue, namely the set of assumptions that are at play whenever life itself becomes the object of a calculative and generalizing discourse. As Guyer points out, insofar as it attempts to register the very 'ability to live', the term 'viability' posits an implicit valuation of life, one that measures any actual or potential life only with reference to a predetermined and normative idea of what 'life' should be. In suspending the link between language and its putative outcomes – the guarantee of 'life' in general – poetry is able to question the norms of productivity that govern our conceptions of life and its generation, norms that arguably extend to biopolitical theory too.

This is how we see the state of the field at the moment. Furthering the line of enquiry opened by Guyer's reading of Johnson, however, we might question whether its own premises might still be too grounded in a preconceived, and hence deconstructable, distinction. Does the claim that poetry is peculiarly suited to traverse the rhetorical, psychical and political itself result in a kind of idealization of poetry as *genre*, one at odds with the material nature of both poetic language and maternity? In what (pre)conceptions about productivity, both bodily and poetic, do such theories continue to be grounded? A terminological issue might encapsulate these reservations. As we have seen, Guyer is hopeful that the 'biopoetics' of her book's title would be able to register the ineradicable role of the poetic in biopolitics. Guyer seems less attentive, however, to the logic of figuration or 'literalization' that drives Johnson's essay and which we have begun to elucidate above. Johnson shows how every act of animation and apostrophe is also a 'literalization', which prevents such acts from giving rise to a generalized link between poetry and life. Yet with the conceptual apotheosis of 'biopoetics', Guyer threatens to consolidate and idealize lyric, as a genre, for its own sake, rather than recognizing lyric's (always singular) capacity to attune us to the problems accompanying all discourses 'about' life. With due attentiveness to this potential shortcoming, Isabel A. Moore uses the term 'biopoetics' in a more reproving register, deployed in a critical reading of recent intersections between poetry and animism (her particular target being Paul Muldoon's *Faber Book of Beasts*):

> I use the term 'biopoetics' to describe the entry of these animist or life-and-death figures into critical accounts and poetic defenses of lyric, which repeatedly collapse the genre's survival with our own. While poetic language has traditionally been granted the power to animate (and therefore to deface), biopoetic discourse seeks to bring the genre itself to life in and as language: more the impossible animation of lyric than the hyperbole of lyric animation. Biopoetic discourse reads its genre as if living its own parallel life, and so as the continuation of human species life by other means.[13]

This, as we see it, is the problem that faces us. How to probe the link between poetry and politics, and attend to the question of literalization, without inadvertently succumbing to an idealization of the lyric, of the kind in which Guyer's text arguably results? It is at this point, we think, that a prolonged consideration of the various realities of childbirth, stillbirth, abortion and miscarriage becomes important.

At a point in her essay that goes somewhat unelaborated, Johnson comments upon the first line of Lucille Clifton's 'the lost baby poem', which runs 'the time I dropped your almost body down'. 'By choosing the word "dropped"', Johnson writes, 'Clifton renders it unclear whether the child has been lost through abortion or through miscarriage.'[14] Johnson, whose deconstructive *nous* maintains that 'there is politics precisely because there is undecidability', specifies why this ambiguity is so important:

> When a woman speaks about the death of children in any sense other than that of pure loss, a powerful taboo is being violated. The indistinguishability of miscarriage and abortion in the Clifton poem indeed points to the notion that *any* death of a child is perceived as a crime committed by the mother, something a mother ought by definition to be able to prevent.[15]

Johnson here highlights and condemns the kind of discursive calculations that inevitably and violently attribute blame to a mother in response to a loss, no matter the circumstances. Yet Clifton's radical poetic insight, Johnson shows, is that such misattributions paradoxically foment a genuinely political possibility, in that they decouple the mother from an imposed passivity according to which she can only experience 'pure loss', the other side of the coin, as it were, from an idealized, 'successful' birth.[16] By refusing to determinately categorize the different ways that the 'death of a child' can occur, Johnson – via Clifton – shows how poetry can interrupt discursive and temporal norms that value only productivity, a possibility explored in greater detail in the texts under scrutiny in the remainder of this chapter. However, as we seek to show while our readings unfold, this 'indistinguishability', so central to the political stakes of Johnson's essay, arguably glosses over the important material differences between abortion, stillbirth and miscarriage, each of which may be experienced, understood or articulated as *specific* interruptions to the norms of capitalist (re)productivity, events that – like the linguistic parts that comprise 'biopoetics' – cannot necessarily be collapsed into one another. After attending to a number of poems that trouble the distinctions between these experiences of loss, then, the conclusion of our essay will consider Sandeep Parmar's 'An Uncommon Language', a text whose hybrid form responds to the lack of poems specifically about miscarriage. How might the tentative notion of a 'poetics of miscarriage' – hinted at in Johnson's essay, but hardly itself 'literalized' – allow us more rigorously to identify and challenge the norms of maternal productivity, which play a more important role in capitalist production, and in biopolitical theory, than previously recognized?

*

> All the connectives of right recall
> have grown askew. I know
> a child could have lived, that
> my body was cut. This cut
> my memory half-sealed but glued
> the edges together awry.
> The skin is distorted, the scar-tissue
> does the damage, the accounts are wrong.[17]

So begins Denise Riley's 'A shortened set', first published in her 1993 collection *Mop Mop Georgette*. The poem is urgently concerned with the distinction between 'feeling' and 'thought': the mind, unable to process the absence of the foetus, and experiencing the speaker's own altered body as a composite in which 'the accounts are wrong', has itself grown erroneously 'askew'. The poem identifies abortion as an intentional, or at least intentionally known or remembered, act ('I know / a child could have lived, that / my body was cut') but soon spirals out and away from identifiably personal testimony: 'your feelings, I mean mine, are common to us all'. As if presaging the problems identified above concerning the collapse of poetry and life into 'biopoetics', the opening stanza ends with a reference to the simultaneous force and threat of poetry, self-consciously registered as a danger in relation to both the poet and the world: 'Now / steady me against inaccuracy, a lyric urge / to showing-off. The easy knife / is in my hand again. Protect me.' The poem here is directed less at the foetus than at the reader or listener, conjured and addressed in the moment of reading by a deictic 'Now' wary of lyric's all too 'easy' self-aggrandizing tendencies. The transference of the 'knife' from an implement used on the passive body of the speaker to one wielded by them effects a shift, akin to that identified in Johnson's reading of Clifton, from the straightforward narrative chronology of biography or life-writing to a more unwieldy and disruptive poetic temporality.

Such a strategy, which deploys the resources of 'lyric' at the same time as ironizing its generic stability, is present throughout Riley's writing practice. In her theoretical writing, Riley complicates not only the idea of a stable lyric self, but the notion of the body as an originary point for writing.[18] In a 1995 interview with Romana Huk, Riley identifies 'A shortened set' as one of the 'few instances in the poems where there is a naturalized female body'.[19] Riley goes on to define the body in the centre of that text as a 'confessional' body, but notes that it is held together artificially, a site of welding rather than recuperation: 'it's written in terms of accuracy of memory, needing to try to get back to the site of original injury in order to cut it apart and restitch it.' In the same answer, Riley goes on to offer another example of the 'naturalized' female body in her work: 'There's one miscarriage poem back in *Dry Air*, but then again it's very much connected to conceptions of lying, or the failure to sustain something.' For Riley, then, the question of 'naturalization' is linked closely to reproduction; both of the poems she identifies are to do with thwarted or interrupted gestational processes. The reproductive body itself, however, according to her own lyric schema, can never be 'naturally' articulated, enforcing a distinction between the product of articulation (the poem) and the experience of reproduction, which can never be accurately described. The question, then, is how or whether – if even the 'naturalized' body is artificial, and its articulation inevitably compromised – a linguistic space can ever be created that allows for the distinction between the intentional ending of a pregnancy and an unintentional one.

It is not immediately clear where in 1985's *Dry Air* one can find the 'miscarriage poem' that Riley identifies; reading the collection with the goal of discovering it, almost every lyric feels like it could be the text in question. A few pages from the end of the collection, positioned between 'What I do', with its undercurrent of violence – 'My / death still will / skip on' – and the uncanny pastoral 'families / strung out across / the fields' of 'To the fields', is a poem called 'No', which begins:

All the towels are red
the navy towel and the black
blood-soaked
and the white dress has slipped
to the bloodied floor.[20]

Here, the biological fact of the loss of a pregnancy becomes all-encompassing; blood, isolated in the middle of the stanza, absorbs all textures and all colours into itself. In the second verse, this disarray extends to the temporal confusion of miscarriage, as Riley introduces a second-person address:

This one you lose you could not love.
You were deceived, your flat blood knew
to open its bright factual eye.
This that you leak you never grew.

The tone initially feels reminiscent of other lyrics of loss, like Elizabeth Jennings's 'For a child born dead', with its address to a being both capable and incapable of action: 'you could not come, and yet, you go.'[21] Unlike Jennings's address to the child, however, Riley's shift from the neutral third person of the first stanza to the second stanza's 'you' instead facilitates a more complex exploration of agency and loss, again not dissimilar to Clifton's 'the lost baby poem'. Riley's address oscillates between blame – 'this one you lose you could not love' – and the assertion that the woman herself was 'deceived' by her own biological matter, her 'flat blood's' knowledge of something other than the pregnancy's progression. The poem's final stanza furthers this confusion of body and self, knowledge and guilt:

The officer is at the scarlet door.
Here is his evidence. Some body lied.
That body's mine but I am in it.
And I am it and I have lied.

The purposefully clunky, riddle-like lines move through the verse, as if drawing out a kind of equation: 'some body' becomes, in the following line, a body that simultaneously belongs to and is inhabited by, but crucially is not at one with, the miscarrying speaker. The final line then elides the 'I' and the 'it' of the body together: 'And I am it and I have lied.' Where, then, is the lie? The miscarriage itself? The poem? Rather than confirming either possibility, Riley instead seems to consider the 'lie' as positioned somewhere between the body and its (failure of) communication. Whilst one part of the body – the part understood by the speaker with their capacity for 'love' – prepares for the child's arrival, another biological part, here signified by the 'flat blood', knew that the new life could never be sustained. It is within this lyric language, then, in this tension between I and not-I, between self, body, speaker, and text, that the event of the miscarriage can exist: lyric's long history of problematizing the personal becomes, here, the only temporal plane in which a full account of this loss can occur.

*

In staging an embodied speaker's relationship to an abortion and a miscarriage respectively, 'A shortened set' and 'No' together demonstrate a linguistic capacity for articulating the temporal complexities of ended pregnancies. In both cases, Riley self-consciously negotiates the relationship between poetic form, lyric genre and the undecidable event of loss, intensifying the line of enquiry initiated by Clifton and Johnson. Alice Notley's 2018 poem 'What Is "Conscious"', on the other hand, almost erases the intentionality of an event (or its remembering) altogether, alerting us to poetry's capacity to articulate wholly different configurations of space and time. The poem relates an 'awful dream / that there were two swimming pools indoors / and in one my baby was suddenly bloodied then disappeared'.[22] The poem's title, 'What Is "Conscious"', as well as distancing the speaker from the 'conscious' act of abortion (or its conscious recollection, or its self-conscious lyric retelling), contains within it the suggestion that the obliquely described event could in fact be a miscarriage, which, depending on the stage of the pregnancy, often occurs without the person in question ever being aware they were pregnant. More troublingly perhaps, it also reminds us of the questions wielded by pro-life campaigners to advocate for the rollback of reproductive rights: when does life begin? What is conscious?

Notley's multifaceted suspension of consciousness distances the speaker's experience from temporal conditions almost entirely. Rather than experiencing time as a dislocation from her own body, as Riley does, Notley's speaker here realizes that 'there had been something not really linearly / but in the way of dreams integral' in her experience of events. The dream's 'integrity', or immanent wholeness, allows for the speaker to take part in a conversation with a 'you', figured not as a specific object or non-I called into being by apostrophic language, but as a dry emissary of the universe itself:

'You're telling me in front of all these people – you the universe
are telling me my baby died'   'You mean
you didn't know'   'Doesn't matter   It's the only thing here'
I wake up crying.   And isn't it the only thing here?

When she seeks to overturn the event or 'scenario' of the death, however, or at least express a desire for a different outcome, the speaker's target ('you') is quite different:

anything any other scenario
as long as the baby doesn't have to die
in the primal pool   if you say this is raw
I reply by whose rules   by whose definition of life
are you asking what poetry is and if it's of use?
nothing's of use!

Notley's speaker admits that her desire to avert the event of the child's death is naive or 'raw' but only, it is hinted, from the perspective of a 'you' that has stultified the relation between poetry and living by means of a 'definition of life' and a set of 'rules'. The exclamation 'nothing's of use!' can certainly be read as a nihilistic lament directed against a universe that has allowed the death of her baby, yet the context of the remark suggests that the speaker's problem is not with the universe – with the cruelty of the event itself – than with the assumption that poetry ought to be able to make 'use' of the event. Though the speaker comes to mock her own fatalism ('But I'm just babbling') the poem attempts throughout to articulate, by means of line breaks and blank space – a deliberate non-use of space, we might say – an eventual perspective of the universe as a 'vanity' that decouples poetry from any use whatsoever. Notley thus teases out poetry's own resilience to the kind of idealization effected by the concept of 'biopoetics'.

The universe's indifference to the poetic and material – productive and reproductive – concerns of its inhabitants is foundational, too, to Peter Riley's

Birth Prospectus. The End of Us (originally published in 1977 in the *Grosseteste Review X* and published in revised form in 2007). The sequence mourns, or attempts to mourn, the loss of Riley's stillborn daughter, addressed in its very first lines:

> Little spinner, you are too clever
> and connect right over. That is
> the end of you, lost in ardour.[23]

In his essay about the sequence, Riley provides relevant biographical detail:

> In 1975 my wife was delivered of a dead baby girl in Stepping Hill Hospital, which is what the whole thing is about. That is what is announced in poem 1. Poems 1-7 reiterate the event, and the still-born child is the 'you' addressed intermittently throughout, the little spinner, the figure of the still point of unlimited potential, the nothing that accounts for all. Everything that is perceived in the poem: land, stars, creatures, everything, is perceived through this death, which guides perception through the world.[24]

From its title onwards – where the productive optimism of 'birth prospectus' is stifled both by the full stops that seal off its movements and by the doubled but deadened 'us' that ends each half – Riley's *Birth Prospectus* attempts to mourn the loss of the child without interpreting the event merely as the failure to fulfil a determined 'purpose' or 'end'.[25] The sequence is important, therefore, for the directness with which it alerts us to forms of existence and experience that elude the temporal norms of capitalist productivity. This happens, above all, through a complex and irreducibly ambiguous exploration of the 'nature' of the event. The second stanza of the first poem parenthetically accepts the facticity (or 'this'-ness) of the stillbirth as 'natural', according to a posited equilibrium in which the 'surplus of energy' generated by the child's life and death contributes to the universe's balance, ironically figured as transactional:

> Because of this (which is natural)
> a surplus of energy builds into the
> grass and the trees of the forest
> elegantly describe themselves as
> interim customers, under contract
> to the oceanic combine.
> It all stays.

To a certain extent, the poem's ironic move into the vocabulary of economy and production jars, despite the veiling elegance of Riley's sibilant 'forests' and 'grass'. The child is transformed into 'surplus' energy, and even the landscape succumbs to 'contract', to 'custom', and the dangerous double edge of 'combine', which could refer to a harvesting mechanism or to the furtherance of commercial interests, culminating in the balancing pathos of '[i]t all stays'. However, in allowing for the 'natural' character of stillbirth, the parenthetical clause of the first line and the stanza's subsequent imagery could be said to perform a somewhat different task, suspending an important distinction posited by Deleule and Guéry between 'the body most generally understood as such, the animal body' and the body that is 'named productive'.[26] The authors of *The Productive Body* propose that 'all the acts of animal bodies are referred to their nature as living beings, not as producers', but Riley's sequence makes room for an alternative possibility: not only can the world's natural elements be productive, human existence can be unproductive. Or, alternatively put, the unproductivity of human life can be understood as productive, at least when an instance of non-reproduction, such as stillbirth, is allowed to be understood as 'natural', and when the norms of capitalist production are concurrently ironized. From this alternative perspective allowed by the poem, we can read '[i]t all stays' (qualified in the next stanza by '[o]r begs to') as a statement of remembrance that defies the co-option of life into an economic process. The life and death of the child, held in impossible equilibrium in a 'natural' and truly an economic space, colour all knowledge, all perception, from this point onwards.

None of this seeks to idealize lyric as genre, however. In his commentary on the poem, Riley stresses how its compromise between openness and closure formed a deliberate rejoinder to lyric poetry's self-conscious epistemology, what he terms 'the knowingness of the knowing poets': 'They knew they had the gift which spread their discourse over and above all other human discourses because they had comprehended it all in its absence, but the baby died. They knew that by pushing imagination into apocalyptic violence they were saving the world by default, but the baby died.' In its depiction of such poetries 'adhering like fury to a denial of / social intercourse', *Birth Prospectus* dramatizes what we have earlier read as the tendency for 'lyric' to close itself off against 'literalizations' in its attempt at generic self-presence. (Nevertheless,

Riley is unable to entirely cast aside these strategies, since his images for the linguistic non-productions of the 'knowing poets' – 'There's not an ounce in it'; 'a knob / of congealed blood' – also demand to be read as images of the stillborn child.) Instead of ruminating in its linguistic self-enclosure like 'a wasp trapped in the instep', the poem instead offers a precarious 'love' that wagers 'our ungainliness against the possible gain'. Despite its potential unproductivity, even the possibility that it might never be read, poetry is simply 'worth writing', Riley proposes:

> Or only that it is worth writing
> for no eyes to see and as dully and
> imageless as it comes (like a swallow
> between the rustling and complaining
> roots of our patience) as
> flat as that, that living furthers.

The penultimate poem of the sequence indeed endeavours to accept that poetry is unable to cut itself off from other social discourses, while at the same time continuing to register, as do the theoretical insights of Johnson and Guyer, how the framing of loss *as* a 'debate' enforces value judgements that implicitly render certain lives discardable: 'We in our partial and twisted end / to end time have the vulgarity / to debate various degrees of your / expendability from all sides.' Both the framing of loss as a 'debate' about productivity and the self-consciously 'poetic' renouncement of the social world enforce a denial of temporality, a denial of the common 'natural' status of the human and non-human world, and a denial of time itself.

*

What lessons can such poetic attempts to salvage 'time', apparently against our own productive and reproductive 'ends', hold? In *Enduring Time*, Lisa Baraitser poses a similar question with regard to the temporality of care or 'maintenance' work, in which the often overlapping times of grief and maternity bear a prominent role. The necessity of considering the multiple relations between time, work and labour, however, leads Baraitser to consider whether the forms of analysis most commonly associated with social reproduction theory might themselves reproduce the reduction of time to productivity. Baraitser notes:

Beyond the sociological analysis of mother's time, the question remains, however, as to whether there is something distinct about maternal time *qua* time; whether the time involved in this particular relation of care can tell us something about time itself.[27]

Citing a succinct question posed by Stella Sandford ('What category of labour can bear the association with the maternal in the phrase "maternal labour" without swallowing it up?'), Baraitser considers how alternate experiences of time can be acknowledged, without being subsumed into the (necessary) abstraction that any recognition of labour's social form demands.[28] If poetry, as we have sought to claim, constitutes a resource for thinking through these questions, we might consider parallels between the threat Sandford recognizes in the phrase 'maternal labour' and the problem we have attempted to identify in the neologism 'biopoetics'. Both terms voice a productive and necessary tension, yet both also threaten to dissolve that tension through establishing an implicit hierarchy: just as 'biopoetics' seems to furtively advance the generic ends of lyric theory, 'maternal labour' might simply collapse the specificity of maternal experience into a productive form that inevitably transforms its character. Needless to say, an extensive investigation of relevant theories of social reproduction is beyond the scope of this chapter. In moving towards an ineluctably provisional conclusion, however, we hope to consider how recent attempts to theorize a poetics of miscarriage might harbour the lessons of the poetry we have previously considered, while at the same time situating them within a defined social, historical and bodily experience.

In 2012, Denise Riley published a short book-length essay, *Time Lived, without Its Flow*, which put forward an account of a specifically maternal experience of time (one that necessitates in turn a recognition and consideration of the 'paternal' idioms of Peter Riley's text, concerned as they are with constructing a lyric temporality of a grief that is necessarily premised on someone else's body). *Time Lived, without Its Flow*, which recounts the state of 'arrested temporality' that Riley experienced after the death of her son, figures the time of bereavement as a kind of pregnancy in reverse: 'As if a pregnancy had by now been wound backwards past the point of conception and away into its pre-existence.'[29]

Riley, both in the text and in an interview with Baraitser, describes the essay as an intentional redress to the absence of literary representation for a state that is 'not rare but for many is lived daily'.[30] The idea that the very existence of a text can perform a recuperative role, locating grief within a shareable framework, is also explored in Sandeep Parmar's 2018 essay 'An Uncommon Language', which advocates specifically for a poetry of, about or in response to miscarriage. Situating itself in relation to an absent canon, Parmar's text more directly raises the problems of time, maternity and production addressed above: 'how might poems about miscarriage, its silence, broaden our picture of maternity, a range of experiences, too often co-opted by the logic and language of productivity?'[31] Parmar develops this insight with reference to the few examples of the genre there are, including Clifton's 'the lost baby poem' and Dorothea Lasky's 'The Miscarriage', with its refrain 'Work harder!', said to speak 'to the exhausting demands on women's lives and bodies from a (western capitalist) society bent on the forward momentum of (re)production'. As these remarks indicate, however, the possibility of establishing a canon of 'miscarriage poetry' (as this clumsy nomenclature betrays) is by no means a given, since the very (re)productive frameworks against which such poetry brushes are the same ones that render its attempts at articulation null and void. In distinction to more 'definable' kinds of grief, that which follows miscarriage – a loss that pre-empts life – is forced to tarry with its own failure to become vocal, productive, recognized. Any 'poetics of miscarriage', then, would be defined by a paradox. It would be a *poeisis* of that which does not bring any recognizable or countable product into being, but that cannot, nevertheless, be ignored. It necessitates alternative forms of articulation and commonality:

> Death is real; what happened to you is not this but some unspeakable loss. A fact that cannot be explained by the framework of life, its order. You have no language of your own, only a remote vocabulary, borrowed from mourning mothers.

Despite its advocacy for a lyric mode of miscarriage, a large part of 'An Uncommon Language' is written in prose, allowing for a more localized perspective on maternal experience. In the first, essayistic section of the text, Parmar catalogues the violence contained within the machinery of care that places blame, or at least a kind of generalized shame, on the expectant mother who makes 'the wrong decisions', a clearly racialized form of harm: 'Not quite

English. The NHS leaflets piled thick in your palm. The hostile posters on the wards threatening those without legal status.' Elucidating the everyday reality of the proliferating discourses that, as suggested by Johnson, turn maternity into an arena of (retractable) rights and (punishable) individual choices, Parmar notes that:

> When a woman with certain privileges is about to give birth there's a slog of learning. Guides in print and thousands of websites. Most of which do not entertain other outcomes. Gradually, you pick it up, the knack of counting your life in weeks. Consider buying one of the many new books on motherhood, mostly by middle-class white women. You learn what it means to [redacted].

The labour of preparation – 'a slog of learning' – both requires the expectant mother to radically alter her own understanding of her body's temporality ('counting your life in weeks') and refuses to acknowledge the precarity or *a* chronology of pregnancy: in the contemporary Western narrative of maternity, risk is absorbed into the smooth facade of late capitalist efficiency, with mortal fears and hopes necessarily repressed.[32]

The specificity of miscarriage, then, concerns not only a particular modality of time but a particular experience of space. Parmar's text is thus set into relief, and differentiated, against two of the poems we have addressed already, Notley's 'What Is "Conscious"' and Peter Riley's *Birth Prospectus*. Notley's text concludes: 'Let it all happen collapse and fly out of your- / selves the only sticking together's of the mole- / cules of soul to tell each other we ex- / ist that's all the universe is vanity.' *Birth Prospectus* finds solace in realizing that 'no one has any better space than / the details you find inscribed / on the walls of your cell'. Whereas both Notley and Riley articulate the possibility of living and writing after loss by making ironic peace with an indifferent, yet hospitable, universe, Parmar's speaker experiences the specific institutional spaces of maternity as hostilely classed and racialized. The prevailing logic that orders the specifically medical arena of loss is no equalizer, a fact that elicits a series of generic, formal and spatiotemporal poetic variations as the text reaches its tentative conclusion.

Near the end of 'An Uncommon Language', after the line 'You stop talking to your selves', Parmar organizes her text into recognizable stanzas, as if the essay form, unable to progress past the barriers of unknowing presented by miscarriage, has to abandon its own discursive paradigms.[33] The address itself starts to splinter, as the body becomes not 'mine' or 'yours' but 'the woman's body', a representative of inherited trauma containing not only the curtailed time of the child but ancestral time, too: '*Her body is a graveyard*, A says. M explains: *miscarriages haunt women down generations*.' As the space of the body coalesces with that of the graveyard – 'What grew in you is not you but a shroud / and any idiot knows a shroud' – time and space collapse into one another anew, and ever again, in formations that disrupt the co-option of maternal loss into a capitalist ideal of intelligible productivity. Moving from the empty room of the hospital to a village that 'smells of blood and panic', the individual body of the speaker contains both the time of its ancestors and the inherited trauma of colonialism, a bodiless 'pulse' that traverses the past and present:

> My grandmother, who died giving birth,
> explains what makes carnelian so red.
> I assumed it was the iron in its veins
> that made the Romans stamp their profiles
> onto its brittle clots. Pulse of empire.

The living and the dead are merged together, as English and Punjabi combine in a dialogue with ghosts:

> *Don't say that / I never visited you.*
> A ghost is as good a family / as you may get.
> *Va, itni der baad thusi aaye hai?*
> After all this time, you've finally come?

Marked by the impossibility of medical salvation and a move into an enclosed, vacant space of loss, Parmar's generic shifts refuse, in the end, consolatory definition:

> A world gone quiet must be this fact.
> For which there is no precise language.
> The monitor goes off and you are led
> past a succession of mothers to a room marked 'empty'.
> Taxonomies of grief elude the non-mother,
> the un-mothered, the anything-but-this-fact.
> No face no teeth no eyes or balled-up fists.

To light the dark with a particular breathing.
A black lamp beats its wings ashore.
In the dark there is breathing.
After five visits to the hospital, the bruising
of inner elbows stitching themselves to themselves
in obsolescence, the nurses stop saying: sorry for your loss.
I may come to miss these laminated hallways.
I know my way there, to the artefact of losing.

Led past a 'succession of mothers', Parmar's speaker is removed from conventional 'taxonomies' of heritage, lineage and loss, including those that might perpetuate the idealization of lyric, of which we have been wary throughout. At stake is not poetry's generic 'art of losing', but its literalized 'artefact'. Despite eluding such consolations, however, we are led to consider how maternal experience can elude the temporal dominion of the productive present: the speaker has not had a child, but she has not *never* had a child. The absence of the expected child's 'particular breathing' becomes the animating force for other, less recognized forms of life; the opening line of the next stanza asserts that 'in the dark there is breathing'.

Multilingual and generically experimental texts like 'An Uncommon Language' work to simultaneously articulate the temporality of loss and inscribe it – spatially – within an inescapably social, political and historical context. In doing so, they give an equally poetic and political voice to a regularly ignored reality: that pregnancies constitute work which is, very often, non-productive. Although regularly overlooked in biopolitical theory, the weaving of (non-productive) time and (socialized) space that characterizes Parmar's work also punctuates theoretical texts that attend to capitalism's violently heterogeneous forms. In her claim that modernity and coloniality are 'constitutive of each other', Baraitser shows in her work on maternal time how capitalist production 'operates through the enforcement of a particular conception of time that then comes to mediate forms of relating to, and representing, the world'.[34] Drawing on the 'multiplicity of times and temporalities' pervading the work of Aníbal Quijano, Walter Mignolo, Dipesh Chakrabarty and Silvia Federici, Baraitser leans on the 'chronobiopolitical' insights of recent scholarship to recognize the global variety of capitalism's contemporary forms and to identify the multiplicity of alternatives to it.

A biopolitics attendant to multiple temporalities would not necessarily avoid the oversights that we have associated with Deleule and Guéry's *The Productive Body* or with other texts that recognize human reproduction as a source of metaphor rather than a site of temporally and productively heterogeneous experience. Nor would it necessarily dissolve the problems we identify with 'biopoetics' and its potential idealization of lyric. Nevertheless, an awareness of the role that hitherto marginalized spatial and temporal frameworks play – both in the biopolitical matrix of production, reproduction and the human body *and* in anti-capitalist practices of resistance – ought to inform our ongoing political and theoretical activity, particularly as we come to recognize, as is necessary, the importance of non-productive maternal experiences. As we hope to have shown, poetry, despite the apparently intractable possibility that it might 'collapse the genre's survival with our own', and so maintain by other means the capitalist logic of intelligible productivity, is uniquely positioned to alert us to these unrecognized modes of space, time, life and loss.

Notes

1   Samuel Solomon, *Lyric Pedagogy and Marxist-Feminism: Social Reproduction and the Institutions of Poetry* (London: Bloomsbury, 2019).

2   Barbara Johnson, 'Apostrophe, Animation, and Abortion', *Diacritics* 16, no. 1 (1986): 29.

3   Johnson, 'Apostrophe', 31.

4   Johnson, 'Apostrophe', 32.

5   Johnson, 'Apostrophe', 38.

6   Johnson, 'Apostrophe', 38.

7   Johnson, 'Apostrophe', 32.

8   Sara Guyer, *Reading with John Clare: Biopoetics, Sovereignty, Romanticism* (New York: Fordham University Press, 2015), 14.

9   Guyer, *Reading with John Clare*, 7.

10 For a concise elaboration of another version of this problem, which played out in Foucault's quarrel with Jacques Derrida, see Peter Fenves, 'Derrida and History: Some Questions Derrida Pursues in His Early Writings', in *Jacques Derrida and the Humanities: A Critical Reader*, ed. Tom Cohen (Cambridge: Cambridge University Press, 2001), 271–95.

11 François Guéry and Didier Deleule, *The Productive Body*, trans. Philip Barnard and Stephen Shapiro (Winchester: Zero Books, 2014), 51. Hereafter *TPB*.

12 See Melanie McDonagh, 'The Irish Anti-Abortion Side Will Lose. There's Nothing Good about That', *The Guardian*, 25 May 2018, https://www.theguardian.com/commentisfree/2018/may/25/yes-irish-pro-abortion-side-politial-class-media-illiberal-view; Breda O'Brien, 'Reasons to Vote No in the Abortion Referendum', *The Irish Times*, 19 May 2018, https://www.irishtimes.com/opinion/reasons-to-vote-no-in-the-abortion-referendum-1.3500375.

13 Isabel A. Moore, 'The Ends of Lyric's Animal Life; or, Why Did the Hedgehog Cross the Road?', in *Against Life*, ed. Alastair Hunt and Stephanie Youngblood (Chicago: Northwestern University Press), 163.

14 Johnson, 'Apostrophe', 36.

15 Johnson, 'Apostrophe', 38.

16 The ambiguity that accompanies this decentring of morality and rights (whereby what matters is *not* whether the mother has made a deliberate choice, but the way the event is, inevitably, rhetorically figured) animates much of Lee Edelman's *No Future: Queer Theory and the Death Drive* (Durham and London: Duke University Press, 2004).

17 Denise Riley, 'A Shortened Set', in *Selected Poems* (London: Reality Street Editions, 2000), 36.

18 See especially the fifth chapter of Denise Riley, *'Am I That Name?': Feminism and the Category of 'Women' in History* (Basingstoke and London: MacMillan, 1988); *The Words of Selves: Identification, Solidarity, Irony* (Stanford, CA: Stanford University Press, 2000).

19 Romana Huk and Denise Riley, 'In Conversation with Denise Riley', *PN Review* 103, no. 5 (1995). Since page numbers are unavailable for the online edition of this interview, we have omitted further footnotes when referring to this text.

20 Denise Riley, *Dry Air* (London: Virago, 1985), 51.

21 Elizabeth Jennings, 'For a Child Born Dead', in *Selected Poems*, ed. Rebecca Watts (Manchester: Carcanet, 1979), 28.

22 Alice Notley, 'What Is "Conscious"', *Datableed* 9, https://www.datableedzine.com/alice-notley-issue-9.

23 Peter Riley, *Birth Prospectus. The End of Us* (Colchester: Intercapillary Editions, 2007). Since page numbers are unavailable for the existing edition of this work, we have omitted further footnotes when referring to this text. Before this 'final' revision of the sequence, the fourth and fifth sections were reproduced in Peter Riley, *Passing Measures: Poems, 1966–1990* (Manchester: Carcanet, 2000) as 'Clouds and Birds over Wolfscote' and 'Boletus under Narrowdale'.

24   Peter Riley, 'Comment on Michael Haslam's Essay', *Intercapillary Space*, http://
     intercapillaryspace.blogspot.com/2007/10/peter-riley-comment-on-michael-
     haslams.html

25   See Helen Charman, 'Parental Elegy: Language in Extremis', *King's Review,*
     October 2018, https://www.kingsreview.co.uk/essays/parental-elegy-language-in-
     extremis.

26   *TPB*, 58.

27   Lisa Baraitser, *Enduring Time* (London: Bloomsbury, 2017), 74. The feminist
     Marxist collective Wages against Housework's famous declaration that 'Every
     miscarriage is a workplace accident' exemplifies this potential erasure of the
     possibility of miscarriage itself to be an instance that defies or disrupts, in
     Baraitser's terms, 'the capitalist everyday': the figuration of miscarriage here
     is part of the broader reading of gestational work as work. See Silvia Federici,
     Revolution at Point Zero: Housework, Reproduction, and Feminist Struggle
     (Oakland: PM Press, 2012), 15.

28   Stella Sandford, 'What Is Maternal Labour?', *Studies in the Maternal* 3, no. 2
     (2011): 2.

29   Denise Riley, *Time Lived, without Its Flow* (London: Capsule Editions, 2012), 23.

30   Riley, *Time Lived*, 7. See also 'Lisa Baraitser in Conversation with Denise Riley',
     Studies in the Maternal 8, no. 1 (2016): 5.

31   Sandeep Parmar, 'An Uncommon Language', *The Poetry Review* 108, no. 3 (2018),
     https://poetrysociety.org.uk/essay-an-uncommon-language-by-sandeep-parmar.
     Since page numbers are unavailable for the online edition of Parmar's essay, we
     have omitted further footnotes when referring to this text.

32   Many recent studies have shown that maternal healthcare provision in the UK is
     institutionally racist, with Black women particularly affected. See Amali Lokugamage,
     'Maternal Mortality – Undoing Systemic Biases and Privileges', *The BMJ Opinion*,
     8 April 2019, https://blogs.bmj.com/bmj/2019/04/08/amali-lokugamage-maternal-
     mortality-undoing-systemic-biases-and-privileges; Javaid Muglu et al., 'Risks of
     Stillbirth and Neonatal Death with Advancing Gestation at Term: A Systematic
     Review and Meta-Analysis of Cohort Studies of 15 million Pregnancies', *PLoS
     Medicine* 16, no. 7 (2019) https://doi.org/10.1371/journal.pmed.1002838.

33   For Parmar's theoretical work problematizing the lyric subject, see 'Not a British
     Subject: Race and Poetry in the UK', *LA Review of Books*, 6 December 2016,
     https://lareviewofbooks.org/article/not-a-british-subject-race-and-poetry-in-the-
     uk/; *Threads*, with Bhanu Kapil and Nisha Ramayya (London: Clinic, 2018).

34   Baraitser, *Enduring Time*, 3–4.

10

(Re)productive data-bodies: Privacy, inequality and anti-abortion politics in the age of tech-capitalism

Grace Tillyard

This chapter examines the digitized strategies of anti-abortion groups and how the data-bodies of people seeking abortion care are being (re)privatized and made productive in the age of tech-capitalism.[1] At the heart of this analysis lie emerging collaborations between for-profit marketing agencies and US-based global anti-abortion groups. Specifically, it draws attention to the recent move by commercial marketing agencies to partner with anti-abortion groups by compiling and selling data sets to pro-life clients. The data equips them with the necessary tools to predict and identify who might be seeking abortion care. As a result, anti-abortion groups are expanding and targeting their messaging through bespoke data-intensive technologies. Corporate tech companies, meanwhile, reap profits from these digital ventures, monetizing purpose-built predictive data sets.[2]

Anti-abortion digital technologies offer an important pathway for analyzing the ways that tech-capitalism (re)configures different bodies, turning them into a source of profit. In *The Productive Body*, Didier Deleule and François Guéry, following Marx, examine the ways that the body is conceptualized and made to produce surplus-value under capitalism.[3] Insisting on the interrelations between human beings and technological means of production, Deleule and Guéry chart the 'conversion of human material into productive form' through the stages of capitalism.[4] Writing in 1972, the authors argue that under capitalism bodies are progressively re-imagined in terms of their economic productivity and collectively organized to produce profit. These observations are pertinent to our data-driven contemporary and invite fresh thinking around the ways that digital technologies, as Donna Haraway claims, 'are the crucial tools re-crafting our bodies'[5] within a profit-driven system. First, digital and algorithmic technologies reassemble bodies into data-commodities.[6] These technologies have material-semiotic effects, producing 'data-bodies' through tools, data flows and infrastructures (material) that simultaneously generate and convey meaning (semiotic). In turn, these 'data-bodies' are made productive by feeding the mechanisms of tech and tech-capitalism. For profit marketing agencies and anti-abortion strategies illustrate these complex entanglements: they mobilize computational technologies to produce data bodies that are bought and sold by tech companies, political groups and state institutions for political and economic ends. This chapter focuses on this convergence of anti-abortion and tech-capitalist agendas, addressing the important questions it raises about how bodies, and *some* reproductive bodies specifically, are being reconfigured through for-profit digital infrastructures. Appraising these anti-abortion technologies, this chapter also revisits Guéry and Deleule's intervention, inviting a broader reflection into the changing relationship between tech-capitalism, data-flows, digital devices and (re) productive bodies.

Data technologies and anti-abortion politics

In recent years, a plethora of data-intensive technologies have been developed by anti-abortion groups in the United States and disseminated across global pro-life networks. As sociologist Jessie Daniels demonstrates, in the earlier days of the internet anti-abortion groups developed web spaces, known as 'cloaked sites', that claimed to provide medically accurate information about reproductive healthcare and abortion whilst concealing a political agenda.[7] In more recent years, pro-life groups have developed and honed marketing and data-intensive technologies to expand their message and reach. These digital tools include Search Engine Optimization (SEO), a technology that enhances the visibility of anti-abortion websites and pro-life counselling facilities in web browsers.[8] Anti-abortion groups also make use of ad-tech to reconfigure the geographies of abortion care, deploying targeted advertisements to deter prospective service users and obstruct access to abortion care facilities. Web mapping services, such as Google maps, are another digital tool used to camouflage and disguise religious counselling facilities as functioning abortion clinics. These digital tools are also (…).[9] These digital tools are also costly, with transnational pro-life organizations such as Care Net and Heartbeat International spending more than $18,000 per month on pay-per-click advertising campaigns.[10]

It stands to reason that data-intensive technologies and targeted marketing are an attractive enhancement for the well-funded and -organized global anti-abortion movement.[11] In the United States, and globally, anti-abortion groups have for decades hampered access to care through conservative law making, by disseminating medically inaccurate information and physically blockading abortion clinics.[12] A central pillar of these anti-abortion organizational efforts in the United States, and elsewhere, are Crisis Pregnancy Centres (CPCs). CPCs are organizations with the objective of deterring people with unintended pregnancies who might be seeking abortion care. Their aim is to prevent abortions by persuading people to carry the pregnancy to term or consider adoption.[13] In the United States, CPCs have been operational since the 1960s and are known to disguise themselves as legitimate reproductive healthcare facilities to deceive prospective service users.[14] Data-intensive technologies and targeted advertisements provide a powerful tool to expand these tactics and infrastructures into the digital realm, propagating anti-abortion information and content across a globalizing network. Digital infrastructures assembled by anti-abortion groups and CPCs thus function as a web of networks combining digital devices, people, organizations, and knowledge that attempt to (re) define and control reproductive bodies marked as 'risky' for their social and political agendas.

The targets of both online and offline anti-abortion tactics are so-called 'abortion-minded women', a pro-life signifier for gendered female pregnant people who seek out abortion care.[15] Historically, the pro-life movement used 'abortion-minded woman' as a dubious psychosocial profile to direct their political activities.[16] References to 'abortion-minded women' still proliferate in latter-day anti-abortion blogs, how-to guides and in academic literature.[17] As prominent pro-life advocate Lisa Jacobson writes, anti-abortion groups use the terms 'abortion-minded' and 'abortion-vulnerable' to assess the likelihood that a person will seek an abortion based on stated intentions and other criteria like their attitude towards marriage and heteronormative family structures.[18] In the age of tech-capitalism and the prediction imperative of consumer profiling, however, anti-abortion groups concerned with identifying and differentiating between 'abortion-minded women' and 'non-abortion-minded women' turn to data-driven marketing to target their messaging and services.[19] In turn, this demand from anti-abortion groups and CPCs has pushed private companies and enterprises to develop bespoke data-intensive technologies to satisfy the needs of pro-life groups. An increasing number of corporate marketing companies in the United States now offer a comprehensive suite of services to their anti-abortion clients that include customisable content management systems, targeted paid advertising and app development. As discussed, these purpose-built data collection systems are designed to produce data-bodies that can be subjected to algorithmic scrutiny and the managerial gaze of pro-life groups and digital marketers.

The entanglements of reproductive bodies and labour with tech-capitalism's infrastructures are examined in contemporary scholarship through two main vectors of enquiry: the rise of commercial reproductive app technologies alongside critical considerations of the impact of the platform economy on reproductive and domestic work. Digital sociologists and anthropologists have analysed the increasingly common practices of self-tracking and the commodification of user data through reproductive health mobile applications.[20] As anthropologist Veronica Barassi qualifies, reproductive health apps, and app centric media more broadly, have provoked a number of critical perspectives on the relationship between technologies, users and commodities.[21] Political economic approaches highlight that the participatory cultures engendered by app technologies bolster corporate exploitation of user's digital production.[22] Corporate platform companies benefit, some scholars argue, from the unpaid labour of internet and app users as they generate content and data.[23] In a similar vein, digital sociologist Deborah Lupton has touted the rise of commercially developed tracking apps that monitor fertility and gestation as congruent with an emergent neoliberal order that produce a subject whose 'performances' are quantified in line with the interests of global capital.[24] These critical insights highlight, in line with Guéry and Deleule's concerns, the ways that gestating bodies are made 'productive' by extracting unpaid labour from users, monetizing their data and content.

An adjacent body of work considers the ways in which digital platforms re-configure forms of reproductive labour and care work, exacerbating inequality and subordination through the digitized mechanisms of the 'on-demand economy'. The social and economic relations of the 'gig economy' are mediated through online platforms with wide-ranging implications for the marketization and commodification of reproductive and domestic labour. As household labour is increasingly outsourced by affluent households, algorithmic decision-making and labour allocation coupled with increasing levels of precarity extend the gendered and racialized histories of reproductive and domestic work into the digital era.[25] Reproductive labour is thus recoded, intensified and invisibilized in the digital age. As Neda Atanasoski and Kalindi Vora highlight, emergent technologies and platforms act as intermediary services that connect subscribers with workers who will do domestic labour at times when the household space is empty. Platform infrastructures are thus designed to conceal the fact that historically classed, racialized, and gendered forms of work are still being done by humans. In doing so, they simultaneously extract work out of populations marked for elimination or surplus, including racialized low-wage laborers.[26] Thinking in Guéry and Deleule's terms, then, platformization optimizes, organizes and produces productive bodies that are open to exploitation through low-waged domestic and reproductive work, upon which capitalist production is dependent.

Building on this, the anti-abortion strategies and technologies analysed in this chapter raise further pressing questions. In the first instance, they are tools that extract data from intimate aspects of everyday life for a specific political objective. Rather than intensifying and mediating forms of reproductive labour or unpaid digital work, the intrinsic value of for-profit anti-abortion marketing strategies lies in their ability to construct and contain 'abortion-minded women', an assemblage charged with an explicit social, political and economic agenda. As discussed, on-demand platforms and commercially developed fertility apps are structured by social, political and economic power relations. Anti-abortion technologies, in addition to this, are bespoke tools assembled by an identifiable organized movement. The meeting of ideological and economic agendas in pro-life strategies also has implications for the ways that anti-abortion groups and marketing firms gather, aggregate and share data. This in turn raises important questions about privacy. What do the tools and technologies of anti-abortion groups reveal, then, about the ways in which *some* reproductive bodies are being (re)made, organized and made productive in the data-driven contemporary? What does this reveal about the ways that bodies are being (re)privatized though the mechanisms of tech-capitalism? And finally, what are the implications of these technologies and strategies for debates around privacy in the context of both reproductive politics and information technology?

Data-bodies and tech-capitalism

Before proceeding into a more in-depth discussion of the marketing strategies of anti-abortion groups, I want to briefly flesh out the ontological politics of bodies in relation to digital technologies and tech-capitalism.[27] As Donna Haraway has pointed out, bodies do not end at the skin.[28] Bodies leave behind traces of organic matter, contain other bodies in the form of bacteria and are entangled with broader entities and information flows. Moreover, in the digitized, networked and machinic age, computational and data-intensive technologies challenge the borders and boundaries ascribed to bodies as contained organic entities. Haraway proposes that bodies are semiotic-material entities that contend with advances in digital and information technologies which in turn reshape social relations and (re)make economic structures. Bodies, then, for Haraway are akin to what Deleuze and Guattari conceptualize as *agencement* or assemblages, a merging of organic and inorganic matter.[29] From this standpoint, body-assemblages do not privilege what is considered human over other entities.[30] Rather, assemblages are understood as 'a multiplicity of heterogenous objects, whose unity comes solely from the fact that these items function together, that they "work" together as a functional entity.'[31] Multiple forms of entangled matter can thus be considered bodies including urban spaces, institutions, informational infrastructures and data.

Following this line of reasoning, 'abortion-minded women' constructed by pro-life groups can be conceptualized as data-body assemblages produced through a network of heterogeneous entities that encompass technologies, institutions, material infrastructures and other bodies. This apparatus seeks to control, contain and discipline the data-bodies of so-called abortion-minded women in line with the political and economic objectives of anti-abortion groups and data-marketing agencies. What is more, this ontology also holds implications for our understanding of how data-bodies, and bodies by extension, are being (re)made and made productive in the context of tech-capitalism.

In their analysis of the changing relationship of the biological body to capitalism and expropriation, François Guéry and Didier Deleule argue that the capitalist interweaving of society and the body create the productive body, a body that is organized to produce commodities, and thereby surplus value. Machines are central to Guéry and Deleule's discussion of the productive body, as they chart mechanistic changes to production through the stages of capitalism. They suggest that in the age of large-scale industry, technology does more than merely replace humans in the work process, rather they conceptualize it as a new kind of life in and of itself. In their words, '[t]he machine is not constructed to replace human life… ; rather its function is to augment the power [*pouvoir*] of life itself understood as the development of the process of mastery over nature.'[32] Guéry and Deleule argue that this conceptualization of 'the body-machine' marks an age where human life itself is used to create a new form of labour-power that in turn produces profit.

Read together, Haraway and Guéry and Deleule's interventions elucidate how bodies are reconfigured and made productive by tech-capitalists. As Achille Mbembe qualifies, 'a key feature of our times is the extent to which all societies are organized according to the same principle – the computational.' The computational, according to Mbembe, is a technical system but also a force and energy that 'produces and serializes subjects, objects, phenomena; that splits reason from consciousness and memory, codes and stores data that can be used to manufacture new types of services and devices sold for profit'.[33] As shown by the impact of platformization on domestic and reproductive labour, technological interfaces are designed to organize bodies and optimize certain forms of work, integrating bodies into these networked systems as elements of production. Within these structures of 'heteropatriarchal racial techno-capitalism', as Haraway emphasizes, precarity and labour become increasingly classed, racialized and feminized.[34] This latter point serves also as an important corrective and reminder that 'productive bodies' in the emergent tech-based economy have a specific social location, a point somewhat under-theorized by Guéry and Deleule.

Moreover, capitalism has turned to data, and data-bodies, as a vital source of economic growth.[35] As Shoshana Zuboff's work shows, the platform economy is driven by a capitalist logic of accumulation based on the exploitation of 'behavioural surplus data'.[36] As networked systems collect the data trails of people's comings and goings on the internet, these are harvested, analysed, aggregated into data sets and exploited within a profit-driven system. Extractive mechanisms then mine data in order to build 'predictive products' which foresee human behaviour, and are traded and sold on 'behavioral futures markets'.[37] As Guéry and Deleule anticipated with their body-machine theory, the mechanisms of tech-capitalism render bodies and forms of living-being 'productive' through machinic logic. Surplus value in the data-driven economy, moreover, is not only delivered through the exchange of wages for labour-power and the sale of commodities.[38] Rather, life itself is being annexed to capitalism. Through this process bodies are abstracted into information flows and reassembled into tradable commodities, like the 'abortion-minded women' produced by digital marketers and bought by pro-life groups. These technologies are therefore far from value-neutral. Rather, as Lisa Nakamura cautions, data-gathering through surveillance and computational technologies always creates, 'new gendered, racialized, and abled or disabled bodies through digital means'.[39] The act of dis-aggregating and re-aggregating data, then, not only (re)privatizes bodies, it also reproduces and compounds existing forms of oppression.

Emerging digital and computational technologies pose novel and important challenges, then, as privacy and surveillance scholars note. In particular, networked technologies have implications for informational privacy defined as 'the claim of individuals, groups or institutions to determine for themselves when, how and to what extent information about them is communicated to others'.[40] Undergirded by liberal frameworks of sovereignty, privacy regulations are framed as 'freedom from' harm and exploitation perpetrated by tech-capitalists and state entities.[41] These regulations, however, are always counterbalanced by a profit motive. Given that extracting profit from data-bodies is the force that drives tech-capitalism, companies maintain a 'cyberlibertarian ideology' to prevent any form of oversight or externally imposed constraints that limit data-collection and exploitation.[42] However, the modalities through which platform capitalists (re)privatize data-bodies at the online/offline nexus raise more fundamental questions about the concept of privacy in the digital realm and beyond. While privacy regulations structure the majority of data-protection laws, they also allow tech-capitalists to claim proprietary data as their private property, free from government and community oversight.[43] This contradiction calls into question whether privacy regulations can effectively counterbalance the drive of platform capitalists to privatize and profit from data-bodies.

Constructing 'abortion-minded women'

'Abortion-minded women' are produced by pro-life groups by organizing bodies and deploying data-intensive technologies. A poignant example can be found in the custom-built websites and data collection processes used by anti-abortion group Heartbeat International. Heartbeat, which describes itself as a 'worldwide network of more than 2,700 pro-life pregnancy help organizations', supports the development of web templates designed to target so-called abortion-minded clients.[44] These public-facing websites are developed by Extended Web Services, a private contractor that was set up in 2007 with the specific aim of making sure that anti-abortion groups and CPCs globally have a web presence.[45] Extended Web Services advertise their products publicly stating, 'we are experts at making sure your website is attracting the abortion-minded client and representing your center in a way that will make your clients feel comfortable with the service they will receive.'[46] This marketing exercise is coupled with a streamlined data collection process through Heartbeat International's Next Level Content Management Solution (CMS) and purpose-built app that gather and aggregate personal information that visitors to anti-abortion centres and CPCs are asked to provide. This information includes the person's name and address, ethnicity, medical history, marital status as well as information about their living arrangement. By harnessing the power of these data collection processes, Next Level aims to gather real-time information on CPC users that can be abstracted, centralized and analysed so as to more effectively identify and dissuade 'abortion-minded women'.

In a similar vein, in 2016 a Boston-based marketing company by the name of Copley Advertising pioneered the use of sophisticated mobile surveillance technology to follow people's activities and find out who might consider having an abortion. The company deployed data-gathering technologies and a practice known as mobile 'geofencing' to compile profiles of 'abortion-minded women' and offered them for sale to anti-abortion clients. The large data sets gathered by Copley Advertising included information about the person's gender, race, age and online shopping habits, all acquired through their smartphone ID. The technology allowed anti-abortion groups to target people waiting in reproductive health clinics across the United States, who began to receive unsolicited advertisements on their smartphones persuading them to visit a religious Crisis Pregnancy Centre (CPCs). The company claimed to have 'pinged' nearly three million cell phones on behalf of anti-abortion clients across five US states with the specific intent of dissuading seekers of abortion care.[47]

Geofencing is a practice commonly used in commercial advertising and marketing that creates a virtual border around a location. The geofence records when a respondent crosses the virtual perimeter either to enter or to exit the fenced location and gathers other available data about the person, which in turn triggers an advertisement or a survey. In digital advertising, marketers tailor their ads to very specific groups of consumers by compiling 'personas' based on aggregated data sets that reveal their online activities. Copley Advertising's plan to geofence abortion facilities as well other facilities like methadone clinics mimicked these strategies and was attractive to anti-abortion groups because of its ability to target people who were suspected to be 'abortion-minded'.[48]

The technologies devised by Extended Web Services, Next Level Content Management Solution and Copley Advertising and sold to anti-abortion organizations are emblematic of the way that the landscape of abortion politics in the United States is evolving alongside information infrastructures and the platform industry. The capitalist logic that drives these digital marketing strategies is dictated by prediction models and consumer profiles ordinarily used to understand consumption patterns and geographical movements.[49] Placed in the hands of anti-abortion groups, digital marketing technologies are used to construct 'abortion-minded women', mobilized in turn to produce data-bodies and predict behaviour. Obstructive tactics are thus rephrased through algorithmic and digital technologies into targeted messaging that aim to lure patients away from abortion clinics and into a religious counselling facility. These strategies exemplify, therefore, the convergence and intersection of disciplinary, capitalist and patriarchal power relations that differentially (re) make but also privatize anew gendered female reproductive data-bodies.

First, pro-life assemblages of data-bodies, technologies, discursive flows, capital and human actors produce 'abortion-minded women', embodied data-entities that are managed by anti-abortion groups. Like rogue elements that disrupt the market, the data-bodies of abortion-minded women signify risk and are profiled, monitored and disciplined. As Jasbir Puar emphasizes, data-bodies, understood as bodies assembled through information and statistics, are not only controlled but also produced through information and surveillance technologies.[50] In other words, the computational technologies discussed in this chapter serve the dual function of controlling social groups marked as 'risky' as well as producing new gendered, racialized and classed data-bodies.

This can be seen in the data-collection processes designed by Next Level Content Management System and Copley Advertising that aggregate information on the targeted person's stated race, gender, age, living arrangements and consumer preferences.[51] While it remains unclear what exactly happens to this data, or how it is processed and shared, the socio-economic location of those using abortion services and CPCs is explicitly integral to the production of 'abortion-minded women'. As Faye Ginsburg and Sarah Franklin posit, anti-abortion politics germane to the United States, and circulated through the pro-life network across the globe, are animated by a reproductive politics grounded in white nativism and Christian nationalism that 'structure an overarching grammar of national belonging defined by the preservation of whiteness, biological men and women, heterosexual marriage, and the right to carry one's weapon of choice'.[52] This wider political context speaks to the urgency with which anti-abortion groups seek to profile and quantify exactly *who* is an 'abortion-minded woman'. The emphasis placed by marketing firms on the need to define and know demographics can be understood, therefore, as a move to essentialize the complexities of reproduction into a gendered, classed and racialized data-body. Producing and controlling these assemblages is part and parcel of a project of safeguarding a reproductive futurity intimately bound up in the politics of gender, race, sexuality, class and the pursuit of capitalism.

In the context of this wider politics, data-bodies assembled by marketing agencies and anti-abortion groups have discretely embodied consequences. Targeting pregnant people with marketing intended to divert them to CPC facilities staffed by volunteers that lack medical training and have little medical infrastructure exposes people to potential physical injury and psychological harm.[53] As evidenced by Copley Advertising's explicit strategy of targeting methadone clinics, gendered, sexualized as well as classed assumptions about who is likely to be seeking abortion care structure the design of anti-abortion marketing strategies. Actively targeting and intercepting people with unplanned pregnancies and those who are using methadone clinics has a discreet impact, exposing them to harm and in some cases resulting in an unwanted pregnancy. Obstructive tactics also have distinct impacts on different people. As reproductive justice activists emphasize, interference and deception add another significant barrier for rural, working class, migrant and communities of colour that already face social, cultural, economic and language barriers to accessing reproductive healthcare and abortion.[54] Simply put, reproductive bodies are differentially (re)materialized through information and data in line with the social and political objectives of anti-abortion groups and broader hegemonic agendas.

This brings us back to the question of how the constructed data-bodies of 'abortion-minded women' are made productive in different ways. Through the mechanisms of tech-capitalism, data-driven marketing agencies organize bodies and re-assemble information flows to produce data that can be sold to anti-abortion clients. Dis-assembling and re-aggregating data sets allow digital marketers to privatize whilst simultaneously producing gendered, sexualized, racialized and classed data-bodies. The profiles of abortion-minded women that include information related to a person's age, gender, living arrangement, race and consumer preferences are the source of profit and means of building targeted anti-abortion marketing tools. In turn, these data-bodies are also productive for the political objectives of anti-abortion groups, providing them with the necessary data to expand their obstructive tactics into the digital realm. 'Abortion-minded women' thus serve a discursive purpose for pro-life groups, essentializing the complexities of decision making into a fixed subjectivity to be managed. Capitalist, disciplinary and patriarchal projects overlap and intersect to produce profit, on the one hand, and technologies of control on the other.

Privacy and abortion politics at the online/offline nexus

The scope and reach of anti-abortion digital technologies prompt a further reflection into the wider frameworks and permissive structures that allow anti-abortion groups and digital marketers to construct and exploit data-bodies. As discussed, the question of privacy is particularly pertinent to anti-abortion technologies of reproductive control given the central role that privacy regulations play in both reproductive politics and tech-capitalism.

Political struggles over bodily autonomy in the context of abortion politics in the United States are historically and currently couched in privacy doctrine. When the New Right 'pro-family' movement rose to prominence in the United States in the 1980s, it consolidated different arenas of white capitalist patriarchal power against perceived threats to the nuclear family, private property and state sovereignty, understood as mutually sustaining structures.[55] The concept of privacy was pivotal to these struggles, as it historically encompassed not only 'free enterprise' and 'property rights' but also the right of white male property owners to control the domestic space, their spouse and children. As political scientist Rosalind Petchesky hypothesizes, privacy doctrine was born from conservative ideas and values around localized and state power structures.[56] State sovereignty, conceived as a form of privacy, permitted patriarchal control over the household whilst also protecting private wealth by creating a buffer to federal laws and taxation policies. Abortion was a prime target of this New Right political formation because of its perceived threat to white patriarchal supremacy and heteronormative family structures.[57] Alongside this, as Dorothy Roberts points out, liberal notions of privacy conceptualized as freedom *from* government interference were actively denied to welfare recipients raising children, many of whom were low-income, Black women and people of colour.[58] This loss of privacy, according to Roberts, permitted state intrusion into the lives of welfare recipients and allowed conditions to be placed on welfare benefits. Historically and currently, therefore, privacy regulations have been deployed selectively to safeguard private wealth and patriarchal control, whilst also being a tool of racialized, gendered and classed reproductive regulation.

This history is significant not only for reproductive politics in their current digital iteration but also for highlighting how single-issue abortion politics centred on privacy doctrine play out within a wider arena of conservative and liberal political power. Privacy doctrine also structured the strategies of liberal feminists whose campaigns for reproductive rights culminated in the landmark *Roe vs Wade* decision that legalized abortion. The 1973 Supreme Court legislation designated abortion as a 'private matter' between a physician and patient. As Marlene Gerber Fried explains, 'Roe vs Wade was not the first step of a feminist agenda of reproductive control; it turned out to be the only step, defended by appeals to the right to privacy – the importance of keeping the government out of our personal lives – and religious tolerance.'[59] By adopting this strategy, the predominantly middle-class and white reproductive rights movement that had fought to guarantee the right to abortion laid the groundwork for the New Right and anti-abortion advocates to restrict government funding to cover abortion costs.

In the digital age these logics are recoded through information flows, devices, targeted and misleading advertisements and geofences. As the obstructive strategies of anti-abortion groups become technologically integrated, the question of privacy regulations surfaces once more. The ease with which anti-abortion groups and digital marketing agencies construct and privatize the data-bodies of 'abortion-minded women' might initially appear as yet another infraction on rights to data-privacy and reproductive autonomy. However, the effectiveness of the data-intensive strategies devised by Extended Web Services, Next Level Content Management Solution and Copley Advertising is altogether unsurprising when we consider that anti-abortion politics and the political-economic infrastructures of the tech industry are produced within the same set of white, capitalist and patriarchal power relations. From this standpoint, the privatization and control of data-bodies through bespoke technologies cannot simply be attributable to the skill of anti-abortion groups; rather, it is actively enabled by privacy doctrine that frame anti-abortion politics and tech-capitalism alike. Exploiting the fact that liberal-patriarchal notions of 'privacy' protect some not others, antiabortion groups and marketing agencies profit politically and economically from the abjection of people seeking abortion care, aided and abetted by the protections afforded by the tech-corporatocracy.

A reliance, therefore, on greater privacy protections to curtail the data-exploits of anti-abortion marketers will be just as ineffective as greater privacy regulations have been for safeguarding abortion access and reproductive autonomy for marginalized groups and communities. Given that privacy functions as a tool to enable accumulation of private wealth and patriarchal power in the domestic sphere, it is a protection that gendered, racialized, sexualized bodies, and data-bodies by extension, rarely enjoy. Reliance, therefore, on liberal frameworks of autonomy and data-protection that seek 'freedom from' harm ignores the fact that privacy is not granted equally to all. For all these reasons, as feminist surveillance studies scholar Rachael Hall points out, the objective must be to identify and combat new forms of discrimination that are practised in relation to categories of privilege, access and risk.[60]

Conclusion

I conclude with a reminder that while the complex sociotechnical assemblages at play in these discussions may appear novel, data extraction for the purposes of reproductive and population control is an ongoing project rooted in capitalist, white supremacist, imperialist and patriarchal exploits.[61] The data-intensive technologies assembled by anti-abortion groups and discussed in this chapter are an iteration of this ongoing history and offer a closer look at how strategies of reproductive control inform and are informed by the social and economic relations of tech-capitalism. The construction of 'abortion-minded women' by pro-life groups and marketing agencies offers, in my view, an important pathway for re-thinking the relationship between data-flows, digital devices, reproductive bodies and the changing capitalist economy. Thinking with data-bodies as an analytic demonstrates that the personas of 'abortion-minded women' produced through technological, material and discursive flows are material-semiotic agencies mobilized by technology or, as Haraway puts it, a 'myth and [a] tool [that] mutually constitute each other'.[62] Once assembled, as Guéry and Deleule propose, data-bodies are organized to produce profit through the mechanisms of tech-capitalism and machinic logic. The production and monetization of 'abortion-minded women' thus highlight the ways that some reproductive bodies are being monetarily and ideologically exploited by white, capitalist and patriarchal projects in the digital age.

Building on this, the anti-abortion marketing strategies discussed in this chapter offer some important insights for scholarship on reproductive politics and the evolution of capitalism alike. First, tech-capitalism makes reproductive data-bodies 'productive' not only through the exchange of wages for labour-power through the on-demand economy or by exploiting unpaid digital labour. Rather, reproductive life itself is annexed to capitalism, broken down into information flows and reassembled into tradable data commodities. The strategic partnership between anti-abortion groups and data-brokers demonstrates how material-semiotic data-bodies are not only converted into a productive form, as Guéry and Deleule highlight, they are also (re)made for ideological and monetary purposes. In line with this reasoning, the second conclusive point that emerges from this analysis is that 'abortion-minded women' are (re)made through computational technology into gendered, racialized, classed and abled or disabled bodies. In the process of transforming reproductive bodies and behaviour into data, anti-abortion marketing firms compound existing forms of oppression. This is evidenced by their explicit strategies to gather data on people's race, gender, economic status, sexuality, living arrangements and by targeting methadone clinics. The ways in which different data-bodies, and bodies by extension, are (re)privatized and made productive under tech-capitalism are therefore differential and contingent on race, gender, class, ability, geographical location and other social locations.

Finally, the technologies and strategies of anti-abortion groups in this discussion expose important fault lines that run through conceptualizations of privacy, positioned in liberal frameworks as a cornerstone of reproductive autonomy and data-protection. Thinking with data-bodies, and how they are made productive under tech-capitalism, makes evident the fallacies of privacy protections in the context of a system premised on the privatization of data-bodies and the accumulation of private wealth. Given that privacy protections enable both the strategies of anti-abortion groups and the accumulation of wealth by platform capitalists, invocations of 'more' or 'better' privacy will do little, if nothing, to combat the emerging forms of exploitation and accumulation documented in this chapter.

Notes

1   When discussing gestation, pregnancy and abortion care I use 'pregnant person' to denote pregnant women, men and non-binary persons who include trans-masculine people and trans men.

2   Sharona Coutts, 'Anti-Choice Groups Use Smartphone Surveillance to Target "Abortion-Minded Women" during Clinic Visits', *Rewire News Group*, 2016, https://rewirenewsgroup.com/article/2016/05/25/anti-choice-groups-deploy-smartphone-surveillance-target-abortion-minded-women-clinic-visits/; Amy G. Bryant et al., 'Crisis Pregnancy Center Websites: Information, Misinformation and Disinformation', *Contraception* 90, no. 6 (1 December 2014): 601–5; Jessie Daniels, 'From Crisis Pregnancy Centers to TeenBreaks.Com: Anti-Abortion Activism's Use of Cloaked Websites', in *Cyberactivism on the Participatory Web*, ed. Martha McCaughey, 140–54 (London: Routledge, 2014); Privacy International, 'How Anti-Abortion Activism Is Exploiting Data', 2019, http://privacyinternational.org/long-read/3096/how-anti-abortion-activism-exploiting-data

3   François Guéry and Didier Deleule, *The Productive Body*, trans. Philip Barnard and Stephen M. Shapiro (Winchester, UK: Zero Books, 2014). Hereafter *TPB*.

4   *TPB*, 52.

5   Here I am referring to Haraway's conceptualization of material-semiotic actors and more broadly to feminist technoscience conceptualizations of technology as producing material-semiotic worlds comprising both meaning *and* matter. See Donna Jeanne Haraway, *Simians, Cyborgs, and Women: The Reinvention of Nature* (New York: Routledge, 1991), 164.

6   Nick Srnicek, *Tech-Capitalism*, Theory Redux (Cambridge: Polity, 2017).

7   Daniels, 'From Crisis Pregnancy Centers to TeenBreaks.Com'.

8   SEO is a process of enhancing the visibility of a website or webpage in a search engine's unpaid results and is intimately connected to information architectures and algorithms made by Google. The search engine 'crawls' or reads the website's content and algorithmically evaluates whether it is relevant to what the searcher is looking for. The results are then indexed by relevance so as to appear in an order that supposedly matches the searcher's query. See Sergey Brin and Lawrence Page, 'The Anatomy of a Large-Scale Hypertextual Web Search Engine', *Computer Networks and ISDN Systems*, Proceedings of the Seventh International World Wide Web Conference, 30, no. 1 (April 1998): 107–17.

9   Bryant et al., 'Crisis Pregnancy Center Websites'; Laurie Fullerton, 'Advertiser Barred from Geo-Targeting Anti-Abortion Ads in Landmark Ruling', *The Drum*, 2017, https://www.thedrum.com/news/2017/04/04/advertiser-barred-geo-targeting-anti-abortion-ads-landmark-ruling.

10   NARAL, 'Crisis Pregnancy Centers: The Insidious Threat to Reproductive Freedom', 2015, https://www.prochoiceamerica.org/wp-content/uploads/2017/04/cpc-report-2015.pdf.

11   The critique in this chapter of the tactics of anti-abortion groups does not extend to those who hold prolife opinions. The decision whether or not to seek abortion care and political contentions over abortion more broadly are not the focus of this analysis. Rather, this chapter critiques the coercive and deceptive strategies, digital and otherwise, used by some anti-abortion groups.

12   The National Abortion Federation recorded an escalation of hostility in 2018, with incidents of obstruction rising from 1,700 in 2017 to 3,038 in the following year (National Abortion Federation 2017). In addition to intended physical obstruction, researchers have also documented that protestors cause psychological distress to clinic users. See Diana Greene Foster et al., 'Effect of Abortion Protesters on Women's Emotional Response to Abortion', *Contraception* 87, no. 1 (January 2013): 81–7.

13   Karissa Haugeberg, *Women against Abortion: Inside the Largest Moral Reform Movement of the Twentieth Century* (Urbana: University of Illinois Press, 2017).

14   Joanne D. Rosen, 'The Public Health Risks of Crisis Pregnancy Centers', *Perspectives on Sexual and Reproductive Health* 44, no. 3 (2012): 201–5; Foster et al., 'Effect of Abortion Protesters on Women's Emotional Response to Abortion'.

15   See note 1.

16   Jacobson, 'The Abortion-Minded Woman'.

17   Choose Life, 'How To Reach the Abortion-Minded Woman' (blog), 2021, https://www.chooselifemarketing.com/reaching-the-abortion-minded-woman/; Betsy Liliana Cote, 'Retrospective Comparative Analysis of the Socio-Demographic Characteristics of Pregnant Abortion-Minded Clients versus Pregnant Non-Abortion-Minded Clients in a Crisis Pregnancy Center in Montgomery County, Ohio', Master's Culminating Experience, Wright State University, Ohio, 2006.

18   Jacobson, 'The Abortion-Minded Woman', https://www.heartbeatservices.org/pdf/Abortion_Minded_Women.pdf.

19   I use 'tech-capitalism or Srnicek's term, 'tech-capitalism', over Zuboff's 'surveillance capitalism' to describe the social and economic relations of the

data-driven age. This is because I align with criticisms raised by Nicholas Mirzoeff and others, who point out that Zuboff's claim that the rise of Silicon Valley has precipitated the age of surveillance capitalism fails, 'to account for its long role in generating and sustaining racial surveillance capitalism on stolen land in the plantation and the factory'. In other words, racialized, gendered and classed surveillance capitalism long predates the rise of commercial technology companies and platforms. See Nicholas Mirzoeff, 'Artificial Vision, White Space and Racial Surveillance Capitalism', *AI & Society* (November 2020).

20 Josie Hamper, '"Catching Ovulation": Exploring Women's Use of Fertility Tracking Apps as a Reproductive Technology', *Body & Society* 26, no. 3 (September 2020): 3–30; Deborah Lupton, '"Mastering Your Fertility": The Digitised Reproductive Citizen', in *Negotiating Digital Citizenship: Control, Contest and Culture*, ed. Anthony McCosker, Sonja Vivienne and Amelia Johns (London: Rowman & Littlefield International, 2016); Sophia Alice Johnson, '"Maternal Devices", Social Media and the Self-Management of Pregnancy, Mothering and Child Health', *Societies* 4, no. 2 (June 2014): 330–50; Deborah Lupton, 'Quantified Sex: A Critical Analysis of Sexual and Reproductive Self-Tracking Using Apps', *Culture, Health & Sexuality* 17, no. 4 (April 2015): 440–53.

21 Veronica Barassi, 'BabyVeillance? Expecting Parents, Online Surveillance and the Cultural Specificity of Pregnancy Apps', *Social Media + Society* 3, no. 2 (April 2017).

22 In addition to these political economic perspectives, scholars that focus on the social, cultural as well as economic discourses of digital self-tracking highlight how fertility app use complicates the social cultural distinctions between assisted and natural conception by using digital data-driven fertility monitoring methods in order to aid 'natural' conception. As Josie Hamper posits, the proliferation of digital and networked tools that manage fertility further complicates the continuously evolving intersections between bodies, technologies and reproduction. See Hamper, '"Catching Ovulation"'.

23 Michael S. Daubs and Vincent R. Manzerolle, 'App-Centric Mobile Media and Commoditization: Implications for the Future of the Open Web', *Mobile Media & Communication* 4, no. 1 (January 2016): 52–68; Christian Fuchs, *Digital Labour and Karl Marx* (New York: Routledge, 2014).

24 Lupton, 'Quantified Sex'; Lupton, '"Mastering Your Fertility"'.

25 Antonio Aloisi, 'Commoditized Workers: Case Study Research on Labor Law Issues Arising from a Set of on-Demand/Gig Economy Platforms', *Comparative Labor Law & Policy Journal* 37 (2016): 653; Niels van Doorn, 'Platform

Labor: On the Gendered and Racialized Exploitation of Low-Income Service Work in the "On-Demand" Economy', *Information, Communication & Society* 20, no. 6 (June 2017): 898–914.

26   Neda Atanasoski and Kalindi Vora, *Surrogate Humanity: Race, Robots, and the Politics of Technological Futures* (Durham: Duke University Press, 2019), 95.

27   I borrow here from Annemarie Mol's discussion of ontological politics. Mol writes, '*Ontological politics* is a composite term. It talks of *ontology* – which in standard philosophical parlance defines what belongs to the real, the conditions of possibility we live with. If the term "ontology" is combined with that of "politics" then this suggests that the conditions of possibility are not given. That reality does not precede the mundane practices in which we interact with it, but is rather shaped within these practices. So the term *politics* works to underline this active mode, this process of shaping, and the fact that its character is both open and contested.' See Annemarie Mol, 'Ontological Politics. A Word and Some Questions', *The Sociological Review* 47, no. 1 (1999): 74–5. The term ontological politics, however, is originally a term introduced by John Law. See John Law, *Aircraft Stories: Decentering the Object in Technoscience* (Durham: Duke University Press, 2002).

28   Haraway, *Simians, Cyborgs, and Women*.

29   Gilles Deleuze and Félix Guattari, *A Thousand Plateaus: Capitalism and Schizophrenia* (Minneapolis: University of Minnesota Press, 1987).

30   Jasbir K. Puar, '"I Would Rather Be a Cyborg than a Goddess": Becoming-Intersectional in Assemblage Theory', *PhiloSOPHIA* 2, no. 1 (2012): 49–66.

31   Paul Patton, 'Metamorpho-Logic: Bodies and Powers in A Thousand Plateaus', *Journal of the British Society for Phenomenology* 25, no. 2 (January 1994): 158.

32   *TPB*, 104.

33   Achille Mbembe, 'Bodies as Borders', *From the European South* 4 (2019): 7–8.

34   Sophie Lewis, 'Cthulhu Plays No Role for Me', *Viewpoint Magazine*, 2017, https://www.viewpointmag.com/2017/05/08/cthulhu-plays-no-role-for-me/.

35   Mbembe, 'Bodies as Borders'; Srnicek, *Tech-Capitalism*; Siva Vaidhyanathan, *The Googlization of Everything: And Why We Should Worry* (Berkeley: University of California Press, 2012); Shoshana Zuboff, *The Age of Surveillance Capitalism: The Fight for a Human Future at the New Frontier of Power* (London: Profile Books, 2019).

36   Behavioural surplus data, according to Zuboff, is data derived from specific and often private aspects of a person's life that contain more information than what is required to improve a product or service. This behavioural surplus is channelled

into manufacturing processes known as machine intelligence to become 'prediction products' that anticipate forms of behaviour. The prediction products are traded in new marketplaces that Zuboff terms behavioural futures markets. See Zuboff, *The Age of Surveillance Capitalism*.

37 Zuboff, *The Age of Surveillance Capitalism*, 8.

38 Christian Fuchs and Marisol Sandoval, 'Digital Workers of the World Unite! A Framework for Critically Theorising and Analysing Digital Labour', *TripleC: Communication, Capitalism & Critique. Open Access Journal for a Global Sustainable Information Society* 12, no. 2 (September 2014).

39 Lisa Nakamura, 'Blaming, Shaming and the Feminization of Social Media', in *Feminist Surveillance Studies*, ed. Rachel E. Dubrofsky and Shoshana Magnet (Durham: Duke University Press, 2015), 221.

40 Ian Kerr, Valerie M. Steeves and Carole Lucock, (eds.), *Lessons from the Identity Trail: Anonymity, Privacy, and Identity in a Networked Society* (Oxford: Oxford University Press, 2009), xxvii.

41 Political philosophy defines 'freedom' or 'liberty' in a positive and negative sense. Negative liberty (freedom from) is understood as the absence of obstacles or constraints. The emphasis here lies with the degree to which individuals or groups are subject to interference from external bodies. Positive liberty (freedom to), by contrast, refers to what you can actually do to realizes one's fundamental purposes. The emphasis here lies more with internal factors affecting the degree to which individuals or groups act autonomously.

42 Zuboff, *The Age of Surveillance Capitalism*.

43 Rosalind P. Petchesky, 'Antiabortion, Antifeminism, and the Rise of the New Right', *Feminist Studies* 7, no. 2 (1981): 206–46; Christian Fuchs, 'Towards an Alternative Concept of Privacy', *Journal of Information, Communication and Ethics in Society* 9, no. 4 (January 2011): 220–37.

44 Heartbeat International, 'Our Mission & Vision', 2021, https://www.heartbeatinternational.org/about/our-passion.

45 Privacy International, 'How Anti-Abortion Activism Is Exploiting Data'.

46 Extended Web Services, 'About – Extend Web Services', 2021, https://extendwebservices.com/about; Privacy International, 'How Anti-Abortion Activism Is Exploiting Data'.

47 Coutts, 'Anti-Choice Groups Use Smartphone Surveillance to Target "Abortion-Minded Women" during Clinic Visits'.

48 Coutts, 'Anti-Choice Groups Use Smartphone Surveillance to Target "Abortion-Minded Women" during Clinic Visits'.

49	There is a large body of literature that looks at predictive modelling under capitalism and the way that these practices rely on the creation of specific types of digital subjectivity and constructed 'personas'. See Goriunova, 'The Digital Subject: People as Data as Persons', *Theory, Culture & Society* 36, no. 6 (November 2019): 125–4; Adrian Mackenzie, 'The Production of Prediction: What Does Machine Learning Want?', *European Journal of Cultural Studies* 18, nos. 4–5 (August 2015): 429–45.

50	Jasbir K. Puar, *The Right to Maim: Debility, Capacity, Disability* (Durham: Duke University Press, 2017).

51	Privacy International, 'How Anti-Abortion Activism Is Exploiting Data'.

52	Franklin and Ginsburg, 'Reproductive Politics in the Age of Trump and Brexit', 4.

53	Rosen, 'The Public Health Risks of Crisis Pregnancy Centers'.

54	The reproductive justice framework has its roots in Black and Chicanx feminist theory and movements. It draws attention to social justice issues such as state violence, policing, gentrification, housing and welfare reform, immigration policies as well as just and equitable access to healthcare and reproductive technologies. The movement, founded by Black feminist grassroots activists in the south of the United States, was formulated precisely in response to the limitations of the strategies employed by the mainstream movement for reproductive rights. See Loretta Ross and Rickie Solinger, *Reproductive Justice: An Introduction* (Oakland: University of California Press, 2017); Loretta Ross et al., (eds.), *Radical Reproductive Justice: Foundations, Theory, Practice, Critique* (New York: The Feminist Press at The City University of New York, 2017); Dorothy Roberts, *Killing the Black Body: Race, Reproduction, and the Meaning of Liberty* (New York: Pantheon Books, 1997); National Latina Institute for Reproductive Justice, 'NLIRH: "No One Should Be Deceived When They Are Seeking Healthcare – It's That Simple"', *National Latina Institute for Reproductive Justice* (blog), 2018, https://www.latinainstitute.org/en/nlirh-%E2%80%9Cno-one-should-be-deceived-when-they-are-seeking-healthcare-%E2%80%93-it%E2%80%99s-simple%E2%80%9D.

55	Rosalind P. Petchesky, *Abortion and Woman's Choice: The State, Sexuality, and Reproductive Freedom* (Boston: Northeastern University Press, 1990).

56	Petchesky, 'Antiabortion, Antifeminism, and the Rise of the New Right'.

57	Franklin and Ginsburg, 'Reproductive Politics in the Age of Trump and Brexit'.

58	Roberts, *Killing the Black Body*.

59	Marlene Gerber Fried, 'Transforming the Reproductive Rights Movement: The Post-Webster Agenda', in *From Abortion to Reproductive Freedom: Transforming a Movement*, ed. Marlene Gerber Fried (Boston: South End Press, 1990), 6.

60 Rachel Hall, 'Terror and the Female Grotesque: Introducing Full-Body Scanners to U.S. Airports', in *Feminist Surveillance Studies*, ed. Rachel E. Dubrofsky and Shoshana Magnet (Durham: Duke University Press, 2015), 127–149.

61 As Michelle Murphy's work elucidates, population control programmes spearheaded by the United States and other countries during the 1960s and 1970s were driven by calculations that devalued lives or labelled them as not worth living based on their estimated contribution to the macro-economy. According to Murphy these calculations of the 'disposability' of life were intimately bound up with notions of gender, race, caste and poverty. See Michelle Murphy, *The Economization of Life* (Durham and London: Duke University Press, 2017). See also Nicole Shepard for an analysis of the continuities between racialized, gendered, sexualized and classed surveillance practices and 'big-data' surveillance Nicole Shepard, 'Big Data and Sexual Surveillance' (Association for Progressive Communication, 2018), https://www.apc.org/sites/default/files/BigDataSexualSurveillance_0.pdf.

62 Haraway, *Simians, Cyborgs, and Women*, 164.

11

Algorithmic capitalism, digital machinofacture and the productive body

Stephen Shapiro and Philip Barnard

When it appeared in 1972, Guéry and Deleule's *The Productive Body* staged a key turn in the thought and culture associated with French Maoism.[1] The text's basic claim builds on Marx's notion that capital has progressed by instituting a particular kind of alienation, wherein productive knowledge is separated from workers, and claimed as originating from (managerial) capital. This appropriation of skills and contemplative purpose is crucial to capital both historically, as a means of degrading artisan control over and protection of technical skills, and in the contemporary moment, as a way of disempowering labourers' awareness of a production process that they could interrupt in search of better wages and class power. Capitalists have seized control over the 'mysteries' and knowledge of production in order to claim they are the 'real' workers who make profit, while presenting labourers as little more than pieces of inanimate material to be purchased and used up. In short, Guéry and Deleule argued that all forms of collective, human achievement, the social body, become degraded as they are turned into a productive body, one that labours insentiently in the service of the endless accumulation of profit.

This faithful and fairly conventional exegesis of Marx's *Capital* was tied, however, to the period's extension of concerns about the post-war rise of the information economy and the way it included a critique of the institutional sites of knowledge production, especially the university. This interrogation of the power relations inherent in the apparatuses, or *dispositifs*, of knowledge-production, likened the school to the factory, as an edu-factory. While the period's critiques of the university included discussions such as Pierre

Bourdieu's *The Inheritors: French Students and Their Relation to Culture* [*Les Héritiers: les étudiants et la culture*, 1964] or Jürgen Habermas's *Legitimation Crisis* [*Legitimationsprobleme im Spätkapitalismus*, 1973] – to choose only two titles from a host of others, including gender and racial critiques – the figure that initially towered over the debate was Louis Althusser. In essays and books dating from the mid-1960s onwards (e.g. from 'Freud and Lacan' in 1964 to the 'Ideological State Apparatuses' essay in 1969), Althusser sought to intertwine Lacanian and semiotic models with historical materialism in order to construct a theory of ideology and thereby claim Marxism *as a science*, a pure form of thought.[2]

In retrospect, Althusser's gambit was replete with internal tensions as it was increasingly seen as complicit with the French Communist Party's containment of the diffuse energies of May 1968, and especially as it mirrored authorities' and bosses' claims that they knew how to organize society better than the insurgent students and workers. One counter-reply to Althusser appeared with the rise of French Maoism, a movement that had less to do with actually existing China than with intellectual and political positions among students and intellectuals who rallied themselves under Sinological slogans. One strand sought to establish a new coalition between students and workers via an analogy that compared industrial de-skilling to what was occurring in educational institutions, especially as concerned the effects of educational streaming and the mythology of meritocratic talent as the primary factor in gaining admission to elite universities. Guéry and Deleule's *The Productive Body* was located within this movement in ways that would also appeal to Foucault with his own writing on discipline and institutional *dispositifs* throughout the 1970s. Here Foucault argued for a definition of apparatus as that which represents the conjuncture of a total institution, professional-managerial evaluation, material architecture and categories of knowledge. Throughout the modern, roughly post-1800 phase, Foucault felt that the various *dispositifs* began to mimic each other's procedures: 'Is it surprising that prisons resemble factories, schools, barracks, hospitals, which all resemble prisons?'[3] These apparatuses not only operated in similar ways, but they also became interconnected to form a larger system that 'produced' a new mode of disciplinary power relations.

Although the Frankfurt School was simply less well known during the 1970s in French circles, and in a European Community that was not as well connected in informational terms as it is today, and so had little or no contemporary relation to French Maoist discourses, it seems to share a critique of seemingly value-free knowledge ('Enlightenment rationality') with them. But these approaches differ in two key ways. First, much of Adorno and Horkheimer's work focused on the (mass) cultural industries as the chief agents of subordination through manipulated consumption. Marcuse famously called this the onset of One-Dimensional Man.[4] French Maoism, as a tendency, still pitched its critiques around the sphere of production, even as they expanded this locus to include education, for instance. This emphasis on production, however broadly conceived, stemmed from their sense that the era of Fordist manufacture and its linkage of monopoly capital with statist regulation, the features that preoccupied the Frankfurt School, were becoming eclipsed by a new phase of post-mass industrial manufacture, variously identified as one of informatics, post-Fordism or the decline of military Keynesianism. The new phase of capitalism only seemed to be a turn towards domination by consumption, because its emerging features did not depend on mass-scale fabrication and natural extraction industries.

Consequently, if another phase of capitalism or mode of production was afoot, then it would also be necessary to return to Marx's writings to regain a compass of response, even if these re-readings would need to innovate in their analyses, given the rise of a form of capitalism that Marx did not live to see, let alone fully explore. While these returns to Marx were, of necessity, experimental and tentative in their first formulations, the gesture also differentiated French Marxism from the Frankfurt School, which did not feel as compelled to scour Marx's lesser-known writings, like the *Grundrisse*, for inspiration.

Hence arises one of the paradoxes of the early 1970s. For just as the incipient pulses of de-industrialization in the West began to be perceived and experienced, French left thinking became more fascinated with the mode of large-scale machinery than it had been for several decades. If Maoism had its roots in rural capitalism, *French* Maoism foregrounded the industrial shop-floor. This dual, we might even say (to use a slogan of that time) schizophrenic, approach – on the one hand, sensing the demise of post-war Fordism, while on the other, returning to the concepts developed to describe its emergence – became the catalyst (or problematic) for a fecund host of theoretical assays to arise. In this way, Foucault drew on Marx's writing on machinery in *Capital*, Volume I, for many of his conceptions of discipline.[5] Similarly, Guéry and Deleule look to *Capital*, Volume I, for their outline of the split between managerial and labouring functions.

Here, our introduction to *The Productive Body* perhaps did not highlight, as much as it might have, the ways in which the text related to Deleuze and Guattari's own efforts to deploy Marx on machinery, in their *Anti-Oedipus* [*Capitalisme et Schizophrénie 1. L'Anti-Œdipe*, 1972]. For Guéry acknowledges that they had heard some of *Anti-Oedipus'* earlier formulations in Deleuze's lectures at the time. In particular, terms like 'assemblage' (Deleuze and Guattari's neologism for Marx's 'large-scale industry', as the concatenation of industrial processes as an increasingly interwoven unit) or the 'body-without-organs', for the lived experience of life within such an automaton (a term close to Guéry's 'incorporated body' (*le corps incorporé*), belong to the ongoing mesh of the period's interventions.[6]

The focus on machinery also belongs to a more classical reading of Marx, as seen with Eden and Ceder [Gertrude Mary Davenport] Paul's 1933 translation of *Capital* volume 1. In their translation, the Pauls use the recently minted term 'machinofacture' to render Marx's *des maschinenmäßigen Betriebs*.[7] Here Marx is speaking not of machine production in the most primary or basic sense, but of the drive or compulsion to be or act like a machine. The Pauls' use of the neologism similarly contrasts large-scale industry with the prior age of manufacture, which still has linkages to artisanal manual skill, rather than machinic instruments, like the 'slide rest', that supersedes the individual variation of a worker's bodily movements.[8] By distinguishing between production that still includes co-operation and detail or specialized labour and the new economies of scale imposed by large-scale industry, as it compels more and more production processes to adapt to and adopt the procedures of automation, the Pauls' translation helps us realize that Deleuze and Guattari's use of machinic assemblages may hew more closely to Marx's meaning that many of their later anglophone followers realized. In a similar fashion, Guéry and Deleule's comments on the body-machine resonate with some of the concerns in *Anti-Oedipus*.

On the other hand, the proximity of *The Productive Body*'s language to that of *Anti-Oedipus*, as well as the two texts' mutual distance from Lacan and

Althusser, can easily mask an important divergence, albeit an incompletely telegraphed one, in the two pairs of collaborators' arguments and direction. On the one hand, Guéry and Deleule stick more closely to a recognizable Marxist framework and their enquiries are more legible in that conventional framework, especially by non-francophone readers, since they are clearly embedded within *Capital*'s familiarities. On the other, *The Productive Body* is perhaps more prescient and forward thinking than *Anti-Oedipus* in its perception of the relationship between managerial information monopolization and the rise of precarious labour, or what was then still called 'temp work'.[9]

*

This insight into the connection between managerialism, information control and the hollowing out of Fordist-era job securities, we want to argue, is part of what makes *The Productive Body* a text that remains important to read today, in ways that go far beyond its interest for a history of left ideas in 1970s France. For in ways that were perhaps not easy to perceive at the time, it can be read as an initial notice of, and investigation into, the emerging phase of neoliberalism, the one defined by the post-1970s crisis, which also attracted Foucault's later interest as he turned from the question of discipline, in *Discipline and Punish*, to that of governmentality, for example in the 1978–9 *Collège de France* seminar, *The Birth of Biopolitics*.[10] Guéry and Deleule note that the division between so-called mental management and the productive body has resulted in a more modern form of the production of a surplus army of reserve labour with the rise and normalization of precarious and contingent labour. Referring to the now-replaced logo of the employment agency *Manpower* – Da Vinci's famous 'Vitruvian Man' image of the body-in-extension while also in containment – Guéry and Deleule indicate the rise of contingent labour as part of capitalism's strategic response to worker resistance in the 1970s. In precarious labour, the labourers' created unfamiliarity with the work process, their structured *discognition*, is extended from its industrial state, where it consisted simply in being made unaware of the entire process of a commodity's manufacture within the larger sphere of production, to a wider and deeper disconnection from any knowledge about the possibility of their 'right' to sell their labour consistently. Here, discognition expands to include not simply the confrontation over the level of wages, but the very predictability of any labour exchange for wages at all. Guéry and Deleule suggest the role that information technology and techniques will play in this new or transformed mode of unemployment in the age of deepening neoliberalism.

Discussions of neoliberalism have tended to sort themselves into two main streams: Marxist-inspired enquiries into neoliberalism's degradation of work conditions, job security and means of exploitation; and Foucauldian-motivated enquiries into the means of shaping subaltern and docile subjectivities. As we have elsewhere argued, 'To overcome this antimony, we recall Michel Aglietta's useful consideration, in his discussion of the crisis of Fordism and the onset of a new regime (which in 1998 he still called "globalization"), of the necessary intertwining between an economic regime of accumulation and a sociocultural mode of regulation.'[11]

Here we seek to intertwine the two approaches by focusing, in the first instance, on neoliberalism's attack on civil society as the bourgeois form of the collective body. As Marx argued firmly in 'On the Jewish Question' [*Zur Judenfrage*, 1844], liberalism produced civil society as the mechanism that would interrelate the social reproduction of the bourgeoisie, which had now firmly become the dominant class in the age of machinofacture, with the rise of capitalism.[12] As Immanuel Wallerstein argued, the rise of liberalism was inextricably connected to the emergence of popular nationalism and racism as elementary constituent features of the nineteenth-century (and later) capitalist world-system.[13] Throughout the nineteenth century, civil society's enormous shaping weight and force, especially through its deployment of public-private divisions, allowed for crucial pressure releases, or characteristic contradictions, accounting, for example, for how figures like Charles Dickens could simultaneously act both as fierce critics of heartless capitalism and as proponents of bourgeois civil society and the reconstruction of the domestic household.

Beginning in the early and mid-twentieth century, and partly in response to the destructive tendencies of far-right nationalist populism, which threatened the continued existence of capitalism, neoliberal practices and ideology took a hostile attitude to 'civil society', as well as to any group or mass cultural form. In the second phase of neoliberalism (beginning roughly from the mid-1960s as prelude, and fully emergent by the early 1970s), the advent of new information technology allowed for the first wave of attempts to degrade the social body via a renewed professional-managerial assault on workers' collective rights. This occurred not least through the persistent disaggregation of Fordist-era vertical production, a form that had come to terms with a basic set of workers' collective labour rights. The post-Fordist disassembly (or deterritorialization) of the workplace allowed for a new 'freedom' from the locale of production through the rise of casualized or precarious labour conditions, a usually forcible ejection from job security that operated as a contemporary form of enclosure. Here Foucault's notion of disciplinary power both captured and mistook the effects of casualizing the workforce in the ways that *The Productive Body*, however, had better noticed.

The sociopathic nature of neoliberalism sought not only to consistently undermine and erode all forms of civil society, on which the liberal *homo economicus* was based and guaranteed, but promoted a new subject, *homo astutus*, the rigorously isolating and calculating individual of Ayn Rand-like Game Theory.[14] For example, John Nash and his colleagues' Game Theory experiment, 'Fuck You Buddy' (later renamed 'So Long Sucker'), trains its players to become hyper-attuned to a capitalist FOMO (fear of missing out) and the risk of losing the best moment to betray one's partner in order to reap the greatest advantage or profit.[15] Neoliberal calculation of optimal competition at the individual level demolishes many of the constituent features of liberalism's social body. For classical political economy, exchange was meant to be 'civil' and mutually satisfying. Smith's very definition of human-ness, after all, is exchange as a requirement based on human inter-dependency: 'Nobody ever saw a dog make a fair and deliberate exchange of one bone for another with another dog. Nobody ever saw one animal by its gestures and natural cries signify to another, this is mine, that yours; I am willing to give this for that.'[16]

In contrast to Smith's vision of selfish desires interlacing through the act of mutually satisfying exchange, the Randian individual must engage in continual competition with all others, where there will be losers. Here neoliberal subjectivity, as mythologized in the contemporary television 'reality show' format from *Survivor* onwards, is decidedly agonistic (to use Arendtian language) and antagonistic: winner takes all, every person for themselves. Even Marx felt that to compete by out-calculating your capitalist exchanger was not a dominant gesture in his era's form of capitalism, as capitalist cheating was a motive directed at the working class.[17] Foucault seemed to conversely argue that, in the rise of discipline as co-dependent with nineteenth-century capitalism, the middle-class first enacted these procedures on itself. However, this was done in bad faith, since the middle classes, according to Foucault, knew that they could protect themselves from the new juridical-penal system and evade its strictures by buying themselves out of surveillance.[18]

Neoliberalism, instead, favours the rise of a constant competitor within and against the middle class. Neoliberal practices in the Anglophone lands were initially designed to fragment the working class and contain the empowerment of rising and increasingly restive subaltern groups like women and non-whites. Yet the destruction of working-class solidarity and gains (aka 'entitlements') that had been built up and institutionalized in the post-1945 period had more or less achieved its goals by the mid-1990s, especially after the 1989 fall of the Berlin Wall and China's development of private markets and trade with the West for commercial ventures, both of which opened up cheaper East European and East Asian labour that could compete against the wage levels of the Western labouring class.[19]

A key feature of this process, throughout this period, was the way in which cognitive awareness as a tactical advantage against other capitalists was acceptable (especially through the theft of trade processes and manufacture 'secrets'). Information was made into a weapon for both inter-capitalist competition and the disempowerment of workers. In this manner, *The Productive Body* saw that the mode of separation of knowledge from production was entering a new phase of struggle. And, from a particularly Parisian or Franco-Maoist perspective, this struggle against the particular scission that the rise of contingent labour represents would be one that could be shared by factory workers and bourgeois university students alike. Thus *The Productive Body* suggests the lineaments of a new left popular front, a coalition ready to be assembled in function of the shared or mutual damages caused by the notion that knowledge is something that capitalism makes autonomously.

*

Today, a new bridge between classes may be emerging through resistance to what Mario Carpo has called the second digital turn.[20] The outline of this new coalition or hegemonic bloc involves the entanglement of neoliberal capitalism, algorithmic (or data) governmentality, worker precarity, monopolization and the return to quasi-artisanal detail labour.

By the mid-1990s, neoliberal tactics began to transform and be turned against the middle class itself. The middle bourgeoisie now found that they had lost the benefits of neoliberalism and that it was beginning to cannibalize their own privileges and lifeworld. This phase ran until the crisis of 2008–11. Against expectations that the financial shock of 2008 would make it plain to all that neoliberalism had run its course and was now a zombie concept waiting to be abandoned in favour of something else, and much to the amazement of many academic commentators, the post-2008–11 phase instead *accelerated* and *amplified* neoliberal policies.

Although neoliberalism's resilience as a mechanism of inequality involves several factors, the one we focus on here is the rise of algorithmic governmentality, as exemplified by the infiltration of social networks into everyday life, tech-capitalism's creation of new and more intensive forms of precarious labour (Uber, Lyft, Deliveroo, etc.), and the expansion of quasi-enclosure through the massification of rentier ownership (Airbnb, WeWork, etc.). We do not use 'algorithm' as a technical definition of a kind of mathemesis, but instead as an apparatus (*dispositif*), a mode of regulation occurring through the implementation of dynamic, 'big' data within social life.

Antoinette Rouvroy explains the relationship between algorithmic big data and a new governmentality. She argues that vast new arrays of digitization do not simply amplify the mechanisms of control by the State or corporations, but have the effect of creating a new historical subject. According to Rouvroy, we are now experiencing the rise of 'data behaviourism', which is based on the 'implicit belief... that provided one has access to massive amounts of raw data... one might be able to anticipate most phenomena (including human behaviours)... thanks to relatively simple algorithms... without having to consider either causes or intentions'.[21] The object of these algorithms is not to outline an integral subject but rather to seek traces and fragments of actions that exist below the signature of the individual. The particle-wave actant that Big Data frames, as it combines the particles of sub-individual, often indiscernible, correlations in order to create a supra-individual wave or data profile, has the purpose of both instilling competition within people and framing a subjectivity that is not primarily organized by the predicates of liberalism's civil society, its public–private divide and its constructions of interiority. Given the dynamic inputs of data as they approach real-time reporting, the process means that no experience is gained by playing the game, since each game's results feed back into the initial parameters and thereby change its predictive outcomes. For example, while we know that surge pricing is now often in effect on digital pricing platforms, neither the timing nor the duration of these surges is ever predictable on the basis of our last experience of them. Likewise, workers on precarious labour contracts, the so-called zero-hour contracts, may be called on to work at any time, or not at all. In this way, labourers experience class exploitation, in the absence of wage exchange, since they must dedicate their time to waiting for the possibility of being formally exploited through waged work. This new form of regulation is significantly different from earlier forms of neoliberalism, which sought to establish *homo astutus* as a rational calculator of the best investments of their own human capital. Within the algorithmic *dispositif*, the individual is made bereft of any basis on which to gauge the profitability of their decisions. The antagonism towards others that Nash's game theory used is now directed inwards to create a radical uncertainty and loss of self-calculation for all.

The implications of algorithms as a new dominant *dispositif* have until now been most thoroughly explored within the field of architecture.[22] While the vocabulary of architectural innovations within the first digital turn (sectioning, tessellating, folding, contouring and forming) is tremendously useful for thinking about the emerging formations of subjectivity, we want to tease out one implication involving the end of Fordist mass culture that has become only recently intelligible.[23] Mario Carpo argues that the rise of computerization has eroded the need for information compression.[24] Because humans' cognitive capacity is limited, we have historically developed mechanisms to handle data in a compressed fashion. One example would be the reliance on mathematical equations (e.g. $E=MC^2$) that allow us to extrapolate results from a limited number of required inputs. A computer does not require these sorts of equations, since it operates efficiently through brute application, processing each possibility until one answer seems to work or satisfy the requirements of a solution. The rise in computational power alongside the cheapening of data storage, retrieval and transmission means that various compression formats of the first digital turn are decreasingly necessary. For instance, the 'lossy' MP3 format gave up data richness for smaller file size, a reduction gained by removing data and relying on extrapolation methods to fill in what had been eliminated. Such a trade-off is now less necessary as files can be 'lossless', large and without data compression equations.[25]

This turn to 'lossless' data, often stored in 'cloud' networks, has several implications for how we approach the problem of the productive body today. First, it allows for a mode of regulation that is vastly different from that of the Fordist era, which relied on mass industrial analogues of information compression through standardized moulds, die-tools and homogeneous materials. The Fordist phase depended on the production of a 'mass' object through the mechanical reproduction of industrial and everyday processes in order to generate economies of scale, to create a mass from a (more or less) single framework. Mass industry was tied to large formations that were registered at every level of society. For example, far-right politics was tied to the notion of a mass population in ways that are different from Romantic-era nationalism. Most Western economies moved to a mode of social regulation that depended on the growth of mass bureaucracies, forbearance with large trade unions, mass standardized education, mass housing (either of urban modernist tower blocks or of suburban cookie-cutter tracts) and so on. The Frankfurt School saw these new formations and wrote on the arrival of mass culture industries. Yet as Cambridge Analytica's Alexander Nix said about mass culture, in a 2016 Concordia Summit talk on Big Data, 'Blanket advertising – the idea that a hundred million people receive the same piece of direct mail, the same television advert, the same digital advert – is dead. My children will certainly never, ever understand this concept of mass communication. Today, communication is becoming increasingly targeted, individualized for every single person in this room.'[26]

However, the Fordist regime of accumulation and mode of regulation, already fairly dismantled by decades of neoliberalism, is far more significantly made residual or obsolete through a host of interconnected means and modes of production involving new technologies linked to algorithmic-driven fabrication. Carpo argues that the advance of computerization and new modes of file-to-factory fabrication, often involving 3-D printing, which does not require an equation, since it can duplicate objects from a holistic scan, have reduced the need for economies of scale. The transformation of fabrication, here, means that it no longer matters whether 1,000 or 10,000 copies will be made. The lack of necessity for mass production introduces an era of large-scale customization, built upon the voxel, as the smallest unit containing unique variation, rather than the mass-produced unit of homogeneous moulding. Similarly, algorithmic governmentality, where control or messaging can be attuned to the level of the sub-individual as Nix suggests, no longer requires the standardized demographics of the last century. These algorithmic and voxellating transformations thus represent a new historical phase of capitalism, far different from both Fordist-era and earlier moments of insurgent neoliberalism. These changes likewise have several implications for a history of the productive body, but the feature we wish to highlight is the scrambling of the familiar sequence of capitalist development in favour of one that has a more combined and uneven form.

Marx spoke about the separation of cognition from the working classes, and this is a core question in *The Productive Body*. Tremendous effort was put into preventing the working class from having knowledge about how objects are made, in order to deny them survival skills that might allow them to endure periods of industrial rebellion, or, more simply, that might lessen their reliance on the commercial market for their goods. Inside the sphere of production, the 'mysteries' of artisan training become appropriated and turned into industrial 'secrets' that managers claim as their own 'labour' in the production of commodities. These processes occurred throughout the late eighteenth century and onwards through the nineteenth. In this sense, the rise of algorithmic labour and tech-capitalism returns to or restores these older conditions, as experiential knowledge is removed from individuals, but this removal is now even more extensive and operates in every sphere of life – production, consumption and distribution. The microtuning made possible by algorithms, along with the loss of need for economies of scale, functions like the proliferation of instruments for each act in detail labour, in that technically sophisticated operations can now exist for miniscule procedures concerning the individual. This is a form of absolute-value production and formal subjection that predates large-scale industry, wherein workers had to adjust to the scale of monstrous automata. The mechanisms of the contemporary era, however, bend and contort the individual more precisely, in ways similar to the proliferation of specialized instruments for each act in the process of production, a multiplication of tools that leads to the division of labour that so fascinated Adam Smith.

On the other hand, the *temporality* of this contemporary transformation echoes less the late-eighteenth- and early-nineteenth-century, and, more, late-nineteenth-century formations, given the current moment's tremendous concentration of monopoly capital and rise of social inequality. Gérard Duménil and Dominique Lévy argue that the late nineteenth century began a managerial revolution through the separation of ownership and management.[27] They consequently see capitalism as now shaped by a knowable pattern of cyclical crises as a result of this late-nineteenth-century division of ownership and management. However, many aspects of the new tech industries remove this historical division with their organization by CEO ownership of firms, especially with the use of large blocks of stocks in lieu of salary to executives. Similarly, the rise of 3-D printing that allows for easier design-to-fabrication flows challenges the prior modern-era fragmentation of the master-builder into an architect, who makes outlines or blueprints, and an on-site foreperson, who executes the compressed blueprint and ensures the model's fabrication in real-site presence. The separation of the architect, who compresses information into a blueprint's standardized representation of information, and the constructor begins to vanish when the architect can feed their virtual plans directly into a 3-D fabrication device. Likewise, in contemporary television, we now see streaming services restoring the vertical integration of production and distribution through an emergent Big Studio system (now under the names of Disney, Netflix, Amazon and Apple) in ways that have not been seen since the early and mid-twentieth century. We also are witnessing the collapse of the Humanist-oriented research university's separation from vocational training through a neoliberal assault on the humanities as insufficiently enthusiastic about ensuring the production of human capital and reproduction of accumulation for accumulation's sake.

In this situation, is the best way to approach an analysis of contemporary capitalism via considerations of late-eighteenth-century modes of detail labour's multifarious instrumentation, or rather of the late nineteenth century's concentration of capital? Perhaps both are currently true in a phase that simultaneously utilizes several formerly sequential moments from the history of capitalism. The certainties of a legacy of left sequentialist historiography, which insists on a linear move from one dominant form to another, need to be questioned when we currently exist in a period that summons features of multiple dominant phases to operate simultaneously. If such temporal catachresis is occurring with capitalism, then perhaps we ought to reconsider our own critical apparatus in analogous ways. Restoring *The Productive Body* to our reading lists is thus not a gesture of left antiquarianism, since it is a text that captures our moment's heterogeneity as it rearticulates and reanimates features of both nineteenth-century machinofacture and twentieth-century emerging informatics. We may look to Guéry and Deleule's study as a set of tools for rebuilding a new cultural materialism, a new historical materialism and a new Marx for the conditions of combined and uneven development we face today.

Notes

1   François Guéry and Didier Deleule, *The Productive Body* (Winchester: Zero Books, 2014). Hereafter *TPB*.
2   Louis Althusser, *Lenin and Philosophy and Other Essays* [1968], trans. Ben Brewster (New York: Monthly Review Books, 1971), 127–219.
3   Michel Foucault, *Discipline and Punish: The Birth of the Prison* [1975], trans. Alan Sheridan (New York: Vintage Books, 1995), 228.
4   Herbert Marcuse, *One-Dimensional Man: Studies in the Ideology of Advanced Industrial Society* (Boston: Beacon Press, 1964).
5   Michel Foucault, 'The Mesh of Power' trans. Christopher Chitty, *Viewpoint* (12 September 2012), https://www.viewpointmag.com/2012/09/12/the-mesh-of-power. See also the prior translation, 'The Meshes of Power', trans. Gerald Moore in *Space, Knowledge and Power: Foucault and Geography*, ed. Jeremy W. Crampton and Stuart Elden (London: Ashgate, 2007), 153–62.
6   *TPB*, 67.
7   Karl Marx, *Capital: A Critique of Political Economy*, Translated from the Fourth German Edition by Eden & Cedar Paul (London: J.M. Dent & Sons, 1933), 418. The neologism was in Anglophone use as early as 1876, for example, in the English translation from German of Franz Reuleaux, *The Kinematics of Machinery*, trans. Alex. B. W. Kennedy (London: Macmillan and Co., 1876); and via the identical French neologism, *machinofacture*, which began appearing in

the 1890s and 1900s, and was promptly transposed into English commentary on and translations of socialist writers such as Adolphe Coste, *L'Expérience des peuples et les prévisions qu'elle autorise* (Paris: Alcan, 1900), and Emile Vandervelde, *Le collectivisme et l'évolution industrielle* (Paris: Société Nouvelle de Librairie et d'Edition, 1904; translated into English, using the neologism, in 1907). Thus, prior to the Pauls' version of *Capital*, the term saw considerable use in English, having apparently appeared by way of translations and importations from German and French.

8   Marx, *Capital* (Fowkes), 503.

9   *TPB*, 66.

10   See Kennedy and Shapiro, 'Introduction', in *Neoliberalism and Contemporary American Literature*, ed. Liam Kennedy and Stephen Shapiro (Hanover, NH: Dartmouth University Press, 2019), 1–21; Stephen Shapiro, 'Foucault, Neoliberalism, Algorithmic Governmentality, and the Loss of Liberal Culture', in *Neoliberalism and Contemporary American Literature*, ed. Liam Kennedy and Stephen Shapiro (Hanover, NH: Dartmouth University Press, 2019), 43–72; and Michel Foucault, *The Birth of Biopolitics: Lectures at the Collège de France, 1978–79* [2004], trans. Graham Burchell, ed. Michel Senellart (New York: Palgrave Macmillan, 2008).

11   Kennedy and Shapiro, 'Introduction', 5. A regime of accumulation is the historically specific 'form of social transformation that increases relative surplus-value under the stable constraints of the most general norms that define absolute surplus-value', while a mode of regulation 'is a set of mediations which ensure that the distortions created by the accumulation of capital are kept within limits which are compatible with social cohesion within each nation'. Michel Aglietta, *A Theory of Capitalist Regulation: The US Experience*, trans. David Fernbach (London: Verso 2015), 68; Michel Aglietta, 'Capitalism at the Turn of the Century: Regulation Theory and the Challenge of Social Change', *New Left Review* 232 (November–December 1998): 44.

12   Karl Marx, 'On the Jewish Question', in *Early Writings*, trans. Rodney Livingstone and Gregor Benton (New York: Vintage, 1975), 211–41.

13   Immanuel Wallerstein, *After Liberalism* (New York: The New Press, 1995); Immanuel Wallerstein, *The Modern World-System IV: Centrist Liberalism Triumphant, 1789–1914* (Berkeley, University of California Press, 2011).

14   Shapiro, 'Foucault, Neoliberalism, Algorithmic Governmentality, and the Loss of Liberal Culture', 45.

15   Mel Hausner, John Forbes Nash, Lloyd S. Shapley and Martin Shubik, 'So Long Sucker, a Four-Person Game', in *Game Theory and Related Approaches to Social*

Behavior: Selections, ed. Martin Shubik (New York: John Wiley & Sons, Inc.), 359–62; See also 'Fuck You Buddy', in *The Trap: Whatever Happened to Our Dream of Freedom*, Adam Curtis, dir. BBC, 2007.

16 Adam Smith, *An Inquiry into the Nature and Causes of the Wealth of Nations*, ed. Edwin Cannan (Chicago: University of Chicago Press, 1976), 17.

17 Marx, *Capital* (Fowkes), 267.

18 Foucault, *Discipline and Punish*, 86–7.

19 Loren Brandt and Thomas G. Rawski, 'China's Great Economic Transformation', in *China's Great Economic Transformation*, ed. Loren Brandt and Thomas G. Rawski (Cambridge: Cambridge University Press, 2008), 1–26.

20 Mario Carpo, *The Second Digital Turn: Design beyond Intelligence* (Cambridge: MIT Press, 2017).

21 Antoinette Rouvroy, 'The End(s) of Critique: Data Behaviourism versus Due Process', in *Privacy, Due Process and the Computational Turn: The Philosophy of Law Meet the Philosophy of Technology*, ed. Mireille Hildebrandt and Katja De Vries (Abingdon: Routledge, 2012), 143.

22 For the most comprehensive entry into these debates, see the interventions within the journal *Architectural Design*, especially the special issues: *Machine Landscapes: Architecture of the Post-Anthropocene Landscape*, guest editor Liam Young, 89, no. 1 (January/February 2019) and *Discrete: Reappraising the Digital in Architecture*, guest editor Gilles Retsin, 89, no. 2 (March/April 2019).

23 Lisa Iwamoto, *Digital Fabrications: Architectural and Material Techniques* (New York: Princeton Architectural Press, 2009); Mario Carpo, ed., *The Digital Turn in Architecture, 1992–2012* (Chichester, UK: John Wiley & Sons Ltd., 2013).

24 Carpo, *The Second Digital Turn*. 19.

25 The television series *Silicon Valley*, which drew closely on actual developments in American technology firms, registers this turn when its software engineer protagonist shifts from trying to bring a new compression technology to market, to seeking a new cloud network that can contain all information without the mediation of reduction methods.

26 Alexander Nix, 'The Power of Big Data and Psychographics', Concordia Summit. https://vimeo.com/212373587.

27 Gérard Duménil and Dominique Lévy, *The Crisis of Neoliberalism* (Cambridge: Harvard University Press, 2011).

Further reading

Franco, 'Bifo' Berardi, *The Soul at Work: From Alienation to Autonomy* (Los Angeles: Semiotext(e), 2009)

Gargi Bhattacharyya, *Rethinking Racial Capitalism: Questions of Reproduction and Survival* (London: Rowman and Littlefield, 2018)

Tithi Bhattacharya (ed.), *Social Reproduction Theory: Remapping Class, Recentring Oppression* (London: Pluto, 2017)

Carl Cederström and Peter Fleming, *Dead Man Working* (Winchester: Zero Books, 2012)

Carl Cederström and André Spicer, *The Wellness Syndrome* (New Jersey: Wiley Books, 2015)

Jonathan Crary, *24/7: Late Capitalism and the Ends of Sleep* (London: Verso, 2014)

Laboria Cuboniks, *The Xenofeminist Manifesto: A Politics for Alienation* (London: Verso, 2018)

Adam Elliott-Cooper, *Black Resistance to British Policing: Racism, Resistance and Social Change* (Manchester: Manchester University Press, 2021)

Susan Ferguson, *Women and Work: Feminism, Labour and Social Reproduction* (London: Pluto, 2020)

Peter Fleming, *The Mythology of Work* (London: Pluto, 2015)

David Frayne, *The Refusal of Work: The Theory and Practice of Resistance to Work* (London: Zed Books, 2015)

Ruth Wilson Gilmore, *Golden Gulag: Prisons, Surplus, Crisis, and Opposition in Globalizing California* (Berkeley: University of California Press, 2007)

Jules Joanne Gleeson and Elle O'Rourke (eds.), *Transgender Marxism* (London: Pluto Press, 2021)

Melissa Gira Grant, *Paying the Whore: The Work of Sex Work* (London and New York: Verso, 2014)

David Graeber, *Bullshit Jobs: A Theory* (London: Penguin, 2019)

François Guéry and Didier Deleuele, *The Productive Body*, trans. Philip Barnard and Stephen Shapiro (Hants: Zero Books, 2014)

Byung-Chul Han, *The Burnout Society* (Stanford: Stanford University Press, 2015)

Helen Hester and Nick Srnicek, *After Work: The Fight for Free Time* (London: Verso, 2020)

Amelia Horgan, *Lost in Work* (London: Pluto, 2021)

Sarah Jaffe, *Work Won't Love You Back: How Devotion to Our Jobs Keeps Us Exhausted, Frustrated, and Alone* (London: Hurst Publishers, 2021)

Phil Jones, *Work without the Worker: Labour in the Age of Tech-capitalism* (London: Verso, 2021)

Matthew Lawrence and Laurie Laybourn-Langton, *A Manifesto for the Age of Environmental Breakdown* (London: Verso, 2021)

Juno Mac and Molly Smith, *Revolting Prostitutes: The Fight for Sex Workers' Rights* (London and New York: Verso, 2018)

Andreas Malm, *The Rise of Steam Power and the Roots of Global Warming* (London: Verso, 2016)

Jodi Melamed, *Represent and Destroy: Rationalizing Violence in the New Racial Capitalism* (Minneapolis: University of Minnesota Press, 2011)

Jason Moore, *Capitalism in the Web of Life: Ecology and the Accumulation of Capital* (London: Verso, 2015)

Ivor Southwood, *Non-Stop Inertia* (Winchester: Zero Books, 2013)

Marina Vishmidt, *Speculation as a Mode of Production: Forms of Value Subjectivity in Art and Capital* (Leiden: Brill, 2018)

Kalindi Vora, *Life Support: Biocapital and the New History of Outsourced Labor* (Minnesota: University of Minnesota Press, 2015)

Jackie Wang, *Carceral Capitalism* (Cambridge and London: MIT Press, 2018)

Kathi Weeks, *The Problem with Work: Feminism, Marxism, Antiwork Politics and Postwork Imaginaries* (Durham: Duke University Press, 2011)

Index